the 50 BEST SCIENCE & TECHNOLOGY STOCKS for CANADIANS

2003 edition

the 50 BEST SCIENCE & TECHNOLOGY STOCKS for CANADIANS

2003 edition

Marco den Ouden

Copyright © 2002 by Marco den Ouden

All rights reserved. No part of this work covered by the copyright herein may be reproduced or used in any form or by any means—graphic, electronic or mechanical—without the prior written permission of the publisher. Any request for photocopying, recording, taping or information storage and retrieval systems of any part of this book shall be directed in writing to CANCOPY, 1 Yonge Street, Suite 1900, Toronto, Ontario, M5E 1E5.

Care has been taken to trace ownership of copyright material contained in this book. The publisher will gladly receive any information that will enable them to rectify any reference or credit line in subsequent editions.

Authors and publisher have used their best efforts in preparing this book. John Wiley & Sons Canada, the sponsor, and the author make no representations or warranties with respect to the accuracy or completeness of the contents of this book and specifically disclaim any implied warranties of merchantability or fitness for a particular purpose. There are no warranties that extend beyond the descriptions contained in this paragraph. No warranty may be created or extended by sales representatives or written sales materials. The accuracy and completeness of the information provided herein and the opinions stated herein are not guaranteed or warranted to produce any specific results, and the advice and strategies contained herein may not be suitable for every individual. Neither John Wiley & Sons Canada, the sponsor, nor the author shall be liable for any loss of profit or any other commercial damages including but not limited to special, incidental, consequential or other damages.

John Wiley & Sons Canada Ltd
22 Worcestor Road
Etobicoke, Ontario
M9W 1L1

National Library of Canada Cataloguing in Publication

den Ouden, Marco
 The 50 best science and technology stocks for Canadians / Marco den Ouden. — 2003 ed.

Includes index.
First published under title: The 50 best Internet stocks for Canadians / Mark Pavan, Gene Walden
 and Tom Shaughnessy.

ISBN 1-55335-022-7

1. Stocks   2. Internet industry—Finance.   I. Benson, Philip. 50 best Internet stocks for Canadians.
II. Title.   III. Title: Fifty best science and technology stocks for Canadians.

HD9696.8.C32D36 2002   332.63'22   C2002-904933-4

Production Credits
Cover and text design: Kyle Gell Design
Printer: Tri-Graphic Printing Ltd.

Printed in Canada

10 9 8 7 6 5 4 3 2 1

In memory of Mom and Dad

CONTENTS

Acknowledgements	ix
Foreword	xi

Introduction — 1

Biology, Medicine, & Environment — 43

Patheon Inc.	44
MDS Inc.	48
ArthroCare Corporation	52
Canadian Medical Laboratories Ltd.	56
Bennett Environmental Inc.	60
Zenon Environmental Inc.	64
Biovail Corporation	68
Forest Laboratories, Inc.	72
Taro Pharmaceutical Industries Inc.	76
Axcan Pharma Inc.	80
Cangene Corporation	84
Paladin Laboratories Inc.	88
Pfizer Inc.	92
Merck & Company, Inc.	96

Energy & Resources — 101

Calpine Corporation	102
Enerchem International Inc.	106
Pason Systems Inc.	110
Canadian Hydro Developers, Inc.	114
Goldcorp Inc.	118
Trican Well Service Ltd.	122

Industry — 127

Magna International Inc.	128
Silent Witness Enterprises Ltd.	132
ADF Group Inc.	136
Bombardier Inc.	140

BW Technologies Ltd. 144
SNC-Lavalin Group Inc. 148
Gennum Corporation 152
Groupe Laperrière & Verreault Inc. 156
Stantec Inc. 160
Winpak Ltd. 164
DuPont Canada Inc. 168
ATS Automation Tooling Systems Inc. 172
CAE Inc. 176
Tesma International Inc. 180
Magellan Aerospace Corporation 184

Information Technology **189**
CGI Group Inc. 190
Microsoft Corporation 194
Siebel Systems, Inc. 198
THQ Inc. 202
Mercury Interactive Corporation 206
Check Point Software Technologies Ltd. 210
Cognos Inc. 214
Network Appliance, Inc. 218
Intel Corporation 222

Telecommunications **227**
Aastra Technologies Ltd. 228
Comverse Technology Inc. 232
Aeroflex Inc. 236
Scientific-Atlanta Inc. 240
DALSA Corporation 244
Cygnal Technologies Corporation 248

Glossary 252
The 50 Best Science & Technology Stocks in Alphabetical Order 255
Index 257

ACKNOWLEDGEMENTS

CDG Books, through their Macmillan Canada imprint, was the publisher of this book last year.

Now, Wiley Canada has taken over the series and has worked diligently to bring the *50 Best* back to your favourite bookstore for another year. Putting together a book is no piece of cake. It takes the hard work of many people besides the author. There are editors, project coordinators, researchers, proofreaders, right on down to the folks who run the actual printing presses. I haven't named all of them here (indeed I don't even know who all of them are), but to any I may have missed, I offer my thanks.

I'd like to thank Joel Gladstone, formerly at CDG, for signing me on for a second year; Susan Girvan, who stick-handled the project until the sale of Macmillan to Wiley was completed; and Robert Harris, who handled the transfer of accounts.

With Wiley I had the pleasure of meeting new people to work with. My thanks to Karen Milner and Abigail Brown who managed the project at Wiley. Thanks also to my editor, Michelle Bullard, who so capably cut down my excessive verbiage to manageable proportions and pointed out areas that needed clarification. Special thanks to Sarah Wight who was my editor last year and this year coordinated, collected, and checked the data for our tables and charts. Once again the Canadian Shareowners Association provided most of the data. Thanks CSA!

Rob Carrick, Ellen Roseman, and Mary Cordeiro made up the *50 Best* Advisory Board and helped me walk the straight and narrow—avoiding stocks that were too speculative or flighty.

As for the actual writing and my approach, I must acknowledge the strong influences of William O'Neil, founder of the CANSLIM approach to investing; Donald Cassidy, author of *It's When You Sell That Counts*, for emphasizing the importance of having a selling plan; and

Patrick McKeough, editor of *The Successful Investor* newsletter, for being Canada's most savvy stock analyst and always an inspiration. Thanks also to David Nielsen, Ross Jardine, and Investools for introducing me to the joys of technical analysis.

Thanks also to personal mentors Raymond Aaron and Ken Ballard of the Raymond Aaron Monthly Mentor program. Raymond honoured me with the Entrepreneur-of-the-Year Award for 2001 and helped me recognize that writing and stock analysis are my passion. Ken is a great friend and has encouraged me to turn my website and newsletter into a paying proposition.

Of course I would be remiss if I did not acknowledge the constant support of my wife Janis Baker. She is always there for me. And my children Adriaan and Sarah are always a joy and inspiration as well. Adriaan himself aspires to be a writer—of fiction. He's a much better writer than I am and he will, one day, be up there with the likes of Douglas Adams and Michael Crichton (his heroes) in the bestseller lists!

The galleys for the book arrived in early October, at exactly the same time my father-in-law came out for a visit. My thanks to Jim Baker for giving up some of our usual Scrabble games so I could finish proofreading and making last minute corrections.

As I noted last year, the Internet played a huge role in writing the book. It is a veritable treasure trove of information and the greatest research tool ever devised. Without it, this book would not have been written.

Finally, I'd like to thank my Mom and Dad for inspiring me to be an independent thinker and encouraging me in whatever I undertook. They were not around to see me become a published author but they would have been proud. They're very much missed.

The book's virtues have been enhanced by all of the above. Any deficiencies, of course, are of my own making.

Happy reading!

Marco den Ouden

FOREWORD

Buying and selling stocks, especially in today's volatile market, can be a daunting task. Few travellers would begin a journey without an up-to-date roadmap, yet every day millions of otherwise prudent people invest in companies they know little or nothing about. *50 Best Science & Technology Stocks for Canadians* is a guide designed to help investors navigate the highways and byways of the stock market. By presenting a carefully selected list of great stocks, *50 Best Science & Technology Stocks for Canadians* helps you identify companies that meet your needs for portfolio return and diversification. In analyzing these companies, the authors have used a database of financial information provided by the research division of the Canadian ShareOwner organization to scrutinize the fundamental information on each firm.

When creating a portfolio, you, as an investor, should select a manageable quantity of perhaps 10–25 stocks with the highest potential for growth. A list such as *50 Best Science & Technology Stocks for Canadians* helps you refine your selection by following a few fundamental principles. Canadian ShareOwner, an educational organization that teaches investors to be self-reliant, advocates a simple set of investment guidelines—proven, time-tested principles that revolve around a prudent investment approach that has withstood the ups and downs of the market.

Canadian ShareOwner's Three Principles of Sensible Investing

1. Buy only the best stocks.

2. Buy in the best way.

3. Sell at the right price.

1. Buy Only the Best Stocks

In order to select the very best stocks for your portfolio, you will need to invest some of your time before you invest your money.

Too often investors buy stocks based on a "hot tip" from a friend or neighbour, or because someone "in the know" has recommended it. The problem with this approach is that "knowledgeable" investors don't always investigate the company, its past performance, fundamentals, or future prospects.

Instead, they listen to advertising designed to convince them they don't have the time, knowledge, or access to information needed to do that homework. Consequently, many retail investors rely on the advice of financial advisors and the resulting poor returns and high fees lead them to seek personal control over their investments. In other words, they graduate to self-reliance.

As a prudent investor, you know it's imperative to buy only the highest quality growth stocks over the longer term. The challenge, then, is learning how to choose those best stocks. While a list like the one in this publication is an excellent starting point, you still must understand the principles of choosing optimum stocks from a relatively large pool.

Fundamental Principles of Stock Valuation

To take control of your financial future you'll need to learn one fundamental principle about stock valuation: over the longer term of at least three to five years, a stock's growth in price is driven by only one thing—growth in the company's earnings per share (or profit). Unless earnings increase, the price can't grow.

To find a stock whose future price will rise, look for a company whose earnings per share will rapidly escalate. Over the longer term, a company's earnings enjoy a rapid rise only if its revenues increase on a regular basis. In other words, the company's sales must be on a continual incline; if its share price is to grow, its future revenues and earnings must grow as well.

The growth chart in ShareOwner's *Stock Study Guide* software presents investors with a company's historical record of revenue and earnings growth. When the revenue and earnings profiles are long, steep and straight, you have found a "Great Company" that is worth further study. But, when the profiles are flat, choppy and trending down (indicating a company that has brought long-term investors a lot of "Grief") you are usually best off moving on and finding another company to study.

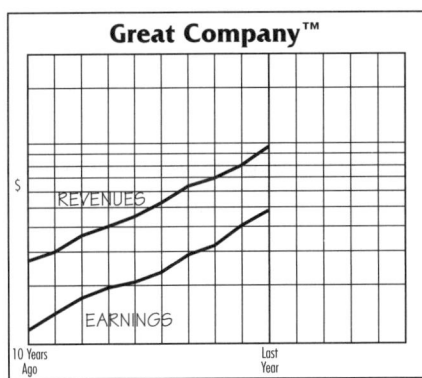
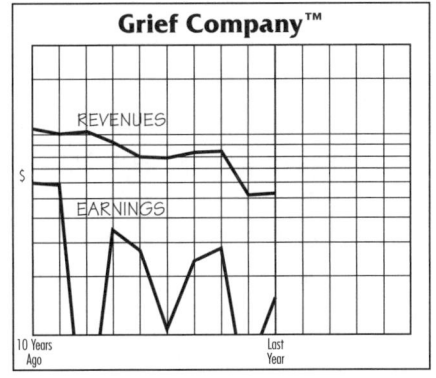

For those firms that qualify as Great Companies, the Guide lets you test the stock's price to see if it is currently on-sale, fairly-priced or over-priced. Of course, the preferred time to buy a stock is when it's not over-priced.

The Guide makes it fast and convenient for you to determine the quality of stocks as they come to your attention from friends, fellow workers, the media or a broker.

2. Buy in the Best Way
Once you have identified a Great Company that's on-sale, you want to add it to your portfolio in the best way—patiently, with a series of modest purchases spread out over several months, quarters and even years. Such a series puts dollar-cost averaging to work, increasing your return and minimizing risk.

Diversify by Price
By using dollar-cost averaging, you make small purchases of a company's shares regularly, over time. The idea is to spread out the amount you invest and take advantage of the natural swings in share pricing. It is best accomplished on a planned, regular basis.

However, the usual brokerage commissions for buying can make dollar-cost averaging prohibitively expensive for small purchases. Canadian ShareOwner makes it possible for investors to buy as many of their 80+ pre-screened securities every 1, 2, or 3 months with commissions that start at about $1 per trade. Plus, all dividends are reinvested automatically for free.

ShareOwner's Low Cost Investing Program (LCIP) allows investors to spread their dollars over many stocks. For example, if you have only $500 to invest every three months, you can specify how much money you want to invest in, 5…10…15… of ShareOwner's pre-screened stocks. For example, you can buy $25 worth of Bombardier, $50 of Loblaws, $150 of Microsoft, etc.

Canadian ShareOwner's pooled purchasing invests according to your specifications, even if it means you are only buying a fraction of one share at a time. Under normal circumstances, this kind of transaction would be impossible because the minimum purchase through any broker is usually a board lot of 100 shares. A single board-lot of high-quality stock can cost in the thousands of dollars. And that single purchase provides no diversification. In addition, Canadian ShareOwner's pooled-purchasing platform allows investors to easily sell their fractional holdings; thus remaining liquid at all times.

Minimize Transaction Costs
One of the big advantages of a self-directed investment plan like the LCIP is saving on the fees, service charges, and commissions that are normally incurred through traditional brokers. Market comparisons suggest that Canadian ShareOwner's unique features—low-cost transactions (starting at about $1 per trade) and free dividend reinvestment, coupled with our educational material—make it one of the best bargains in the investment arena.

Diversify By Sector
It's important to diversify your portfolio by ensuring representation from some of the major market sectors like Financial Services, Communications, Utilities, Consumer Goods, Technology, Resource, Health Care, Food & Beverage and Transportation. For further diversification, or to round out a portfolio, you may wish to consider using some of the Exchange-Traded Index Funds that you can buy through the LCIP. They have low management fees, mirror the performance of certain markets or market sectors and include, among other features, the S&P/TSX 60 Index, The Dow Jones Industrial Average Index, the NASDAQ-100 Index and the S&P 500 Index.

Invest Only What You Can Afford
For the average retail investor, mortgaging the house to build a portfolio, or buying on margin means betting that the market will do exactly what you expect it to do, exactly when you need it to. The market, like

life, does not always follow the paths we dictate. Borrowing makes time your enemy and adds emotional pressure to your decision-making.

It's better, therefore, to adopt a long-term view for building a quality portfolio by investing regularly what you can afford, as cash becomes available—either inside or outside a registered retirement savings plan.

3. Sell at the Right Price

Selling is far more complicated than buying. There are two situations in which you would normally consider selling your stock—one negative, the other positive.

Negative Performance

If the growth, financial or operating fundamentals that first attracted you to a stock have started to decline over the past few quarters, then it is time for careful monitoring and a possible exit. Remember, it was those great fundamentals that led you to buy the stock in the first place. You should also be monitoring whether the market for a company's goods or services is drying up, the competition is trouncing them or other aspects of their prospects have changed dramatically.

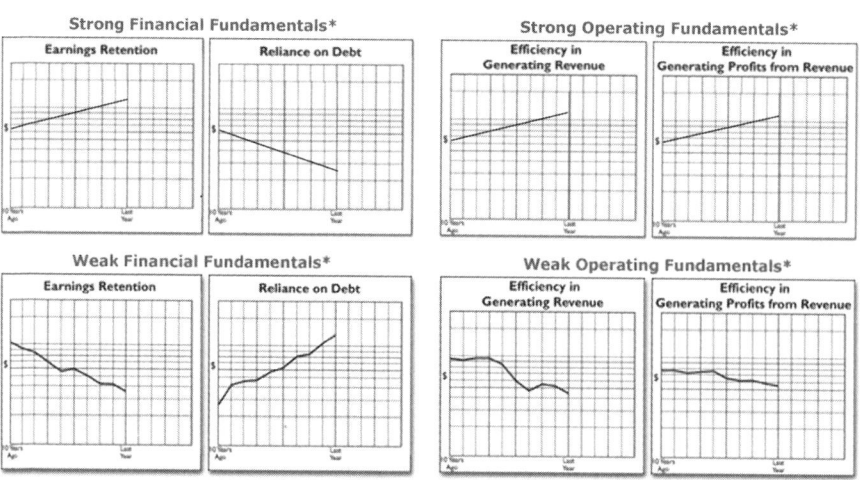

Overvalued Share Price

With the ShareOwner *Guide*, you can determine whether a company's share price has become significantly overvalued due to investor enthusiasm or other market factors. When prices rise to dizzying heights, it is time to reap your profits. Selling even a "Great Stock" when it is overpriced allows you to crystallize profits, while understanding that if the price returns to a reasonable level, you can buy it back.

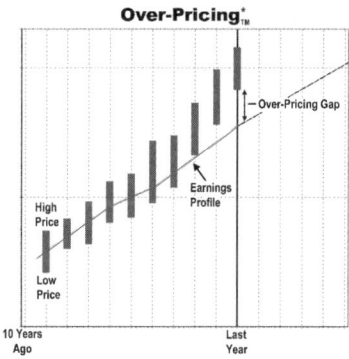

About Canadian ShareOwner

During his tenure as a Professor of Finance at the University of Windsor in Ontario, Founder and President John Bart, Ph.D., discovered the investing principles and education available through the National Association of Investors Corp. in the U.S. In 1987, Dr. Bart founded the Canadian ShareOwner organization to adapt and further develop that education for Canadians.

Today, Canadian ShareOwner provides investors with a suite of educational tools and seminars that are as easily used by both new investors and stock market veterans.

Tool #1—The *Stock Study Guide*: Canadian ShareOwner's *Stock Study Guide* (the "*Guide*") teaches individuals how to identify high-quality growth stocks and to know when to sell them. This powerful investing tool makes it fast and easy for investors to take control of their investing decisions. With the *Guide*, you invest a little of your own time—before you invest your money—to reliably identify stocks with the potential for superior returns.

Tool #2—The Low Cost Investment Program (LCIP): Investors with limited investment dollars often find it difficult to apply fundamental investment principles. The LCIP allows them to practice diversified investing and dollar-cost averaging at minimal cost and reduced risk. Buying commissions start at about $1 per transaction.

Tool #3—The Study Portfolio is an easy way to learn how to build a quality portfolio using the LCIP. Featuring 15 stocks selected from ShareOwner's pre-screened base of the 80+ securities, the Portfolio illustrates the construction and performance of a low-maintenance portfolio designed to produce superior returns. Transaction activities, performance, and decisions are reported in every issue of *ShareOwner* magazine. By its first anniversary in June 2002, the portfolio had produced a positive return of 4.26% against a 3.05% increase in the TSX and a loss of 4.36% in the S&P500.

Tool #4—ShareOwner Magazine: Every issue of *ShareOwner* contains a list of the 80+ high-quality stocks that are available through the LCIP; reports on the Study Portfolio; and, in-depth analysis of two currently interesting "Stocks to Study." Regular columns include "Market Outlooks," written by technical and fundamental analysts; the "Portfolio Coach;" "Tax Planning;" and special features like "Preparing for the Next Bull Market" and "Finding Stocks in the Buy Zone."

Tool #5—www.ShareOwner.com: ShareOwner's website offers an introduction to its investment strategy and a free initial assessment of a stock using its exclusive "Great Stock? Grief Stock? Test." Simply typing a company's name into the Test produces historical revenue and earnings profiles that clearly indicate the stock's record as a Great Stock or a Grief Stock.

Members who take advantage of the full Canadian ShareOwner offering can access simple, straightforward software, information about the fundamentals of equity investing, a regular magazine, and educational seminars. In addition, they can participate in an investment program with extremely low transaction costs and free dividend reinvestment. As a result, individuals and investment clubs can select quality stocks, start investing at a low threshold, manage their own accounts, minimize transaction costs, and design a personal portfolio that matches their own risk profile, time horizon, yield expectation, and desired level of control.

In the fifteen years since its inception, tens of thousands of individual investors have joined Canadian ShareOwner and taken advantage of its investment education programs and database of high-quality stocks. This approach has generated consistently superior results. Since 1987, stocks studied with the *Guide* and featured in *ShareOwner* magazine gained, on average, over three times more than the Toronto Stock Exchange's benchmark index.

A Concluding Word For The Self-Reliant Investor

Self-reliant investors approach equity investing with discipline and prudence. They purchase only the highest-quality stocks when they are "on-sale" and gradually build their positions in Great Companies. Furthermore, they reinvest all dividends to get compounding working and sell when a stock gets overpriced. While proper buying is very important, there is also a time to take profits.

There is no place for emotion in the market. In your life as a self-reliant investor, you must avoid being driven by greed, fear and the herd mentality. And, don't panic when the market turns down—as it inevitably does. Instead, use the opportunity to average down, buying carefully among your chosen high-quality stocks. Then, when the market turns up again—as it always has—you can enjoy the fact that you kept your head while all about you were losing theirs.

I invite you to take advantage of the free stock evaluation opportunities on our web site at www.ShareOwner.com. Use our "Great Stock? Grief Stock? Test" and see for yourself what a high-quality stock looks like. I think you'll get the picture.

Helping private investors earn superior returns since 1987,

John Bart Ph.D., President
Canadian ShareOwner Group

INTRODUCTION

Plus ça change...

"Plus ça change, plus c'est la même chose." *(The more things change, the more they stay the same.)*
                              –Alphonse Karr, *Les Guêpes* – 1849

The above quote from the brilliant French journalist Alphonse Karr, editor of *Le Figaro* and creator of the satirical journal *Les Guêpes*, may seem an unlikely choice as the theme of this book. After all, didn't we go through the terrorist attacks of September 11th? Didn't we witness the collapse of Enron and Worldcom in the largest bankruptcies in history? Heck, everything's changed and the world will never be the same again!

And that is true on some level. The world is constantly changing. We take two steps forward and one step back. Science advances. The standard of living advances. Then events like 9/11 and Enron take us a step back.

But at a very fundamental level, everything stays the same (or rather, everything that goes around, comes around). And that is especially so in the world of stock investing. The principles that guided such geniuses as Jesse Livermore, the brilliant technical analyst who made $100 million shorting the market in 1929, or the completely different value investing principles that guided another genius, Benjamin Graham, and his student, Warren Buffett, remain timeless.

But first, let's look at the events from mid-2001 to mid-2002 to gauge their importance.

A New York State of Mind

A fellow in his mid-30s wearing a tan coat stopped and asked if we were visitors from out of town. He told us he was a stockbroker who worked nearby. In March 2002, my wife, son, and I were standing looking at one of the many makeshift memorials—a block-long expanse of flowers and posters along a fence—near the site of the former World Trade Center.

Bruce told us he was just heading out for work on that fateful day when his wife called out, "Wait. There's something on the news. There's been an explosion." Like most New Yorkers he was glued to his set watching the events unfold. Anguish gave way to horror when the second plane hit.

A neighbour of his, a young woman of 31, died in the destruction. She had just returned to work after having a baby. Her husband has since moved to another part of town. The memories were too painful for him to stay in the same place.

Bruce, in fact, knows three people who died that day. He told us that you'd think in a city of 8 million, probably half didn't know any of the victims. But that is not the case. He personally does not know a single New Yorker who did not know someone who died there.

The wounds are deep and Bruce told us how much he and his fellow New Yorkers appreciated people visiting and paying their respects, not to mention spending a little cash and helping to rebuild the economy. Throughout our chat he rubbed his eyes continually, whether a nervous tick or to fight back tears we could not tell.

That is the human toll of September 11th. It is an event that will be etched in our hearts and minds as long as we live. This terrorist attack on American soil continues to have repercussions. The U.S. moved from a peacetime to a quasi-wartime economy. The airline and related industries got hit with a solid body blow as travel slowed to a trickle. Increased security concerns put another roadblock in the path of free and peaceful trade.

The effect on stock markets was historic. The U.S. markets were closed in the immediate aftermath of the terrorist attacks, but when they reopened on September 16, the Dow Jones Industrial Average went into its sharpest weekly decline since 1933, and the second worst since 1915, as it plunged 14.3 percent.

That, in fact, marked the nadir of the stock market for 2001. The Dow bottomed at 7,296.93 on September 21. The NASDAQ dropped to 1,387.06 that day. And the TSE hit bottom at 6,513.13. Putting substance to Nathan Rothschild's advice to buy when there is blood in the streets (unfortunately quite literally), the market soared in subsequent weeks with the Dow closing at 10,021.5 by year-end, a gain of 37.3 percent. The NASDAQ did even better, climbing 40.6 percent by New Year's. And even the TSE soared 18.0 percent. It had not slumped as badly to begin with, hence the smaller gain. The stocks in last year's book, incidentally, joined in this advance, increasing an average of 41.9 percent from September 2001 to year-end, beating all three of the above indices.

But a more significant event for investors emerged in October. And this, among other things, was about to put the kibosh to the market's advance in the first half of 2002.

The Collapse of Enron

Energy-trading giant Enron was the seventh-largest publicly-traded company in America and the 16th-largest in the world. But its apparent success had come about through some fancy accounting shenanigans that hid over a billion dollars in debt. It buried this debt in the accounts of special partnerships. At the same time, funds raised through venture capital issues were added to the bottom line as profits.

When this debt was brought to light in October 2001, Enron's stock price collapsed and so did its credit rating. Unable to secure additional credit, the company went bankrupt in December 2001. At the time it was the largest corporate bankruptcy in history. You can find the entire fascinating history on the BBC website—http://news.bbc.co.uk/hi/english/static/in_depth/business/2002/enron/timeline/default.stm

The lasting significance of this was that it made investors nervous and distrustful of corporate reporting. Whenever a company's stock staggered due to alleged or perceived accounting irregularities, the headlines called it "Enronitis." Sometimes this was short-lived as the company managed to convince the skeptical public it was on the up-and-up. But, as often, the concerns were justified and the affected stocks plunged and dragged down the rest of the market. Companies like WorldCom, which avoided reporting a $4-billion loss and surpassed Enron as the largest bankruptcy in history when it died, and even that paragon of probity and good taste, Martha Stewart, tried the patience of a weary investing public.

Nevertheless, the call went out for more transparency in accounting practices. One change that emerged was a new way of accounting for amortization of goodwill. Namely, it was not to be amortized if the goodwill was still an asset of the company. That, of course, just made good sense. A corporate brand name doesn't decline in value from year to year, so why should the company be able to depreciate it as an expense? The jury is still out on employee stock options at this writing with some demanding that they be expensed while others, notably in the high tech industries, insisting that unexpensed employee stock options are a necessary tool for cash-strapped start-ups to attract talented workers. Some companies are voluntarily expensing options and some are not, but it is not law at this stage.

With the pressing of criminal charges against former executives of WorldCom and Adelphia, the accounting scandals of 2001 and 2002 took their final grim turn. New legislation in the U.S. hopes to nip future transgressions in the bud by having CEOs and CFOs sign off on corporate accounts, certifying that they are proper and fully disclose the state of a company's finances.

But Enron and 9/11 were hardly the only events to affect investors over the year. Many elite companies of the dot-com era continued to post billion-dollar losses. In the third quarter to March 31, 2002, JDS Uniphase reported a US$4.3-billion loss on revenues of just US$261.8 million. But that was a far sight better than the same quarter the year before, when the company posted an unprecedented loss of US$41.8 billion!

Amazingly enough, the story reporting the third-quarter JDS Uniphase loss cited a bank analyst who maintained a "hold" rating on the stock, which brings us to the next significant event for investors.

The Investigation of Merrill Lynch

On May 22, 2002, Merrill Lynch, the huge Wall Street brokerage firm, agreed to pay US$100 million in penalties to forestall criminal charges in allegations of breach of trust and fiduciary responsibility by the company.

The company had been under investigation by New York state Attorney General Eliot Spitzer for alleged conflict of interest between Merrill Lynch's analysts, who promoted stock issues to the public, and the company's investment-banking arm, which handled lucrative new stock issues.

It came out that analysts who wrote glowing reports on stocks being handled by the investment-banking arm often disparaged these stocks privately, sometimes even going so far as to call them "a piece of crap."

One such analyst was Henry Blodgett, who quietly accepted a multi-million dollar golden parachute to leave Merrill. Blodgett became an Internet guru and one of the highest paid analysts on Wall Street during the dot-com frenzy. And true to form for many analysts, he just couldn't say the word "sell."

His sorry record? In January 2001, of 107 Internet stocks Blodgett had touted, only one had gone up. One! The second-best stock in the bunch was down 30 percent. As one wag put it, "An orangutan throwing a dart at a stock page would have done far better."

At the time he still wouldn't issue a sell order on any of them. The closest he came was a "near-term neutral" call on eToys just prior to its total collapse into penny stock status. Blodgett is hardly the only offender. There is a general tendency in Wall Street analyst circles to disdain the "s" word.

Morgan Stanley Dean Witter analyst, Mary Meeker, who pulled in US$15 million in 2000 as an Internet guru, remained bullish in January 2001 despite her 11 Internet stock recommendations being down an average of 83 percent from their highs.

In his book *It's When You Sell That Counts*, Donald Cassidy, a senior analyst with Lipper Analytical Services, says that all of the following analyst buzzwords should be interpreted as "sell."

- Hold
- Accumulate
- Long-Term Buy
- Market Performer
- Market Weight
- Perform in Line
- Underperform
- Underweight

And the most dangerous word here, he argues, is *hold*. "In fact, *hold*," he says, "really should generally be interpreted as meaning *do not hold*."

Perhaps the New York Attorney General's investigation will put an end to this fraud. But I'm skeptical—and so should you be—of what professional analysts recommend.

So What's the Upshot Here?

The more things change, the more they stay the same. First, September 11th. In the short to medium term, the threat of more domestic terrorist attacks remains high. In the long term, the war on terrorism and heightened concerns about security should ultimately lead to a safer world. Why? Because new methods of detecting terrorism and nipping it in the bud are being developed—and by science and technology companies at that. The fragile peace that existed domestically before 9/11 will ultimately give way to enhanced security.

The Enron debacle has led to an increased interest in sound accounting principles and full and honest disclosure by corporations of their financial status. This has led to improved accounting practices with respect to the treatment of amortization of goodwill and the handling of employee stock options, not to mention an increased demand for transparency in reporting.

The Merrill Lynch case is leading to an end to conflict of interest in the brokerage business, as well as more honest and balanced analyst coverage. I've noticed considerably less reluctance on the part of analysts to issue sell recommendations in the first half of 2002.

Plus ça change, plus c'est la même chose. In the end the public wants domestic peace and security, honest accounting, and honest brokers—just as they always have. And ultimately, this is what we get back to.

Is the Bear Market Over?

The question that lingers for investors is whether the bear market of the last two years is over. At mid-2002, the average price/earnings multiple (P/E) on the major stock indices remained excessively high. But this can be explained by the fact that earnings have been falling faster than stock prices. Should the companies in the doldrums manage to recapture their former earnings, they could be fairly valued or undervalued.

The big question is whether economic recovery is underway as our political leaders would have us believe. At mid-2002 results were uneven. Some companies were recovering and growing earnings again. Still others were reporting continuing losses. And to the extent that earnings were growing, the figures were under a cloud because of the accounting scandals.

Some analysts, the perennial bearish crowd, have predicted this bear market will last much longer than anyone expected. Some have predicted that a complementary bull market in gold will arise (with some speculating on a blow-off top of over $2,000 an ounce).

Still other analysts, such as Vancouver's Bob Hoye and *The Roaring 2000s* author Harry S. Dent have predicted that the market will have bottomed by September or October of 2002, a prelude to an unprecedented boom over the next five years.

My view is that it is pointless to try and predict the market. One should take the market's measure and act accordingly. Be a selective stock picker. Look for stocks that are growing revenues and earnings. Look for stocks that are beating the market—leaders not followers. If they are science and technology stocks, this book should help in finding some winners. And if they are large caps, our companion volume, *The 50 Best Stocks for Canadians*, should be handy. If they are small caps, look to *The 50 Best Small Cap Stocks for Canadians*. And review *The 50 Best Global Stocks* for a cross-section of top stock picks from around the world.

And if they are gold stocks or resource stocks, you'll find one gold stock in this book (yeah, a "high tech" gold stock—cool eh?) and several resource stocks in the companion volumes.

The point is, be aware and be prepared.

The Power of Innovation

Why should we invest in science and technology stocks? There are, after all, many other areas to invest in, from resources to retail.

Science and technology, in fact, offer some of the best opportunities for investors in the marketplace. The reason is the power of innovation. The sole distributor of a product or service commands a distinct market advantage and a unique profit opportunity. Many science and technology companies are on the cutting edge of development—innovating and bringing new products to market. Being first with a product, particularly one protected by patents, gives a company a quasi-monopoly position in the market.

Sometimes this advantage translates into a long-term market dominance that makes the company a giant among its fellows. Consider Intel Corp. In 1971 Intel developed the microprocessor, the key building block of every personal computer. Its first application was in a calculator developed by the Japanese company Busicom. A few years later, the fourth generation of microprocessor, the famous 8086-8088 line, went into IBM's new personal computer.

What did this mean for investors? Quite simply, it created many a millionaire. Someone lucky enough or smart enough to have invested US$10,000 when the company went public in 1972 would have netted US$4,784,580 on September 21, 2001, at the NASDAQ bottom for 2001. At Intel's peak she would have pulled down a cool US$18,752,014.

But what if she had missed Intel in 1972, or even when IBM came out with the PC in 1978? By early October 1987, Intel stock had risen 31-fold from its launch price. Then came the crash, and Intel plunged from US$62.75 to a low of US$27.00, a 57-percent drop in three weeks. An investor at that point could have thought, "Well, I guess this one's peaked. Too late to get in now." Or she could have seen it as an opportunity: Intel on sale! If she had plunked down US$10,000 at that point, she could have made over US$1,344,444 at the August 2000 peak. Selling on September 21, 2001, she still would have netted US$343,035.

Many technology stocks reached a similar point in 2001 and 2002. They are on sale. Some have risen threefold or fivefold or even eightfold, and will be going up even more. Still others will sputter and fail.

There's no doubt that investing in science and technology stocks can be volatile. But later in this introduction we'll discuss ways to increase your probability of success in this and any market.

What Is a Science and Technology Stock?

Last year I went into a detailed discussion of what exactly we meant by a science and technology stock. Rather than repeating it here, suffice to say that I argued that the category shouldn't be confined to computers, information technology, and telecommunications, as was often implied in the buzzwords "tech wreck" or "Internet bubble." Nor should it include companies that were often regarded as technology stocks because they used the Internet to communicate and sell products. Amazon.com, we concluded, was not a technology company but a book retailer.

We came up with the following definition:

Science and technology companies are companies that are developing new ways of doing things and advancing the state of knowledge. Usually they have a budget for research and development, and often they hold patents on technology they have developed. Science and technology companies are innovators discovering new scientific knowledge and inventing new products and techniques. They make a significant portion of their revenues by developing or exploiting science and technology.

That would also include companies that are technology-driven, such as broadcasting and electronic data and information systems, even if they do not engage directly in research and development. Such companies promote the development of technology by being the customers for the inventors, innovators, and developers.

This definition also includes companies supplying other businesses with support services involving technological expertise. These companies must stay on the cutting edge or die. This includes many companies involved in outsourcing, whether in pharmaceutical manufacturing, oil industry services, or information technology.

We included the energy industry, as some electricity-generating companies are technology-driven, even if they bring in technology developed outside the company. Companies such as Calpine are revolutionizing the business, bringing modern, clean, natural-gas-fuelled plants online to replace the coal-burning dinosaurs that many utilities still use. Others, such as Canadian Hydro Developers, are exploring alternative sources of energy: geothermal, wind power, or recycled waste.

This year we added engineering companies, which generally do not invent products or develop new technology, but often develop innovative ways of implementing technology and also must stay on the cutting edge of changes in technology. And we added resources to the mix when we discovered a mining company that used technology in such an innovative way that it was named one of the Top 50 Champions of Innovation by *Fast Company* magazine.

In this book I have divided the stocks into broad categories, defining five sectors that cover specific areas of the science and technology economy. To some extent, these sectors are independent of each other, and spreading investments across the categories will minimize risk.

- **Biology, Medicine, & Environment** Includes biotechnology, pharmaceuticals, research labs, technical medical services, and environmental remediation.
- **Energy & Resources** Includes electricity generation, alternative energy, and energy industry support services, but not including oil or mining companies except for Calpine Corporation, the one mining company we noted above.
- **Industry** Includes aircraft technology and maintenance, automotive engineering, general industrial engineering, and civil engineering, as well as chemicals, plastics, and materials science.
- **Information Technology** Includes computer hardware, software, and Internet applications.
- **Telecommunications** Includes infrastructure developers, equipment developers and manufacturers, telephony technology, Internet service providers, broadcasting, and video technology.

Selecting the 50 Best

Science and technology stocks come in many flavours and colours, as I've noted. What characteristics should we look for to find the real winners to invest in? It comes down to two things: growth and profits.

These two factors, while ultimately crucial, may not be necessary in the short run. In fact, a science and technology company in its early stages often runs at a loss as it grows and develops. Growth alone—plus hype and hope—is often enough to move the stock price of a start-up upwards.

And then there are companies heavily involved in research, particularly in the biotechnology field, who may not have revenues, let alone earnings, as they work on product development. They survive on their capital, or on return on invested capital, as research progresses. The share price of these companies may go up considerably just on the promise that their research will be successful and lucrative products will be available in the future. Such companies, while interesting, are too speculative to be included in this book.

Although it doesn't always hold true in the short term, there is a long-term correlation between earnings growth, revenue growth, and share price growth. The minimum criteria for the stocks included in the *50 Best*, as determined by the Advisory Board, reflect this correlation.

- Stocks listed on TSX, NYSE, or NASDAQ for at least three years
- Average 10-year share price growth more than 10 percent annually
- Average 10-year earnings per share growth more than 5 percent annually
- Average 10-year revenue growth more than 5 percent annually
- Not more than one negative return on invested capital in any one of the last 10 years

These are fairly stringent requirements, but many excellent science and technology stocks have less than a 10-year track record, so I also looked for companies with superior revenue, earnings, and share price growth since going public.

Canadians are fortunate in that we have a large and powerful industrial giant next door—the U.S. We're doubly fortunate in that investing in American stocks is a piece of cake: Just call up your broker. (Americans are not as fortunate the other way around—unless they are dual-listed, Canadian stocks are difficult for Americans to buy.) Because of the robustness of the American economy and the tremendous opportunities there, as well as the fact that many Canadians like to buy U.S. stocks, I've included a number of American companies here.

In any event, diversification into some American stocks is not only good exposure to a very strong economy but also affords protection against a declining Canadian dollar. You'll note that many of the Canadian companies covered are international players as well, with revenues derived globally.

How I Chose the 50 Best

Since this is the second year of doing this book, and since I wanted to provide some continuity between the 2002 and 2003 editions, the first part of my selection process was to review last year's picks and see whether they were still worth recommending. Most of them, in fact, were.

Here's how I went about culling the list. First I put together a table of the 50 stocks. Then I entered recent data—the most recent annual revenue numbers, the most recent annual earnings-per-share numbers, and the most recent quarterly earnings per share.

Right off the bat I decided to scratch any companies that lost money in the most recent fiscal year. You don't make a profit, baby, you ain't in the book! The stocks dropped because they suffered losses in their most recent fiscal year are AOL Time Warner, EMC Corp., Solectron, Yahoo!, Sapient, ATI Technologies, Celestica, Internet Security Systems, PMC Sierra, and Research in Motion.

Now, it could be argued that these companies are still excellent prospects because they could recover as the economy recovers. Perhaps. But why not pick stocks that continued to be profitable and in many cases even grew despite a weak economy?

That's 10 dropped stocks. Others that were dropped include takeover subjects C-MAC Industries, which was taken over by Solectron, and

Wescam, which was slated for takeover by L-3 Communications Holdings as the book went to press. BCE Inc. came under a cloud over questionable accounting practices even though it managed to eke out a profit in fiscal 2001. It posted a loss for the trailing 12 months to March 31, 2002 and did not look like it would resolve its problems by 2003, so we dropped it as well.

Also dropped was Cree Inc. which, while profitable in fiscal 2001, posted a significant loss for the trailing 12 months to March 31, 2002 and did not look like it was making progress towards recovery, and The Thomson Corporation, which was marginal in our ratings to begin with. Thomson was downgraded by ace stock-picker Pat McKeough from a buy to a hold for patient investors only in the June 2002 issue of *The Successful Investor*. Call me impatient!

There were a few remaining stocks that were in the iffy category because they had declining revenues or declining earnings or both. But I opted for continuity and decided to keep as many of the previous year's picks as possible. We have been, after all, in a bit of an economic slump, and even the best companies, such as Microsoft and Intel, have faced some difficulties.

Filling the holes with new entries followed a similar pattern to choosing the 50 last year. First, I went through the top 500 stocks on the TSX looking for one-year returns to March 31, 2001. These were stocks that had actually forged ahead and made gains during the NASDAQ bear market. I compiled the data using the excellent filtering tools at Globeinvestor.com (one of my favourite stock research websites). This list contained few technology stocks, heavily dominated instead by gold mining companies, some oil and gas, consumer, and industrial stocks. I then looked through these stocks to select the companies that had grown earnings, revenues, and share price. These were the first stocks on my list.

Second, I went through all the publicly-traded stocks on the Fast 50 lists, employing the same criteria. I also examined other industry lists: *Profit Magazine*'s Profit 100 and *Alberta Venture Magazine*'s 30 Fastest Growing Companies in Alberta.

I also scoured through various magazines for articles on hot stock picks, including *Canadian Business, Smart Money, U.S. News & World Report, Bloomberg Personal Finance, Red Herring,* and *Worth*.

And I used a proprietary search tool at Online Investor Toolbox (http://pro.investortoolbox.com) that looked for stocks with "strong long-term growth." A number of these matched the stocks from the various magazine articles, so those moved up the list. In the end, I narrowed the list to 24 new Canadian companies and 24 new American ones.

I decided that I wanted to increase the number of Canadian companies, and so started by giving the 24 Canadian stocks closer scrutiny. Eleven made the grade. Unfortunately, A.L.I. Technologies, one of my favourites from this list, was bought out by a large American company before we went to press, leaving 10 new Canadian companies. This left room for only four new American companies, although there were a fair number that qualified.

Wescam became the subject of a takeover bid just before press time and I replaced it with one more Canadian company that hadn't qualified originally but started showing its mettle during the summer of 2002 when many tech stocks were slumping. (Dalsa Corp., in case you were wondering.)

Like last year, some of our stocks did not meet all the requirements set out by our Advisory Board. But the exceptions, for the most part, were companies that failed to meet the requirement for no more than one year of negative return on equity. There were a number that had run a few unprofitable years and then turned the corner. Companies that can turn the corner into profitability when the rest of the market is crashing strike me as particularly noteworthy, so I included them. The exceptions to our guidelines are noted in the individual profiles.

How Last Year's Picks Fared

Before we go on, it's worth taking a look at the stocks from last year's book to see how they've fared. It should be noted that the time lag between manuscript and hitting bookstore shelves is about four to five months. This includes the time for editing, revisions, typesetting, proofreading, corrections, printing, warehousing, and shipping to bookstores. It's a lot of work!

Because of this time lag, the stocks are all selected by the end of June in the preceding year. Things can change precipitously in six months. Between manuscript and New Year's 2002 we had the terrorist attacks on America, the Enron debacle, and continuing bad news on the earnings front.

And because of this time lag, I took a varied approach to last year's selections. I picked some stocks because they had shown strength in a down market. I selected others because they had a long history of success but were in a temporary slump, caught up in a general market malaise. And I selected still others because they were high-flying tech wonders that got creamed in the technology rout, but which I figured had the legs to get back up and run for the top of the hill again.

I anticipated that some of these had farther to fall in 2001 before starting on the climb up again. In fact, that proved quite true. The market as a whole hit bottom on September 21, 2001, 10 days after the terrorist attacks on America. That was followed by a superb rally to the end of the year in which our picks participated. As noted earlier, they climbed even higher than the NASDAQ, which was the strongest of the major indices for that period.

The table below gives the performance of the 50 stocks from last year. Although the stocks were selected as my picks for 2002, I've included their performance for 2001, for September 21 to December 31, 2001, from January 1, 2002 to May 31, 2002, and from January 1, 2002 to August 31, 2002. Only eight of the picks from last year were in positive territory by the end of August 2002. That's almost embarrassing, but not surprising considering that the bear market renewed its attack with vigour during July and August. The real test will be to see how they've fared by December 31. I'll publish that information on my website, The Break Out Report, at www.breakoutreport.com in January 2003. The stocks below are listed in alphabetical order.

Company	Symbol	% Change 2001	% Change Sept. 21 to End of 2001	% Change Jan. to End of May 2002	% Change Jan. to End of Aug. 2002
Aastra Technologies Ltd.	AAH	120.69%	107.57%	23.70%	17.55%
AOL Time Warner Inc.	AOL	-7.76%	7.54%	-41.74%	-60.59%
Arthrocare Corp.	ARTC	-8.05%	-23.70%	-37.48%	-24.09%
ATI Technologies Inc.	ATY	135.09%	78.19%	-24.38%	-54.48%
ATS Automation Tooling Systems Inc.	ATA	-15.00%	14.25%	25.00%	-13.53%
Axcan Pharma Inc.	AXP	42.86%	46.10%	2.67%	-23.33%
BCE Inc.	BCE	-16.84%	7.81%	-21.30%	-21.13%
Biovail Corp.	BVF	52.26%	46.42%	-44.05%	-52.32%
Bombardier Inc.	BBD.B	-28.73%	27.71%	-15.33%	-59.39%
BW Technologies Ltd.	BWT	157.23%	77.87%	22.61%	16.63%
CAE Inc.	CAE	-5.16%	40.24%	20.14%	-41.92%
Calpine Corp.	CPN	-62.74%	-26.20%	-42.82%	-70.94%
Canadian Hydro Developers, Inc.	KHD	-31.44%	0.00%	9.76%	1.95%
Canadian Medical Laboratories Ltd.	CLC	11.99%	13.22%	51.82%	59.12%
Celestica Inc.	CLS	-20.99%	68.42%	-29.84%	-43.59%
CGI Group	GIB.A	104.17%	47.24%	-32.90%	-48.65%

Company	Symbol	% Change 2001	% Change Sept. 21 to End of 2001	% Change Jan. to End of May 2002	% Change Jan. to End of Aug. 2002
Check Point Software Technologies Ltd.	CHKP	-55.20%	65.38%	-59.24%	-58.01%
C-MAC (now Solectron Canada)	SCT	-52.72%	20.00%	-31.12%	-67.50%
Cognos Inc.	CSN	41.32%	95.89%	-7.61%	-28.41%
Comverse Technology Inc.	CMVT	-79.41%	-10.81%	-47.03%	-63.43%
Cree, Inc.	CREE	-17.08%	102.89%	-61.03%	-53.29%
DuPont Canada Inc.	DUP.A	55.27%	31.75%	5.50%	-5.46%
EMC Corp.	EMC	-79.79%	20.54%	-46.06%	-49.70%
Forest Laboratories, Inc.	FRX	23.34%	27.43%	-9.91%	-10.92%
Gennum Corp.	GND	10.31%	22.67%	-5.95%	-13.84%
Intel Corp.	INTC	4.62%	62.95%	-12.18%	-47.00%
Internet Security Systems, Inc.	ISSX	-59.13%	146.62%	-47.38%	-52.65%
Magellan Aerospace Corp.	MAL	-14.53%	10.62%	31.80%	-1.00%
Magna International Inc.	MG.A	60.73%	35.07%	7.89%	-2.16%
MDS Inc.	MDS	-14.86%	12.84%	21.43%	29.89%
Merck & Company, Inc.	MRK	-37.20%	-10.50%	-2.89%	-14.08%
Mercury Interactive Corp.	MERQ	-62.35%	72.14%	-0.35%	-25.22%
Microsoft Corp.	MSFT	52.72%	33.27%	-23.15%	-25.92%
Network Appliance, Inc.	NTAP	-65.93%	172.69%	-40.51%	-56.38%
Pason Systems Inc.	PSI	30.94%	13.75%	44.51%	33.52%

Company	Symbol	% Change 2001	% Change Sept. 21 to End of 2001	% Change Jan. to End of May 2002	% Change Jan. to End of Aug. 2002
Patheon Inc.	PTI	-15.82%	56.25%	-14.00%	-4.48%
Pfizer	PFE	-13.37%	11.31%	-13.17%	-16.99%
PMC-Sierra Inc.	PMCS	-72.96%	42.11%	-33.11%	-67.03%
Research In Motion Ltd.	RIM	-68.64%	57.13%	-39.14%	-55.97%
Sapient Corp.	SAPE	-35.34%	103.16%	-80.96%	-83.55%
Siebel Systems, Inc.	SEBL	-58.63%	109.90%	-34.77%	-69.73%
Silent Witness Enterprises Ltd.	SWE	49.36%	17.68%	-22.75%	-32.70%
Solectron Corp.	SLR	-66.73%	12.69%	-28.37%	-67.02%
Tesma International Inc.	TSM.A	20.36%	16.82%	21.18%	2.22%
The Thomson Corp.	TOC	-15.77%	13.10%	3.41%	-12.20%
THQ Inc.	THQI	98.83%	18.92%	-0.96%	-28.51%
Trican Well Service Ltd.	TCW	-8.28%	-13.92%	59.77%	28.87%
Wescam Inc.	WSC	35.29%	50.00%	6.09%	-9.42%
Yahoo! Inc.	YHOO	-40.98%	104.38%	-9.70%	-42.00%
Zenon Environmental Inc.	ZEN	127.03%	37.74%	-8.75%	-5.77%
AVERAGE		2.06%	41.90%	-12.25%	-27.89%

As you can see, the 50 on average returned 2.06 percent in 2001, while the TSE 300 Composite dropped 13.9 percent and the NASDAQ dropped 21.1 percent. This included five stocks that doubled or better in 2001. But as noted, we anticipated some still had to hit bottom before starting up again, and the overall score for 2001 was 20 on the upside with 30 in negative territory

Where it gets interesting is during the last quarter of the year plus a few days (from September 21 to December 31, 2001) when the 50 on average gained 41.9 percent, compared with the TSE, which rose 18.00 percent, and the NASDAQ, which rose 37.0 percent (based on closing prices).

It's important to note from our table just how volatile science and technology stocks can be. Consider the case of Internet Security Systems. Our table shows it climbed 146.62 percent from September 21 to December 31, 2001 and then declined 52.65 percent to the end of August 2002. That's volatile! But what it does not show is that its stock didn't bottom until September 27, when it dropped below $10 and then positively soared, peaking at over $40 in January, for a gain of over 300 percent. That's *really* volatile!

Unfortunately, the mini-boom to the end of 2001 proved to be an interim rally, as stocks (and especially science and technology stocks) began to fall again in the first eight months of 2002. At this writing, it is expected that the markets will continue to tumble, perhaps hitting new lows in September or October before climbing again. That being the case, our 50 stocks for last year dropped from the peak of the late 2001 tech rally through August 31, 2002 by 27.89 percent. This was significantly poorer than the S&P/TSX Composite Index, which lost only 15.8 percent, but better than the NASDAQ, which lost 32.6 percent. That's not a happy result, but not surprising considering the turmoil in the market at the time.

It's interesting to note that the eight stocks that turned up in positive territory at the end of August are all Canadian. None of my American picks did. But in the post 9/11 relief rally, the best performers were all American.

Who Isn't Here

Once again Canada's tech giants, Nortel and JDS Uniphase, are not here. They've been losing ungodly sums of money and a turnaround does not seem to be imminent at the time of writing. In any event, losing money disqualifies the company.

But there are many companies that qualified but are not included. The main reason is that it is not possible for me to research every science and technology stock. There are simply too many of them. So there are probably many good companies of which I am simply not aware.

And to some extent, subjective judgment comes into play. In making my last few selections from a large list of American stocks, I opted to choose a few that I found appealing because of the prospects for the company's technology, or because of a strong Canadian connection or some other reason.

The *50 Best* companies in this book vary from large multinationals to little-known, smaller companies that have been quietly growing revenues and earnings without much fanfare. Many of the Canadian stocks are international in scope, with large markets outside of Canada. Some do 80 percent or more of their business outside of Canada. With some exceptions as noted in their profiles, all of the companies in this book show a strong track record of revenues, earnings, and share price growth. We're pleased to offer them for your consideration.

Using This Book Effectively

As we've seen in the last two years, science and technology stocks can be volatile. Just when you thought it was safe to go back in the water (like around New Year's 2002), the big bad bear takes another bite out of you. So it's worth taking a look at some strategies to improve your chances of success in the stock market. These strategies are good for all stocks but especially so for science and technology stocks.

Diversify

The first thing to consider is your risk tolerance and how much of your portfolio you want to devote to potential high flyers. I believe all investment plans, within the context of a balanced portfolio, should include some science and technology stocks, particularly if you are younger and years away from retirement. These companies, after all, are the ones that will drive the economy in the future. The other books in this series, *The 50 Best Stocks for Canadians*, *The 50 Best Small Cap Stocks for Canadians*, and *The 50 Best Global Stocks for Canadians*, will give you insights into some of Canada's stellar companies in consumer goods and services, manufacturing, finance, resources, and utilities. Diversification across all these sectors is recommended. Science and technology stocks can fall into nearly all of those categories, except finance and resources. As I've already mentioned, I have, in fact, divided up the *50 Best* stocks into five categories to make diversification within this niche possible as well.

These sub-sectors are not always in sync; some may be advancing while others are retreating. Investors who were mostly into communications and Internet-related technology in the first quarter of 2000, and who did not have a selling discipline, would have suffered devastating losses in the following year. But those who diversified, particularly if they diversified into energy and industrial technologies, would have fared quite well.

On the contrarian side, there are some who believe the opposite strategy is preferable—rather than diversify, consolidate. In *The Gorilla Game: An Investor's Guide to Picking Winners in High Technology*, Geoffrey Moore and his co-authors recommend buying several stocks that have a chance of dominating the technology sector, and then as the market develops and one company looks to be emerging as the winner, selling the other stocks to put all your money behind the winner. This philosophy is echoed by Robert Kiyosaki in his *Rich Dad's Guide to Investing*: "Most investors say diversify. The rich investor focuses."

I see merits in both approaches, but it's like comparing apples and oranges in a way. Mr. Moore is talking about consolidating within a specific niche. Mr. Kiyosaki is talking about specialization. Neither recommends putting all of your investment eggs in one basket. Diversify your portfolio across the various economic sectors. And diversify your technology holdings across the various technology categories.

Buy Right

Once you've decided how much of your portfolio to allocate to science and technology stocks, you don't want to just go out and buy all the stocks in this book willy-nilly. For one thing, circumstances may have changed considerably since the book was written.

For another, each stock will appeal to different investors for different reasons. Although we have laid down fairly conservative criteria for inclusion in the *50 Best*, some of the companies are decidedly more conservative than others. There's a big difference between Magna International, a large auto parts manufacturer, and Zenon Environmental, a small company making advanced water filtration systems. One might exhibit slow, steady growth while the other might have dramatic ups and downs. Both are excellent companies with excellent prospects, but an investor with a low tolerance for volatility would be better off with Magna. Even such stalwarts have good and bad times, though.

You may want to buy the more conservative, large cap picks—DuPont Canada, Intel, Microsoft, Pfizer, Merck, or Magna International—to lock into your portfolio with a long-term horizon (although not to completely forget about). One of the other books in this series, *The 50 Best Stocks for Canadians*, focuses on these stocks across a wider range of sectors. Other stocks you'll want to monitor and perhaps sell after a time. Still others among the *50 Best* may no longer be attractive for various reasons: high prices, changing markets, and so on. The commentary on each stock should give you some thoughts on whether it is suitable for you.

An excellent general approach to selecting growth stocks is the CANSLIM approach developed by William O'Neil, founder of *Investors Business Daily*, in his best-selling book *How to Make Money in Stocks.* The appeal of this approach is that it is based, not on theory, but on empirical observation. He studied the top-performing 500 stocks between 1953 and 1993, looking for common threads that distinguished the really big winners from the herd. These common characteristics were CANSLIM, an acronym that stands for:

- **Current Quarterly Earnings Growth** Mr. O'Neil discovered that three-quarters of the top-performing stocks had current quarterly EPS growth of 70 percent before they began their huge advance. At any one time, only about 2 percent of all stocks listed for trading will show such growth, he says, recommending 18 to 20 percent as a minimum standard of growth.
- **Annual Earnings Growth** EPS for each of the last five years should show growth over the previous year. The annual compounded growth rate should be at least 25 percent, but the higher the better. The average of all firms Mr. O'Neil studied was 24 percent a year, but this included the one out of four stocks that were turnaround situations.
- **News** New products, new management, new highs—a new discovery, invention, patent, product, or management often sparks a significant price move. Ninety-five percent of the successes Mr. O'Neil discovered had some significant change before their run-up. His most interesting discovery was that a stock making new highs tends to go higher and a stock making new lows tends to go lower. This goes completely contrary to the general wisdom of "buy low, sell high," and most people resist it. They prefer to look for stocks that have gone down in price and are, supposedly, a bargain. The contrarian (and profitable) position is "buy high, sell higher." In particular, look for stocks making 52-week highs for the first time. Note that many of the companies included in this book have suffered severe price declines in the wake of the technology crash. But many will be approaching the anniversary of their market bottoms in the fall of 2002 and through the

spring and summer of 2003 and may well be hitting 52-week highs again as you read this.

- **Supply and Demand** Simply put, the smaller the number of shares outstanding, the lower the supply, and the more any demand for the stock will move the price upwards. It's not rocket science. Mr. O'Neil says, and I agree wholeheartedly, "The law of supply and demand is more important than all the analyst opinions on Wall Street." He also points out that excessive stock splits (which increase the supply on the market) are not good for a stock's price. Stocks sometimes peak just after a split. Similarly, a company buying back its own shares (and reducing the supply on the market) is a good thing.
- **Leadership** In any industry group, some stocks are clearly the leaders, moving ahead by leaps and bounds. Others are clearly laggards—slow, pokey stocks that just can't keep up. Go for the leaders, not the followers. A strong indicator, in this respect, is a stock's relative price strength—how well the stock is doing against the rest of the market.
- **Institutional Sponsorship** Mr. O'Neil argues that stocks tend to have some institutional sponsorship before they make really big moves. That is, mutual funds, pension funds, insurance companies, and the like should be buying. They provide "big demand." On the other hand, he cautions against excessive sponsorship. By the time every institution owns a stock, he says, it may already be too late to make big profits.
- **Market Direction** Of course, market direction is an important factor. The NASDAQ plunge pulled down many good stocks as well as flighty, speculative issues. Don't swim against the tide. Don't spit into the wind. You get the picture.

To a certain extent, that is the approach I've taken in selecting the stocks in this book, focusing primarily on annual earnings growth and leadership. What the reader will want to consider is current quarterly earnings growth, any news concerning the company, and perhaps market direction. It was pretty obvious what direction parts of the technology market were taking in the last two years, and people bucked the market at their peril. Like the old Bobby Fuller Four song says, "I Fought the Law and the Law Won." If you fight the market, the market will win.

Sell Right

Science and technology stocks can be among the fastest growing and also the most volatile stocks on the market. Consequently, it is worth having a selling plan in place to forestall severe losses (or the vaporization of your paper profits).

An excellent book on the subject is Donald Cassidy's *It's When You Sell That Counts*. A senior analyst with Lipper Analytical Services, he has years of experience observing and working in the markets. His most intriguing argument for having a selling plan is that holding a stock should be an active and not a passive decision. The buy-and-hold philosophy says pick a good stock, buy it, and forget about it. But as Mr. Cassidy points out, even the most stalwart stock may falter at some point. Fundamentals change. Sometimes these are broad fundamentals, such as the changing nature of the economy. Sometimes these are fundamentals within an industry or even a specific company.

Consider the Dow Jones Industrial Average, the venerable measure of stock market performance launched by Charles Dow on May 26, 1896. It started with 12 stocks considered to be solid and representative of the broad market at the time. The Dow Jones Company says that in selecting stocks for the average, it looks "among substantial industrial companies with a history of successful growth and wide interest among investors." It is not a current hot stock list, as the listings are changed infrequently; the aim is "stability of composition."

The Dow was increased to 20 stocks in 1916 and to 30 stocks in 1928, the number it has stayed at ever since. But the same 30? No. In fact, only one stock in the current Dow has been around since 1896—General Electric. Several companies have been removed at some point and later reinstated. GE was removed and reinstated twice before 1928. U.S. Rubber, DuPont, and IBM are others that have been on the list more than once, with IBM removed in 1939 and not rejoining the index until 40 years later. Mr. Cassidy reports that half of the components of the Dow have changed since 1961. The most recent changes were in 1999 when Union Carbide, Sears Roebuck, Goodyear, and Chevron were removed in favour of Home Depot, Intel, Microsoft, and SBC Communications. The point is that these companies, supposedly the most stable and successful in the U.S., are constantly changing. In other words, even the Dow doesn't hold its stocks forever.

A buy-and-hold strategy is particularly problematic in the constantly changing world of technology. Consider the seven largest computer companies in 1984, when the industry was in its youth. Only IBM remains intact, though it underwent some painful problems, including a long-running antitrust battle and the transition from large mainframes to PCs. This supposedly unstoppable dynamo of a stock at one point took a 75 percent hit on its share price. The other six—Burroughs, Sperry, NCR, Digital Equipment, Honeywell, and Control Data—either merged, were taken over by other companies, or changed the nature of their business. All are considered minor players today.

So what selling strategies should the science and technology investor have in place? That depends on the nature of the company and current market conditions, but here are a few suggestions:

- If the stock doubles, consider selling half, particularly if the stock is more speculative. At the same time, you don't want to lose out on potential future gains. So consider this option in conjunction with other factors.
- Sell when fundamentals falter. If a previously profitable company comes in with a bad earnings report or sales are dropping off, put

yourself on alert. If it comes in with a second poor showing, sell if you haven't already done so.
- Sell when trends shift. This was a good tip when the NASDAQ started faltering. Market indices are trend indicators. Some stocks can buck a trend, but beware and be prepared.
- Watch for a blow-off top. Sometimes stocks will experience a sudden and dramatic upswing in price. This is often unsustainable and you may want to be nimble and take quick profits. Then, if the stock still exhibits the fundamentals that made you buy it in the first place, buy back after it drops down in price again.
- Cut your losses short. The full saying is "Cut your losses short and let your winners run," or in other words, set a point below which you will not tolerate further losses. The editors of the Cabot Market Letter, who specialize in growth stocks and use a combination of momentum and fundamentals to select their stocks, recommend selling if any stock gives you a 15 to 20 percent loss. Others recommend a 10 percent limit. But another excellent suggestion is discussed below.

Channel Surfing for Fun and Profit

We're not talking about sitting in front of the tube like a couch potato here. We're talking about stock chart channels. In *It's When You Sell That Counts*, Mr. Cassidy notes that stock prices don't move in a straight line. They go up. They go down. They go up again. On a graph, a stock price makes a zigzag pattern, which trends generally upwards (ideally) or downwards.

Mr. Cassidy does not like the idea of setting some arbitrary point at which to cut your losses based on your purchase price. Rather, he says you should note the stock's recent history. As long as its zigzagging prices stay roughly within the parameters of its channel—its general trend—you should hold on to it. When it clearly breaches the channel, in either direction, you should be prepared for the possibility of selling. If the channel is breached on the upside by a sharp spike accompanied by heavy volume, you are witnessing a possible blow-off top and should consider selling. If the channel is breached on the downside, note any previous resistance points and watch to see if they are breached as well. If so, sell.

For example, Calpine is one of the stocks recommended in this book. I became so enamoured of the stock when I first wrote about it for last year's book that I bought some, just as it neared the top of an up-channel. When the stock fell, I didn't heed my own advice because I got trapped in a common error investors make—don't fall in love with your stock! Calpine is growing at a tremendous rate. There was a huge energy crisis in California. How could it lose? Or so I reasoned. So I bought some more after it had fallen well below the sell point. And it fell further!

If I had followed my own advice, I would have sold the stock when it broke below its trend lines and kept the money on the sidelines waiting for a good buying opportunity (since I still liked the company's story and its fundamentals). I would then have had more stock to profit from when the stock price recovered. The stock has fallen a lot further since last year, caught up in Enronitis as are a lot of energy companies. Nevertheless, it continues to grow revenues and earnings and I've included it again in this book for that reason. (I did sell eventually, bought back when it started moving up again, and sold again on another downswing, making money along the way.)

The House Advantage

Imagine if you could wander into a Las Vegas casino and win or break even 70 percent of the time. And imagine that your average win on all your bets including the losers is 6 percent. Would that be a good deal? You bet it would be!

But, in fact, we don't get such odds in Las Vegas. The casinos have what is called a house advantage. That means that over the long run, the casino always comes out ahead.

According to The Good Gambling Guide (a website at www.thegoodgamblingguide.co.uk) the edge varies from game to game. Here are some house advantages for a variety of games:

- **Roulette** 1.35 percent to 5.26 percent
- **Blackjack** around 1 percent
- **Casino Stud Poker** 2.5 percent
- **Craps** 0.7 percent to 16 percent
- **Progressive Poker** 3.45 percent

The house, in fact, actually pulls in more than that. The house advantage applies to the most conservative betting strategy. When gamblers play long shots, the house advantage increases considerably.

In any event, given the best odds for a player, the house wins 50.7 percent of the time in the most conservative game with the lowest edge—craps.

Many people think of the stock market as a crap shoot—especially in the last two years. And many have been turned off by investing as a result. But you can, in fact, invest in such a way that you have better-than-even odds of winning.

There are, in fact, a number of winning strategies, some outlined in the CANSLIM strategy noted earlier. Others are investing in undervalued stocks à la Warren Buffett. But we're going to look at just one strategy that will give you a winning investment 70 percent of the time.

One of the things Mr. O'Neil notes in his CANSLIM strategy is the positive effect that leadership has on a stock's future prospects. Stocks, like physical objects, tend to conserve momentum. They tend to keep going in the same direction unless acted upon by some outside force, usually a change in the profit picture or revenue prospects.

To measure leadership, O'Neil created a new stock market statistic that he called "relative strength." The measure is a percentile score, like those on SAT tests: A relative strength of 90 indicates the stock is outperforming 90 percent of the other stocks in the market. Mr. O'Neil publishes relative strength numbers for all stocks on the major American markets every week in *Investors Business Daily*.

Such data for Canadian stocks, however, is hard to come by. In fact, it was unknown until I started publishing the relative strength (RS) numbers for the top 500 stocks on the TSX every month-end on my Break Out Report website (www.breakoutreport.com).

In the first quarter of 2002 I decided to investigate what sort of predictive power relative strength has for stocks on the Toronto Stock Exchange. The Top 500 stocks that I chart each month make up about 30 percent of the approximately 1,725 securities listed. This gives them an RS score of around 71 or better, the area recommended by Mr. O'Neil for investors to focus on.

I took the Top 500 stocks for three dates—December 31, 2001, January 31, 2002, and February 28, 2002 and went back to see how the stocks performed over the ensuing month. The results were quite fascinating.

In creating my monthly charts, I list the stock, its symbol, its price at month-end, its RS, and its change in RS from the month before. In preparing my retrospectives, I divided the stocks into groups based on their change in relative strength for the date in question.

Here's an example. On December 31, 2001, BW Technologies, one of our *50 Best*, was the 33rd-best-performing stock for the preceding year. It had an RS of 98.07 (1,712 securities listed minus 33 = 1,679, which divided by 1,712 and multiplied by 100 gives us our RS score of 98.07). The month before it had an RS of 96.54, for a change of 1.53.

For the three months, the turnover of stocks making the Top 500 varied from 77 on February 28, 2002 to a high of 95 on December 31, 2001. New stocks to the Top 500 did not have a change in RS listed because I did not record the RS for every stock the month before, just the Top 500. So "New" was a separate category.

The table below summarizes the average growth for stocks on the Top 500 list for various RS changes for the following month.

RS Change	Dec. 31, 2001	Jan. 31, 2002	Feb. 28, 2002
New	8.91%	7.65%	8.01%
>5	8.33%	8.89%	9.37%
0 to 5	5.72%	5.25%	8.36%
-5 to 0	4.25%	4.91%	5.82%
<-5	5.33%	2.33%	5.46%
All	6.03%	5.71%	7.16%

Note that the Top 500 stocks on the TSX at December 31, 2001 increased by an average of 6.03 percent in the following month. The Top 500 for January 31 increased by 5.71 percent, while the Top 500 for February 28 increased by 7.16 percent.

Moreover, although not shown in the table, I also calculated the percentage of stocks in each category showing a profit. For all the stocks, the success probability ranged from a low of 58.4 percent to a high of 67.4 percent.

Further interesting results are that, despite occasional deviations, the greater the change in relative strength, the greater the average change in stock value. In our table above, stocks in the Top 500 that had increased in RS by five points or more went up anywhere from 8.33 percent to 9.37 percent. Stocks that were new to the Top 500 did almost as well. The success ratio was higher as well, ranging from 61.9 percent to 70.2 percent.

A good number of the stocks each month had no change, and looking at the combined profitable and break-even stocks to get a no-loss ratio we found that there was a 68.6 percent to 73.6 percent chance of breaking even or better on any particular stock in the Top 500.

While three months is not a strong enough sample to draw general conclusions from, it should be noted that these samples covered months when the general market was flat or in a downtrend. It is likely that further studies will show that the pattern continues for most and perhaps all months.

If the theory is correct, then an investor with enough resources to invest in 500 different securities could average 5 percent to 7 percent return each month by staying invested in just the Top 500 and rotating out of stocks leaving the list and into new stocks making the list each month. Compounded, that's a return of anywhere from 80 percent to 125 percent a year, far outperforming the average Canadian equity mutual fund.

I also looked at the three-month performance for the Top 500 stocks on December 31, 2001 and January 31, 2002. The interesting thing here was that the longer time frame brought in a respectable average return of 22.53 percent for all the December 31 stocks and 17.22 percent for all January 31 stocks. But even more interesting was that the probability of success increased to 72.4 percent and 72.6 percent, respectively. The no-loss ratio increased to 79.0 percent and 77.8 percent, respectively.

In the three-month studies, the success ratio for stocks with an RS change greater than 5 was 74.5 percent and 84.3 percent. The no-loss ratio topped 80 percent in both periods. And the average gain for those stocks was 26.14 percent and 23.72 percent, respectively.

Imagine working Las Vegas with such odds! Now that's what I call a House Advantage! (I intend to do more extensive studies covering a wider range of cases and variables, perhaps publishing the results in a book within the next year or two.)

Through a Glass, Brightly

Science and technology is a fascinating subject. The world is changing faster now than ever before. Who would have thought 35 years ago that in 15 years you would be able to telephone your spouse from your car? Who would have thought 15 years ago that in five years you'd be able to transmit written messages live over a new invention called the Internet? Who would have thought five years ago that in two years you'd be able to download all your favourite music from when you were a kid? Who would have thought two years ago that…? Your guess is as good as mine.

Richard McGinn, former CEO of Lucent Technologies said, "You either move with speed or die. It's the converse of 'speed kills.'" Lucent didn't move fast enough to keep pace with Nortel, and it's dying. McGinn no longer works there. And we're not 100 percent sure about Nortel. How can you, a regular investor, keep up with it all? The answer is, you can't. That said, there are some broad trends that investors can consider in making investment decisions.

- **Security** In the wake of 9/11 there has been a strong interest in security and related technologies. Such things as facial recognition technology, surveillance cameras, and military hardware are all experiencing a resurgence. Stocks in our book that could benefit include Dalsa Corporation, Silent Witness, Check Point Software, and Aeroflex.
- **Convergence** This theme of technology guru Nicholas Negroponte is slowly becoming reality—more slowly than many, including myself, anticipated. Two of last year's picks were chosen because of the promise of convergence—AOL Time Warner and BCE Inc. Both have been dropped this year as the promises have not come to fruition and it looks like it may be a few years yet before they do. But we added Scientific-Atlanta, a company growing revenues and earnings in this field. And outsourcer Cygnal Technologies may also be a beneficiary. Neither broke the bank trying to capitalize on this market through mergers or diversification (or as Peter Lynch calls it, diworsification). Both focused on and expanded their expertise—a winning strategy in today's tough market.
- **Outsourcing** In an increasingly competitive world, companies are trying to cut costs while maintaining quality in production. The result is that they are focusing on their core competencies and outsourcing the rest. For example, in June 2001, Laurentian Bank decided to outsource its IT functions to CGI Group.

Laurentian's core competency is banking. Why maintain an extensive IT department when CGI can do it better and more cheaply? So look for companies that provide services to companies that are outsourcing. Others included among the *50 Best* are Patheon, Trican Well Services, Magna International, and Tesma International.

- **The Internet** Despite the demise of many dot-coms, the Internet will become increasingly important in the years ahead, particularly in business. Look for companies that are facilitating e-commerce in particular, such as Siebel, Cognos, or Mercury Interactive, all included in this book.
- **Nanotechnology** Things will get smaller and smaller. Flatbed computer screens and television screens will become common. Companies involved in video technology that are featured in this book include Gennum Corporation, Dalsa Corporation and Silent Witness.
- **Energy** U.S. consumption of electricity is growing by 3 percent a year, and energy will be a growth industry in all its facets in the years to come. Power companies and technical support services for resource companies will continue to be in high demand. And environmental concerns will continue to fuel demand for alternative energy technology. You will find some great companies in the Energy section such as Calpine and Canadian Hydro Developers.
- **Medical breakthroughs** An aging population will place even more demands on our health care system. There will be increasing urgency to develop cures for diseases associated with aging. Seek out pharmaceutical companies with established products and large research and development budgets, as well as medical outsourcing companies, all of which you will find in the expanded Biology, Medicine, and Environment section.

To keep up with future trends and ideas, here are a few handy on-line resources:

- The Future File (www.futurefile.com): Canadian broadcaster and futurist Tod Maffin's website
- Dr. Tomorrow (www.drtomorrow.com): Another Canadian futurist, Frank Ogden
- Canadian Biotech News (www.canadianbiotechnews.com)
- MIT Technology Review (www.technologyreview.com)
- Red Herring (www.redherring.com)
- Wired (www.wired.com)

Using the Internet to Research a Stock

The overviews in this book are short—500 to 625 words each. I've tried to make them interesting and informative, but it is difficult to do a company justice in such a short space. The historical financial data in each profile will be difficult to find anywhere else, but before you invest, you will also want a sense of the current state of the company. If my discussion gives you an interest in a particular stock, check it out further.

Nearly all the research for this book was done online using the Internet. It is an impressive resource, but using it effectively can be a challenge. Company websites are listed in each *50 Best* profile so that you can read further about the company's business and management. Many corporate websites have two-page fact sheets that offer a quick overview. Then go to the Investors or Financials section and download the most recent annual report. Nearly every company now has its annual report available online in PDF format, often several years' worth. Some corporate sites also include analyst reports. If so, check them out. Corporate websites are usually the best sources for in-depth studies, but their quality does vary.

General investing websites such as Globeinvestor.com and Advice for Investors are excellent for quick and easy access to key information. Let me conclude with a list of handy websites you can use to do your own research. Go to town. Have fun.

General Resources

- The Break Out Report (www.breakoutreport.com): My own website, which links to all the resources below.
- Globeinvestor.com (www.globeinvestor.com): The best all-around investing website for Canadians. You can check out company profiles, three-year performance statistics, and stock charts. The News section for each stock features headlines, including recent quarterly reports where you can check how a company is doing in the short term. And you can keep up with such things as option chains and institutional ownership with the fee-based GlobeinvestorGOLD.
- Equity Research Center (www.equityresearchcenter.com): This excellent site focuses specifically on Canadian technology stocks.
- Advice for Investors (www.adviceforinvestors.com): Formerly called Carlson Online, this site includes links to news from the major wire services, to Sedar profiles and documents, and to company websites. Again, this site has lots of useful information for free, as well as premium fee-based services.
- Sedar (www.sedar.com): The government's corporate document database, Sedar is the repository for all mandatory company filings, including annual reports.
- Toronto Stock Exchange (www.tsx.ca): The TSX is a superb website with many useful resources.
- Big Charts (www.bigcharts.com): The best site for historical pricing information—use the prefix CA: for Canadian stocks.
- Technology Review (www.technologyreview.com): This magazine from MIT includes a patent scorecard as well as an annual listing of the top innovators under 35.
- Canadian Shareowner (www.shareowner.com): Home of the Stock Study Guide, a subscription service.
- Online Investor Toolbox (me.investortoolbox.com/welcome.html): This is a subscription website that provides perhaps the best technical analysis tools available today.

Stock Lists
- Re$earch Infosource (www.researchinfosource.com): Lists the top 100 companies for R&D spending in Canada.
- Fast 50 (www.deloitte.ca/en/Industries/techcomm/fast50/winners02.asp)
- Fast 500 (www.public.deloitte.com/fast500/index.shtm)
- Branham 300 (www.branham.ca/branham300/index.php)
- Profit 100 (www.profitguide.com/profit100)
- Fortune 100 (www.fortune.com): Select 100 Fastest-Growing under Companies.
- T-Net 100 (www.bctechnology.com/frameset_tnet100.html)
- Alberta's Fastest Growing Companies (www.albertaventure.com/best)
- Top 500 Stocks on the TSX (www.breakoutreport.com/relstrength/blrs1.htm): My own monthly compilation of the Top 500 stocks for one year performance arranged both sequentially and alphabetically.

Newsletters
- The Successful Investor (www.thesuccessfulinvestor.com)
- The FutureStock Review (www.keystocks.com)
- The Cabot Market Letter (www.cabot.net)
- Canadian Biotech News (www.canadianbiotechnews.com)
- Hager Technology Research (www.fredhager.com)
- The Break Out Report (www.breakoutreport.com)

How the Book Is Arranged

You'll find the stocks in this book arranged by broad market sector: Biology, Medicine, and Environment; Energy and Resources; Industry; Information Technology; and Telecommunications. The number of stocks in each varies from a low of six in the Energy and Telecommunications sections to a high of 15 in the Industry section.

Each profile begins with the basic facts about the company and its management. A short table gives the stock a rating of up to five stars on each of three measurable growth criteria: revenue, EPS, and share price. Here's how the star ratings were assigned: The minimum average growth rates for inclusion in the book were 5 percent annual revenue growth, 5 percent annual EPS growth, and 10 percent annual share price growth over the last 10 years. Using my trusty spreadsheet program, I calculated that 5 percent annual growth for 10 years was equivalent to a total 62.89 percent increase. Ten percent meant 159.4 percent cumulative change. Fifteen percent annually translated to 304.6 percent, 20 percent to 519.2 percent, and 25 percent to 831.3 percent.

Since we're looking for big growth with science and technology, I decided that achieving 5 percent growth in any category warranted one star; 10 percent, two stars; 15 percent, three stars; 20 percent, four stars; and 25 percent, five stars. Then I calculated the percentage increases from 10 years ago to the most recent complete fiscal year and awarded stars accordingly. For younger companies with less than 10 years' history, I used the data from the first available year as the starting point. So a six-year-old company with three stars in, say, revenue growth, actually grew at significantly greater than 15 percent annual growth to achieve an increase of 304.6 percent in its sales. This balanced out the fact that companies often grow much faster in their early years with the lack of a longer track record. The number of stars for revenue, EPS, and share price growth were then added to get an overall star rating.

Following the ratings table is general company background, followed by two sections. "Opportunities and Challenges" looks at the reasons I expect the stock to grow and discusses any negatives facing the company that may add risk to the investment. For stocks that were in last year's book, I moved some of the opportunities information to the profile and updated the opportunities section with an update on the news of the last year. "Financial Highlights" identifies the more important developments reflected in the financial table that closes the profile and shows a company's results over the past 10 years.

About Me

In 1997, I became the guide for Investing: Canada at About.com, the sixth most popular web portal in North America, according to Media Metrix. About.com (then called the Mining Company, with the slogan, "We mine the Net so you don't have to") asked me to cover the entire gamut of investing for Canadians rather than just mutual funds, which was my primary interest at the time. That sounded like a pretty tall order, but I was game, passed their trials, and managed the Investing: Canada site until September 2001 when the company laid off 300 of its guides in a cost-cutting reorganization. (It was, after all, a dot-com and bleeding red ink.) That included nearly all the Canadian topic sites including mine.

Over the years at About, I came to prefer stock investing and have read extensively on the subject. During the Internet boom, I created a Canadian Internet Index and profiled many Canadian Internet stocks. Then I started profiling stocks that had hit new highs and were generating solid earnings growth. My former About.com website was re-launched as The Break Out Report (www.breakoutreport.com) in January 2002.

I have no professional connection with any brokerage house or vested interest relating to the stocks reviewed in this book. However, I may own, may have owned, or may own any of them in the future.

Philosophically, I am a hard-core fan of capitalism and its blessings. While preparing this book, I became filled with awe and admiration for the achievements of the people behind these companies—people like J. Armande Bombardier, who loved machines and tinkered in his shop to invent the snowmobile; Robert Noyce and Gordon Moore, who followed their vision and made the modern world of computers possible; Serge Godin and André Imbeau, who turned a small Quebec City business consultancy into a billion-dollar powerhouse; Bill Gates, who dropped out of university to develop Microsoft; Klaus Woerner, who immigrated to Canada and started ATS Automation Tooling Systems; and Frank Stronach, who turned a small machine shop into a multi-billion-dollar automotive empire. There are many, many more.

I was a university student in the late 1960s when self-styled revolutionaries were setting fires on campuses, rioting, and hoping to change the world. But the world has been changed as much if not more by technology and the products and services it enables. In 1974, when the microprocessor was just beginning to have an impact, Intel founder Gordon Moore said, "I'd like to think that we're the real revolutionaries in the world. Things are being revolutionized a lot more by electronics technology than by some political things going on."

So read on about the true revolutionaries. Enjoy.

BIOLOGY, MEDICINE, & ENVIRONMENT

Biomedicine
Patheon Inc.
MDS Inc.
ArthroCare Corporation
Canadian Medical Laboratories Ltd.

Environment
Bennett Environmental Inc.
Zenon Environmental Inc.

Medicine
Biovail Corporation
Forest Laboratories, Inc.
Taro Pharmaceuticals Industries Ltd.
Axcan Pharma Inc.
Cangene Corporation
Paladin Laboratories Inc.
Pfizer Inc.
Merck & Company, Inc.

PATHEON INC.

2100 Syntex Court
Mississauga, ON L5N 7K9

Tel: (905) 821-4001
Fax: (905) 812-6705
www.patheon.com
Symbol: PTI (TSX)

Employees: 2,700
Founded: 1974
Listed: 1981

Chairperson: Peter A. W. Green
President and COO: Nick DiPietro
CEO and CFO: Robert C. Tedford

Share Price Growth	★ ★ ★ ★ ★
Revenue Growth	★ ★ ★ ★ ★
EPS Growth	★ ★ ★
CREE	**13**

About the Company

Patheon provides manufacturing and contract research facilities for the pharmaceutical and biotechnology industries. This includes specialized manufacturing capabilities, formulation development, analytical services, and clinical trial development, as well as commercial manufacturing. In fact, the company manufactures over 600 products ranging from over-the-counter medications to all formulations of prescription drugs, including topical creams, pills, liquids, and injectables.

With six plants in Ontario and four in Europe, the company serves over 100 clients, including 15 of the 20 largest pharmaceutical companies in the world. This impressive client list includes such giants as

Hoffman-La Roche, GlaxoSmithKline, Bristol-Myers Squibb, Johnson & Johnson, Bayer, Amgen, Novartis, Aventis, and Pfizer.

The company has a long history, founded in 1974 in Fort Erie, Ontario, it expanded operations to Burlington in 1982 and started serving the U.S. market in 1990. Since then, the company has grown internally and through acquisition, buying manufacturing facilities from Upjohn Canada, Hoffman La Roche in both Canada and Italy, and Hoechst Marion Roussel in both Britain and France. These takeovers invariably included long-term contracts to continue manufacturing products for the companies selling their plants.

The company's goal is to become the dominant player in pharmaceutical outsourcing. It was ranked 40th out of 500 companies in *Canadian Business* magazine's Investor 500 list published in July 2001.

Opportunities and Challenges

Drugs representing over 50 percent of pharmaceutical sales are coming off patent in the next few years. This is putting intense pressure on leading drug companies to focus on research and development of new products. With the cost of such research averaging over US$600 million per drug, these companies are looking for ways to cut costs by focusing on R&D and marketing. Enter outsourcing. The American market for outsourced drug manufacturing, in fact, is growing at 10 to 12 percent a year.

On top of that, the number of biotechnology companies has doubled in the last five years. These companies are research-focused and looking for ways to bring their products to market without expensive outlays for manufacturing facilities. The solution? Again it is outsourcing.

The company's expansion continues apace with the opening of a new laboratory and expanded warehouse in Toronto in January 2002 and the acquisition of a 144,000-square-foot facility in Ferentino, Italy in February 2002. This plant focuses on a process called lyophilization, which is the freeze-drying of sterile injectable products that are unstable in liquid form. The company plans to double the plant's capacity and become fully operational in the first quarter of 2003.

As with outsourcing companies in the electronics arena (such as Celestica and Solectron), Patheon's success depends on the health and success of its clients. Much of Patheon's growth was fuelled by the acquisition of plants from companies that are now its customers.

Financial Highlights

Patheon's revenues grew by 24.8 percent in fiscal 2001 with earnings per share growing 9.3 percent. The first three quarters of fiscal 2002 showed continued growth with revenues up 38.2 percent and earnings per share up 71.0 percent. Gross earnings were up even more, but a new share issue increased the float by 8 percent, decreasing the EPS figure. The stock was flat for most of 2001 before nosediving in September. Post 9/11, the stock has risen steadily to $13 in mid-April 2002 from a low of around $8.

Value investor Jonathan Wellum of AIC Diversified Canada Fund reported in June 2001 that he had added Patheon to his Fund's portfolio as a solid pick in a weak economy, with potential for growth on economic recovery. He also sees it as a potential takeover candidate. The fund continues to hold an interest in the company.

The solid revenue growth for 2001 saw a star added to our ratings over last year.

Patheon Inc. at a Glance

Fiscal Year-end: October
7-Year Return: 49.3%

	1997	1998	1999	2000	2001	7-Year Growth Average (%)	7-Year Growth Total (%)
Revenue ($ mlns.)	50.7	70.5	127.4	256.3	319.9	49.2	878.5
Net Income ($ mlns.)	2.4	4.0	7.3	13.6	16.3	54.0	1,086.1
Earnings/ Share ($)	0.07	0.12	0.18	0.30	0.33	39.1	450.0
Dividend/ Share ($)	0.00	0.00	0.00	0.00	0.00	–	–
Price/ Earnings	18.6 - 40.0	16.3 - 28.2	15.6 - 66.4	21.2 - 56.2	23.0 - 49.5	–	–

Table data courtesy of  www.shareowner.com

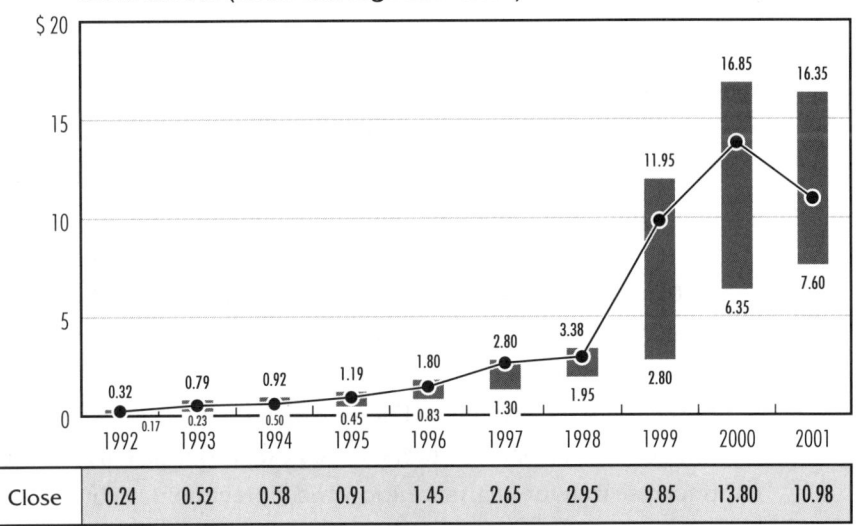

MDS INC.

100 International Boulevard
Toronto, ON M9W 6J6

Tel: (416) 675-7661
Fax: (416) 675-0688
www.mdsintl.com
Symbol: MDS (TSX) (Also MDZ-NYSE)

Employees: 10,376
Founded: 1969
Listed: 1973

Chairperson: Wilfred G. Lewitt
President and CEO: John A. Rogers

Share Price Growth	★ ★ ★
Revenue Growth	★ ★ ★
EPS Growth	★ ★
MDS	**8**

About the Company

MDS Inc. is an international health and life sciences company employing over 10,000 people in more than 20 countries. The health side of the business provides products and services to the health-care industry, such as diagnostic services, managing hospital laboratories as joint ventures, distribution of medical supplies, distribution of emergency medical products, and manufacture of anesthesia equipment for dental and veterinary use.

On the life sciences side, MDS is involved in providing technology and services to manufacturers of medical products. This includes contract research for pharmaceutical and biotechnology companies, sterilization services, the manufacture of specialized analytical instruments, nuclear isotopes for use in diagnostic imaging (MDS is the world's leading supplier of radioisotopes), and products and systems for radiation therapy. MDS's newest venture, launched in 2000, is proteomics research, the study of protein structures for the development of diagnostic tests and new drugs.

In the 30 years of its existence, MDS has grown from offering laboratory services in Canada into a world leader in medical supplies and services, with over 60 percent of its business outside Canada. Expansion has been through internal growth and through acquisitions. The half-billion-dollar acquisition of Phoenix International Life Sciences in 2000 made MDS the third-largest contract research organization in the world. The acquisition has been integrated into MDS Pharma Services.

The company also owns 47 percent of MDS Capital Corporation, a venture capital company that manages a number of public and private investment funds, including the labour-sponsored Canadian Medical Discoveries Fund.

MDS has been listed on the Toronto Stock Exchange since 1973 and was listed on the New York Stock Exchange in 2000.

Opportunities and Challenges

MDS's proprietary AutoLab testing system has increased its efficiency and been a strong element in forging joint ventures to manage hospital laboratories on a contract basis. There are more than 8,000 hospital-based laboratories in the U.S., providing 56 percent of all the diagnostic work done. AutoLab gives MDS the leverage to develop joint ventures in this US$20-billion market—and the company has barely scratched the surface.

The new Proteomics Division is a bold venture into a field in its infancy. MDS's specialized spectrometry instrumentation, among other things, has excited joint venture partners such as the research department of Mt. Sinai Hospital in Toronto. Like the human genome project, proteomics may shed new light on the nature of disease and potential cures.

In 2001, we saw this new division form strategic alliances with Agilent Technologies, IBM Life Sciences, and Abgenix, aimed respectively at development of new research technologies, bioinformation systems, and antibody drugs.

MDS Nordion, the radioisotope division of the company, is building a new cyclotron in Vancouver to meet increasing demand for therapeutic radioisotopes. This will double current capacity at its Vancouver site and is slated to be operational in January 2003.

Financial Highlights

MDS's revenues grew 13.2 percent in 2001, but earnings took a beating, dropping 39.5 percent. The company's core businesses improved both revenues and earnings, but earnings per share were down due to dilution of shares, as new shares were issued in the acquisition of Phoenix International Life Sciences. The new Proteomics section sustained heavy losses in its initial year, reducing overall earnings. But as the company put in its 2001 annual report, "In fiscal 2001, we built a foundation for future growth."

MDS's share price was flat from 1997 through 1999, then took off from $14 to hit a peak of $32 in September 2000. The stock then plunged to almost $16 in June 2001 due to disappointing earnings. But since July 2001, the stock has been in a sustained though volatile uptrend. This trend should continue as the company grows its established divisions and the Proteomics division starts to show results.

Nevertheless, the 10-year performance of the stock declined, dropping it two stars in our ratings.

MDS Inc. at a Glance

Fiscal Year-end: October
10-Year Return: 16.8%

	1997	1998	1999	2000	2001	10-Year Growth Average (%)	10-Year Growth Total (%)
Revenue ($ mlns.)	930.0	1,001.5	1,191.7	1,444.9	1,636.0	16.1	267.8
Net Income ($ mlns.)	64.9	71.8	85.6	89.6	30.7	11.4	52.5
Earnings/ Share ($)	0.58	0.64	0.74	0.70	0.22	8.0	10.0
Dividend/ Share ($)	0.06	0.06	0.07	0.12	0.09	12.0	125.0
Price/ Earnings	16.1 - 30.8	18.8 - 27.0	18.6 - 23.5	18.8 - 46.3	73.2 - 137.5	–	–

Table data courtesy of Canadian Shareowner www.shareowner.com

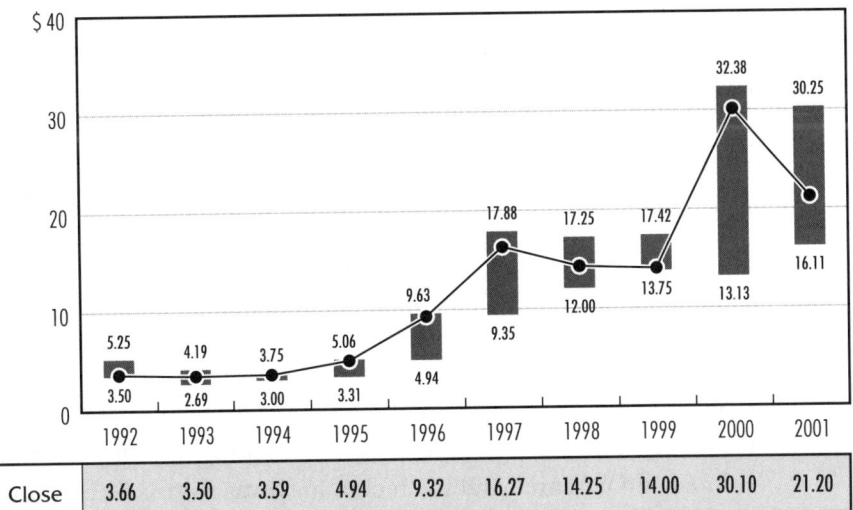

Stock Growth (Fiscal Year High-Low-Close)

| Close | 3.66 | 3.50 | 3.59 | 4.94 | 9.32 | 16.27 | 14.25 | 14.00 | 30.10 | 21.20 |

ARTHROCARE CORPORATION

680 Vaqueros Avenue
Sunnyvale, CA 94085-3523

Tel: (408) 736-0224
Fax: (408) 736-0226
www.arthrocare.com
Symbol: ARTC (NYSE)

Employees: 272
Founded: 1993
Listed: 1996

President and CEO: Michael A. Baker

Share Price Growth	★
Revenue Growth	★ ★ ★ ★ ★
EPS Growth	★
ARTC	**7**

About the Company

ArthroCare, a surgical supply company in Sunnyvale, California, was set up to develop new tools for cardiovascular surgery, but the company's founders made an interesting discovery. Electrical impulses behaved differently when sent through a conductive solution than in the non-conductive environment used by traditional electro-surgical tools.

The old method of electro-surgical tissue removal involved heating tissue to temperatures approaching 400° C, causing it to literally explode or vaporize. This often caused heat damage to surrounding tissue. ArthroCare developed a new method using ionized plasma to disintegrate targeted tissue electro-chemically. This discovery was refined and patented and the technology was named Coblation, a contraction of "cool ablation" (ablation is the technical term for surgical tissue removal). Coblation was found to be particularly useful for surgery on joints, or arthroscopic surgery.

In March 1995, the FDA cleared the company to market its arthroscopic system, and the first products were shipped in August that year. The company now has 20 U.S. and 16 international patents on its system and has found other uses for it. These include spinal surgery, cosmetic surgery, and ear, nose, and throat (ENT) surgery.

ArthroCare was the 34th fastest growing company on Fortune Magazine's Top 100 Growth Companies list published in August 2002.

Opportunities and Challenges

The company believes that Coblation can replace the multiple tools traditionally used in soft tissue surgery with one handy multi-purpose system. The Coblation process is sold as a controller unit with attachable and disposable tools designed for specific purposes.

ArthroCare is continually exploring new avenues of development, introducing a specialized tool for delicate knee surgery and another for head, neck, and ENT surgery in the first quarter of 2001. The company is also working with Boston Scientific to develop Coblation surgical tools for myocardial revascularization, a promising new treatment for heart disease.

In June 2001, the FDA approved the company's Perc-D line of tools for treating herniated discs. This was followed by approval for Coblation-assisted tonsillectomies in August. And in October 2001, the company received approval to market a tool kit known as the Plasma Forceps™ for general surgery procedures, including laparoscopic surgery and endoscopic gynecology. Laparoscopic surgery is a minimally invasive procedure that involves inserting the surgical tool and a small video camera into the body through a small incision, rather than the large conventional surgical cuts that damage skin and muscle. This opens a whole new area of possibilities for use of the Coblation technology.

ArthroCare markets Coblation through a network of distributors worldwide and has licensed Ethicon, a division of Johnson & Johnson, to use the technology for arthroscopy and gynecology. In February 2002 the company licensed ACMI to market products for urology treatments.

Also in 2001, the company began construction on a new manufacturing plant in Costa Rica and moved to establish a sales force in Germany. And in the first quarter of 2002, ArthroCare moved to new facilities. The new plant is expected to be operational in the second half of the year.

ArthroCare has a fascinating and unique product with tremendous potential. Its biggest challenges are to continue developing new uses for the technology and to market it effectively.

Financial Highlights

ArthroCare had losses for its first three years as a public company. However, we allowed this exception to our screening criteria because the progression has been from declining losses to increasing profits, and for a young medical services company this is not unusual. And its EPS more than doubled in 2000.

In 2001, revenues increased 23.2 percent, but earnings declined 36.8 percent. The first half of fiscal 2002 saw revenues up 4.6 percent, but EPS dropped to US$0.08 from US$0.23. This was partly the result of costs incurred with the move to its new location and investment in a direct sales force.

After surging to over US$79 during the technology explosion in 2000, ArthroCare dropped below US$12 in March 2001. The stock subsequently soared to $32 before falling back to below US$10 in June 2002. The stock was back up to $13 by September, and improving margins as the Costa Rican plant comes on stream should pave the way for new gains.

Despite the company's gains in revenue, we downgraded the rating for stock appreciation by two stars and for EPS growth by one star due to its anemic performance.

ArthoCare Corporation at a Glance

Fiscal Year-end: December
6-Year Return: 4%

	1997	1998	1999	2000	2001	7-Year Growth Average (%)	7-Year Growth Total (%)
Revenue (US$ mlns.)	12.8	27.9	48.7	67.6	83.3	504.9	38,121.1
Net Income (US$ mlns.)	-7.69	-2.14	5.5	15.8	10.1	–	–
Earnings/ Share (US$)	-0.44	-0.12	0.27	0.68	0.43	–	–
Dividend/ Share (US$)	0.00	0.00	0.00	0.00	0.00	–	–
Price/ Earnings	-6.0 - 16.8	-42.2 - -95.8	23.6 - 148.1	18.0 - 116.5	27.6 - 76.8	–	–

Table data courtesy of  www.shareowner.com

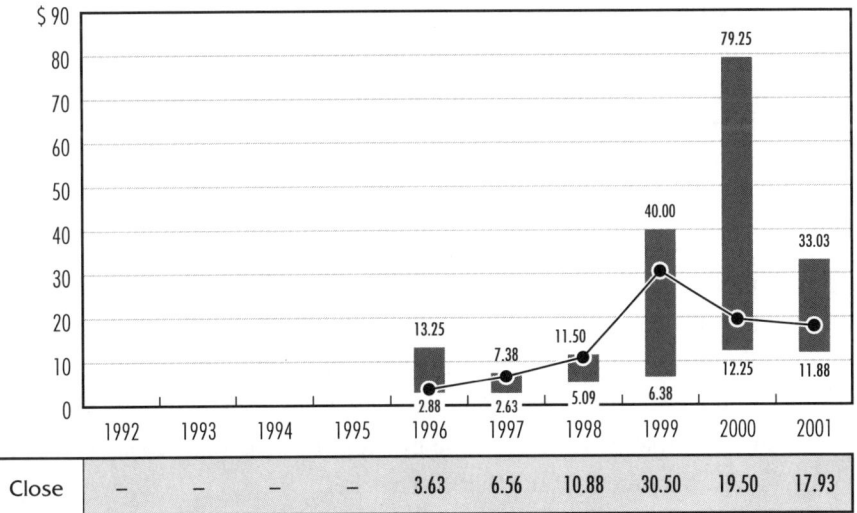

CANADIAN MEDICAL LABORATORIES LTD.

6560 Kennedy Road
Mississauga, ON L5T 2X4

Tel: (905) 565-0043
Fax: (905) 565-1776
www.canmedlab.com
Symbol: CLC (TSX)

Employees: 1,400
Founded: 1971
Incorporated: 1993
Listed: 1996

Chairperson, President, and CEO: John D. Mull, MD

Share Price Growth	★ ★ ★
Revenue Growth	★ ★
EPS Growth	★ ★
CLC	**7**

About the Company

Founded by a doctor to serve doctors, Canadian Medical Laboratories (CML) has grown from modest beginnings to become the largest medical testing laboratory business in Ontario, serving 20,000 to 30,000 patients daily through over 150 facilities. This growth included the acquisition of other laboratories such as Cybermedix Health Services, Excel Bestview, and Med-Chem Health Care. CML offers a complete range of testing services including histology, hematology, biochemistry, cytology, and microbiology. Combined, CML's lab facilities have over 30 percent of the Ontario market.

In 2000, CML launched a new subsidiary, Cipher Pharmaceuticals, to develop innovative new drugs. Their focus is to license drugs in late stages of development and carry them through regulatory approval and on to market.

And in November 2001, CML acquired DC DiagnostiCare, an Edmonton-based company that runs the largest network of non-hospital-based medical imaging clinics in Canada. This move gives the company a presence in the medical imaging market and affords the company the opportunity to leverage its core business to other provinces. Its 141 clinics in five provinces generate $70 million a year in sales.

Canadian Medical Labs has more than tripled annual revenues since 1996. It is consistently profitable, so much so that it actually knocked down $36 million of its long-term debt in fiscal 2000. A further $20 million was knocked off in fiscal 2001, reducing outstanding debt to just $43.9 million.

Opportunities and Challenges

The Cipher Pharmaceuticals subsidiary negotiated four licensing agreements with Galephar Pharmaceutical Research in 2001. It filed its first investigational new drug (IND) application for a lipid-lowering drug in late June 2001 and its second for an asthma treatment in October 2001. An IND for a once-a-day version of Tramadol was filed in January 2002. This all adds up to an auspicious start for a pharmaceutical company in its first year of operation.

The company's core diagnostic business stands to gain from outsourcing by hospitals as government cutbacks on health care force rationalization of services. The province of Ontario increased the cap on spending for diagnostic sources to provide such leeway. In fact, governments across Canada are looking for ways to control costs, and outsourcing of diagnostic testing and medical imaging could increase greatly over the next few years.

CML's attempts to consolidate the clinical research market through strategic acquisitions of Site Management Organizations (SMOs) have not been overly successful. SMOs organize and manage clinical trials for clinical researchers. CML is currently reviewing its options in the (SMO) market and withholding new investment. The SMO market in the U.S. may be abandoned altogether. Clinical research through subsidiary Pharma Medica is now expected to be a niche contributor and not a major contributor to the company's growth.

The challenge for Canadian Medical Laboratories is to leverage its acquisition of DC DiagnostiCare to expand its diagnostic services beyond Ontario. Growth of Cipher Pharmaceuticals will also be a key element in CML's growth plans. Currently the core diagnostic business contributes 84.8 percent of revenues.

Financial Highlights

Canadian Medical Laboratories' fiscal year to September 30, 2001 showed modest revenue growth of 1.3 percent and solid earnings growth of 10.9 percent. But things started to improve considerably in the first quarter of fiscal 2002, with revenues up 16.2 percent and earnings per share up a handsome 54.8 percent.

CML's stock had been trading in a narrow range between $18 to $20 from April to December 2001. Then it started to take off in a sustained growth path to $34 in late August 2002. Continued growth, if it can be achieved, should continue to be reflected in the stock price over the next few years. It is already reflected in the addition of a star for share price growth in our ratings.

Canadian Medical Laboratories Ltd. at a Glance

Fiscal Year-end: September
5-Year Return: 43.8%

	1997	1998	1999	2000	2001	6-Year Growth Average (%)	6-Year Growth Total (%)
Revenue ($ mlns.)	71.0	74.5	130.4	186.0	188.4	31.1	249.5
Net Income ($ mlns.)	7.1	11.3	23.5	32.8	35.4	45.8	470.6
Earnings/ Share ($)	0.46	0.58	1.16	1.54	1.68	42.0	265.2
Dividend/ Share ($)	–	–	–	–	–	–	–
Price/ Earnings	9.8 - 15.8	10.3 - 15.1	4.8 - 21.2	9.1 - 15.6	7.7 - 11.8	–	–

Table data courtesy of ✓Canadian Shareowner www.shareowner.com

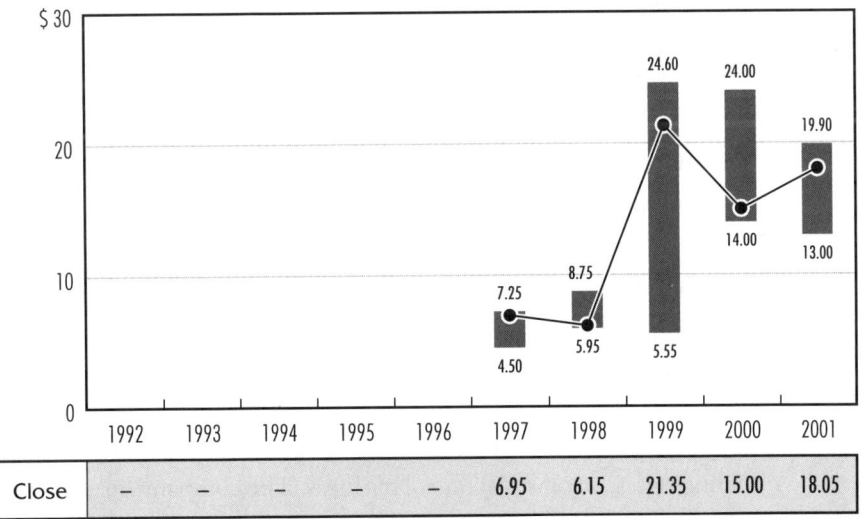

Stock Growth (Fiscal Year High-Low-Close)

* EPS growth figures based on five years. Data for the years 1996–97 from company reports.

BENNETT ENVIRONMENTAL INC.

1540 Cornwall Road, Suite 208
Oakville, ON L6J 7W5

Tel: (905) 339-1540
Fax: (905) 339-0016
www.bennettenv.com
Symbol: BEV (TSX) (Also BEL-AMEX, BEW-Frankfurt)

Employees: 50
Founded: 1993
Listed: 1999

Chairperson and CEO: John A. Bennett
President: Peter Richardson

Share Price Growth	★ ★ ★ ★
Revenue Growth	★ ★ ★
EPS Growth	★ ★ ★ ★ ★
BEV	**12**

About the Company

Environmental remediation may seem to be a relatively modern phenomenon, but Bennett Environmental and its various predecessors have, in fact, been engaged in the business for over 30 years. The company specializes in thermal treatment of hydrocarbon-contaminated soil, including chlorinated hydrocarbons such as PCBs, dioxins, and furans.

Bennett Environmental began in 1993 as an offshoot of Aqua Guard Technologies, an oil spill control business. The company operates one primary facility, the Récupère Sol Inc. plant in St. Ambroise, Quebec, established in 1996. Its Mark IV Thermal Oxidizer operates with 99.99999 percent efficiency. Contaminated soil goes in. Reusable soil comes out. The contaminated soils are incinerated at extremely high temperatures to separate, remove, and destroy the contaminants. Bennett is one of only two facilities permitted to treat PCB contaminated soils in Canada and is authorized to treat contaminated soil from the U.S.

The year 2000 saw Bennett's revenues drop drastically due to increased competition from landfills and inadequate marketing of its services. But the company addressed the problem, forging strategic alliances in August and September that year with Onyx Environmental Services, a subsidiary of the French company Vivendi, and IT Corporation, one of the largest site remediation companies in the U.S. This gave Bennett access to a large U.S. sales network as well as a five-year contract to handle a minimum tonnage of soil remediation contract work.

The company returned to profitability in the first quarter of 2001 after a year in the red. In May 2001, the company announced $38 million of new contracts to run from Q2 2001 through 2002, plus an additional $12 million of projects in contract discussions. Revenues for all of 2000 were only $8 million.

The deals also spurred plans for the building of a second facility in Kirkland Lake, Ontario as well as an upgrade to the St. Ambroise facility. As of September 2002, the review process was ongoing for the Kirkland plant with the building application expected to be delivered to the Environment Minister in November.

Opportunities and Challenges

The last 10 or 20 years has seen increased concern over hazardous waste and its proper disposal. But remediation, particularly the high temperature incineration technology of Bennett Environmental, has several advantages. It eliminates the possibility of the uncovering of contaminants by future generations. It is a permanent solution. And it returns a scarce resource—usable soil—to production.

The market potential is huge. It's estimated that there is US$200 billion worth of clean-up work to be done in the U.S. alone, with 55 million tonnes of PCB-contaminated soil on the U.S. Environmental Protection Agency's priority list. Canada itself has 10,000 toxic waste sites to clean up.

Bennett, through its affiliation with Onyx and IT Corporation, has effectively started to capitalize on this problem. Current annual revenues are still less than $100 million, so the growth potential is staggering.

Bennett's chief challenge is to keep up with the growing demand. It's receiving shipments from throughout Eastern Canada and the Northeastern U.S. as far south as Missouri. The new plant in Kirkland Lake is expected to be constructed and operational by the end of 2003.

Financial Highlights

Bennett had a stellar year in 2001 with revenues up 1,745.8 percent over its anemic showing for 2000. A loss of $0.22 per share turned into a profit of $0.46 per share. In the first quarter to March 30, 2002, the company reported a fifth consecutive quarter of growing revenues and growing earnings.

After trading in a narrow range from $4 to $6 from March 2000 to November 2001, the stock soared to over $30 by May 2002. This blistering pace is not likely to be sustained. In fact, the stock underwent a major correction after May, partly spurred by an extensive maintenance shutdown at the Quebec plant. But long-run growth seems assured.

Bennett Environmental Inc. at a Glance

Fiscal Year-end: December
5-Year Return: 84.0%

	1997	1998	1999	2000	2001	4-Year Growth Average (%)	4-Year Growth Total (%)
Revenue ($ mlns.)	–	5.4	22.1	8.0	23.4	146.1	333.5
Net Income ($ mlns.)	–	0.3	6.3	-2.3	4.7	–	1,513.3
Earnings/ Share ($)	–	0.04	0.62	-0.22	0.46	–	1,050.0
Dividend/ Share ($)	–	–	–	–	–	–	–
Price/ Earnings	–	62.5 - 152.5	7.3 - 19.7	-13.6 - -38.9	7.4 - 22.7	–	–

Table data courtesy of  www.shareowner.com

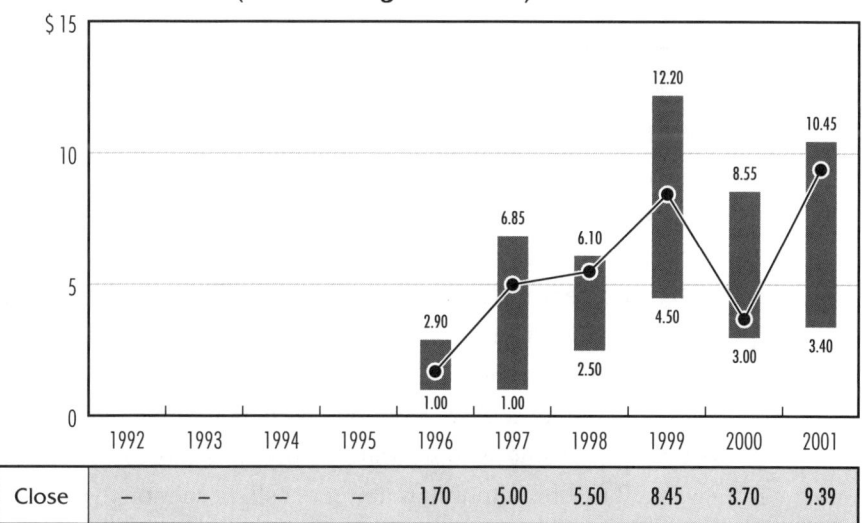

ZENON ENVIRONMENTAL INC.

3239 Dundas Street W.
Oakville, ON L6M 4B2

Tel: (905) 465-3030
Fax: (905) 465-3050
www.zenonenv.com
Symbol: ZEN (TSX)

Employees: 634
Founded: 1980
Listed: 1992

Chairperson and CEO: Andrew Benedek

Share Price Growth	★ ★ ★
Revenue Growth	★ ★ ★
EPS Growth	★ ★ ★ ★ ★
ZEN	11

About the Company

We turn on the tap and out it comes—clean, fresh water. We flush the toilet and there it goes—not so clean, not so fresh water. We tend to take these things for granted. But water, whether it's coming or going, needs to be treated, and Zenon Environmental is one of the leading companies developing and marketing both water purification and waste-water treatment plants.

Zenon's patented ZeeWeed hollow-fibre membrane technology works by reverse osmosis to separate particulates and contaminants from water. The fibres draw in water under slight suction to produce clear, clean drinking water. Fibre pores vary to as little as 0.01 microns in size, small enough to filter out infectious agents like cryptosporidium and giardia.

The ZeeWeed modules can be adapted to existing treatment facilities, allowing for low-cost retrofitting. But many clients have contracted for complete filtration systems from scratch, including the Olivenhain Municipal Water District in Southern California, which completed the largest ultrafiltration water treatment plant in North America in January 2001 using Zenon technology.

Zenon is international in scope, with operations in Latin America, Asia, Europe, and the Middle East where the company has built the world's largest ultrafiltration waste-water treatment plant. It also makes shipboard filtration systems for cruise ships, the merchant marine, and navies.

Opportunities and Challenges

Tragedy struck the town of Walkerton, Ontario, in May 2000 when E. coli infected the water supply: Seven people died and many more became seriously ill. The scandal led to a government inquiry and the establishment of Operation Clean Water, a concerted effort to introduce universal water quality standards in the province.

Walkerton is not an isolated incident. Exactly a year later, three people were reported killed by water-borne bacteria in North Battleford, Saskatchewan. These tragedies have highlighted the problem of aging and inferior infrastructure and the need for remediation.

The town of Collingwood built the first ZeeWeed plant in 1996, and by the end of 2000 there were 22 completed or under design in the province. Ninety percent of Ontario's drinking-water facilities turned to Zenon membrane technology in 2000, including Walkerton.

Although there was a lull in the market in the first half of 2000, Zenon invested heavily in new manufacturing capacity and product development, opening a new head office and assembly plant in June and a major extension to the manufacturing plant in November. The company can now handle over $200 million in sales.

The year 2001 saw continued expansion to the Burlington, Ontario plant and the start of construction on a new plant in Hungary. The latter should double the company's production ability by the end of 2002.

Zenon is poised to be a major player as municipalities around North America and the world re-evaluate their drinking-water and waste-water treatment facilities. But it is looking beyond the municipal market as well with the introduction in 2002 of the new Homespring™ water treatment system for private homes.

Zenon had a backlog of $122 million at the end of 2001, up from $72 million the year before. Despite expanded facilities, Zenon's biggest challenge may well be keeping up with demand. The company's checkered EPS record does not meet the criteria we established for this book, but we have made an exception because of the particular nature of Zenon's business and its strong prospects for the future.

Financial Highlights

Zenon's investment in infrastructure and employees has paid off in spades as revenues soared 47.6 percent for 2001. On top of that, earnings per share jumped to $0.19 a share profit, from a $0.13 a share loss in 2000.

Because of its stock's solid turnaround from its steep fall in 1999, Zenon did the best in our ratings, shooting up seven stars—five in earnings and one each for revenue and share price growth.

Zenon Environmental Inc. at a Glance

Fiscal Year-end: December
9-Year Return: 17.5%

	1997	1998	1999	2000	2001	10-Year Growth Average (%)	10-Year Growth Total (%)
Revenue ($ mlns.)	58.4	77.2	98.8	84.5	124.7	19.9	296.2
Net Income ($ mlns.)	2.2	4.8	2.7	-3.07	4.6	–	–
Earnings/ Share ($)	0.12	0.22	0.12	-0.13	0.19	–	–
Dividend/ Share ($)	–	–	–	–	–	–	–
Price/ Earnings	34.4 - 67.9	30.7 - 65.6	62.5 - 171.9	-43.1 - -96.2	36.3 - 90.3	–	–

Table data courtesy of  www.shareowner.com

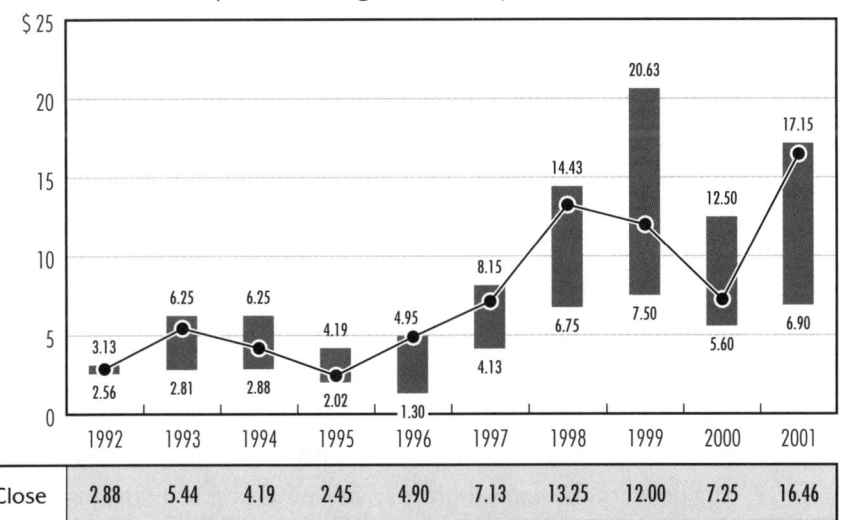

BIOVAIL CORPORATION

7150 Mississauga Road
Mississauga, ON L5L 1J9

Tel: (905) 286-3000
Fax: (905) 286-3050
www.biovail.com

Employees: 1,200
Listed: 1987
Symbol: BVF (TSX) (Also NYSE)

Chairperson and CEO: Eugene N. Melnyk
President: William S. Poole

Share Price Growth	★ ★ ★ ★ ★
Revenue Growth	★ ★ ★ ★ ★
EPS Growth	★ ★ ★ ★
BVF	**14**

About the Company

Unlike drug companies that focus on developing new proprietary drugs, Biovail has focused on drug delivery systems, specifically, oral controlled-release technologies. The company applies these patented technologies to existing medications to develop new branded and generic products. One of the most significant of these technologies is FlashDose®, a rapid dissolving delivery system for patients who have trouble swallowing pills. The tablet dissolves on the tongue and can be swallowed without water.

Controlled-release products are a significant improvement over the same medicine taken say, three times a day. They offer more predictable drug delivery throughout the day, as well as obviating the problem of patients forgetting to take their medicine. Biovail targets successful multiple dosage drugs to create improved once-a-day versions, and it also creates generic versions of drugs whose patents have expired.

The company has commercialized more than 20 different products in Canada, the U.S., and over 55 other countries. Sales in the U.S. are handled through Biovail Pharmaceuticals U.S., a subsidiary developed in 2000 through the acquisition of DJ Pharma. International sales are handled through strategic partners that include Forest Laboratories, Teva Pharmaceuticals, Wyeth-Ayerst, and Rhône Poulenc Rorer. Thirty further products are in the research and development stage with four of them in third-phase trials.

Biovail's contract research organization designs pharmaceutical studies for clients and carries them through to clinical trials. The company's two clinics in downtown Toronto house 230 beds to accommodate a great variety of studies. Equipped with state-of-the-art analytical tools, Biovail Contract Research has been involved in research on dozens of drugs, including the AIDS drug acyclovir.

Biovail was the 26th-largest spender on R&D in Canada in 2001 according to RE$EARCH Infosource.

Opportunities and Challenges

The oral controlled-release pharmaceutical market offers some unique growth opportunities. Biovail has six different controlled-release technology platforms, which gives it the flexibility to customize a wide variety of drugs regardless of their physical, chemical, or clinical properties.

The company has been successful in buying expiring patents from their current owners, then developing a new oral controlled-release form of the patented drug. New patents can then be applied for. This has served to extend the life of a number of patents and forestalled generic competition on these drugs.

In August 2001, Biovail filed a New Drug Application (NDA) for Cardizem® XL, a once-a-day version of the hypertension drug diltiazem. Preliminary approval was granted in June 2002 and product launch is expected in the fourth quarter. October 2001 saw Biovail file an NDA for a FlashDose® version of fluoxetine, marketed as Prozac by Eli Lilly.

Several cross-licensing agreements have been signed with North American and European drug manufacturers including GlaxoSmithKline's Wellbutrin XL, a once-a-day drug for depression, scheduled for mid-2003 launch.

A continuing source of frustration for Biovail has been its protracted patent dispute with generic drug manufacturer Andrx Corp. Each had been suing the other over patent infringement of Biovail's wildly successful drug Tiazac®. But in February 2002, the two companies came to an agreement where Biovail will license its patents on Tiazac® to Andrx in exchange for royalties.

Biovail has a long track record of growth, which looks poised to continue, though some analysts have expressed concern over its high valuation.

Financial Highlights

Biovail continued to show strong growth in 2001, with revenues up 88.6 percent and earnings up 57.0 percent, excluding extraordinary one-time charges. The first half of 2002 saw revenues up 34.7 percent, with earnings up 42.0 percent.

Although there has been some comment in the press on Biovail's high valuation relative to sales, its P/E ratio is not high for a fast growing company. And analyst estimates target Biovail's earnings to double from its 2001 numbers by 2004.

Nevertheless, questions about accounting, anti-trust actions, and lawsuits have made Biovail's stock extremely volatile and investors would do well to pick a good entry point and have an exit strategy.

Biovail Corporation at a Glance

Fiscal Year-end: December
8-Year Return: 70.8%

	1997	1998	1999	2000	2001	9-Year Growth Average (%)	9-Year Growth Total (%)
Revenue ($ mlns.)	99.8	155.6	219.2	437.6	928.9	74.9	6,204.5
Net Income ($ mlns.)	50.3	69.8	77.8	53.1	320.8	–	–
Earnings/ Share ($)	0.47	0.63	0.76	0.37	2.13	–	–
Dividend/ Share ($)	0.00	0.00	0.00	0.00	0.00	–	–
Price/ Earnings	15.1 - 30.0	12.7 - 27.9	15.6 - 45.0	74.3 - 187.8	21.5 - 42.7	–	–

Table data courtesy of *Canadian Shareowner* www.shareowner.com

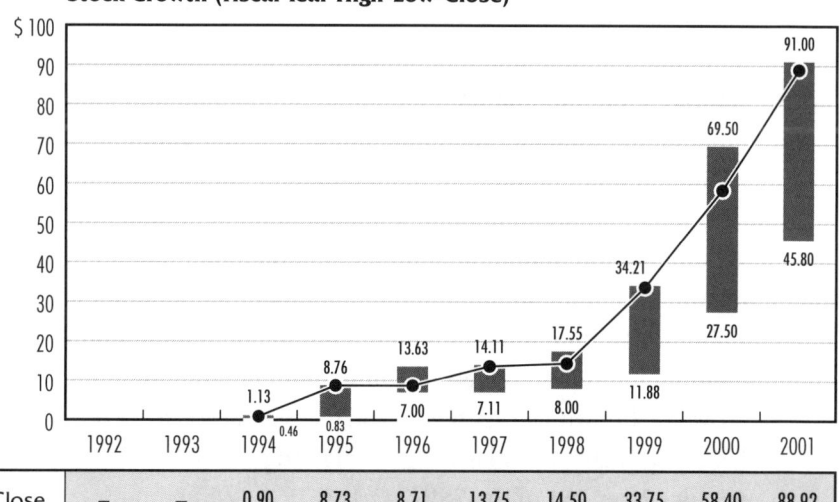

Stock Growth (Fiscal Year High-Low-Close)

Close	1992	1993	1994	1995	1996	1997	1998	1999	2000	2001
	–	–	0.90	8.73	8.71	13.75	14.50	33.75	58.40	88.92

FOREST LABORATORIES, INC.

909 Third Avenue
New York, NY 10022-4731

Tel: (212) 421-7850
Toll Free: (800) 947-5227
www.frx.com
Symbol: FRX (NYSE)

Employees: 2,500
Founded: 1956
Listed: 1967

Chairperson and CEO: Howard Solomon
President and COO: Kenneth E. Goodman

Share Price Growth	★ ★ ★ ★ ★
Revenue Growth	★ ★ ★ ★
EPS Growth	★ ★ ★ ★
FRX	**13**

About the Company

Forest Labs scored a coup of sorts in 1998 when it won the licensing rights to Celexa, a selective serotonin reuptake inhibitor (SSRI) developed by the Danish pharmaceutical firm H. Lundbeck. Celexa competes effectively with such antidepressants as Prozac, Zoloft, and Paxil.

None of the companies with the resources to outbid Forest Labs for the U.S. rights to Celexa nibbled, fearing the market was overcrowded. But with an aggressive and focused sales force, Forest turned Celexa into one of the fastest-growing drugs in America. It now commands 12 percent of the SSRI market.

The drug is differentiated by faster action, less conflict with other drugs, higher response rate, and fewer side effects. Many think it is, in fact, the best of the antidepressants and its market share could grow significantly larger.

Forest Laboratories is an old, well-established drug company with a different approach to R&D. As one analyst put it, its strategy is "minimal R and lots of D." What Forest does (and does extremely well) is negotiate licensing deals for drugs developed by other, often smaller, companies that lack the resources to finish research and bring their products to market.

A good part of its business comes from introducing successful foreign drugs to the American market by shepherding them through the FDA approval process, or serving as the U.S. marketing arm for these products. Celexa is a prime example.

The company maintains nine plants and distribution centers in the U.S. and three in the British isles.

Forest Labs is growing profits at 35 percent annually, far higher than the industry average of 15 percent, and commands a correspondingly high valuation. It was ranked number 14 in *Business Week*'s list of the Top 50 Performers of the S&P 500 in 2001 and number one in health care. It was 26th on *Fortune*'s 2002 list of the fastest growing companies in America and topped US$1.2 billion in sales in fiscal 2001.

Opportunities and Challenges

Forest Labs has a number of products in its production pipeline. A New Drug Application (NDA) was filed in October 2001 for lercanipidine, a medication for hypertension. This was approved in August 2002, and production is expected to begin in the second half of 2003.

December 2001 saw the company sign an agreement with Sankyo Pharma, Japan's second-largest drug company, to promote olmesartan medoxomil, a treatment for hypertension. The FDA approved marketing of the drug in April 2002.

Other drugs in the pipeline include Oxycodone/ibuprofen, a patented combination of the two painkillers, and ALX-0646, a treatment for migraine headaches.

Final approval came in August 2002 for an NDA on Lexapro™, the new generation form of Celexa. Marketing began in September. Celexa is such a huge success that it contributes over two-thirds of the company's revenues. Lexapro should solidify Forest's leadership in this market.

The biggest challenge for Forest is to expand its product line so it is not so dependent on one hugely successful product.

Financial Highlights

Results for Forest Labs' 2002 fiscal year-end to March 31 showed revenues up 32.9 percent, with earnings per share up a whopping 54.2 percent. The first quarter for fiscal 2003 was superb with growth of 33.3 percent and 67.5 percent for revenues and diluted EPS, respectively.

While the computer and telecom sectors were nose-diving from March 2000 to March 2001, Forest Labs stock gained 40.2 percent. After a sharp correction over fears that the company would lose a leading drug, Tiazac, in a patent dispute, Forest's stock price started another steady ascent hitting new highs approaching US$85 in March 2002. After a brief correction, the stock started bouncing off downside resistance at the $70 level in August 2002.

This performance gave the stock one new star for stock price and one new star for EPS in our ratings over last year.

Forest Laboratories, Inc. at a Glance

Fiscal Year-end: March
10-Year Return: 23.6%

	1998	1999	2000	2001	2002	10-Year Growth Average (%)	10-Year Growth Total (%)
Revenue (US$ mlns.)	427.1	546.3	872.8	1,174.5	1,566.6	24.4	448.9
Net Income (US$ mlns.)	57.9	77.2	168.0	224.7	338.0	19.3	425.5
Earnings/ Share (US$)	0.35	0.45	0.96	1.23	1.82	16.3	420.0
Dividend/ Share (US$)	–	–	–	–	–	–	–
Price/ Earnings	22.9 - 54.3	35.6 - 65.4	21.5 - 45.4	30.4 - 58.6	29.4 - 46.7	–	–

Table data courtesy of  www.shareowner.com

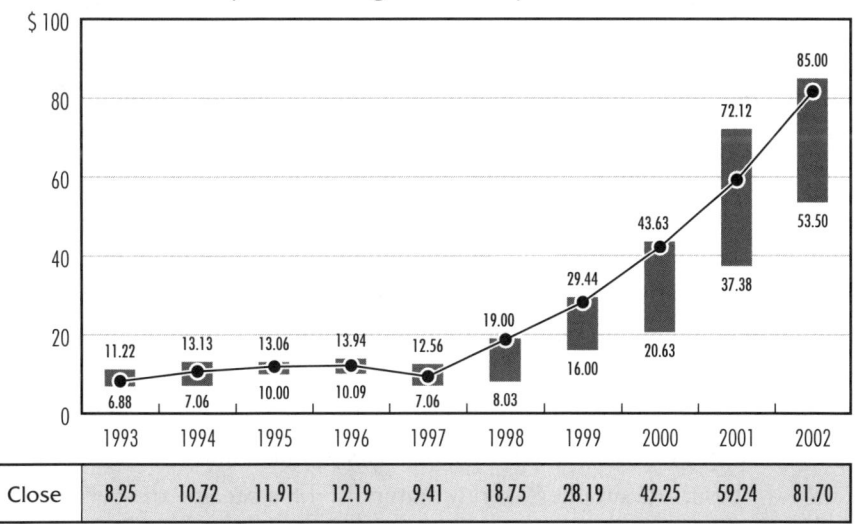

TARO PHARMACEUTICAL INDUSTRIES LTD.

5 Skyline Drive
Hawthorne, NY 10532

Tel (U.S.): (914) 345-9001
Tel (Canada): (905) 791-TARO
Tel (Israel): 011-972-4-847-5700
www.taro.com

Employees: 600
Founded: 1950
Listed: 1961
Symbol: TARO (NASDAQ)

Chairperson: Barrie Levitt
President: Aaron Levitt

Share Price Growth	★ ★ ★ ★
Revenue Growth	★ ★ ★ ★
EPS Growth	★ ★ ★ ★ ★
TARO	**13**

About the Company

Taro (a contraction of "taasiya rokchit," Hebrew for pharmaceutical industry) was founded in 1950 in Israel by a group of Israeli pharmacists and American physicians. In 1961 it went public with an initial public offering, and for 10 years it made and sold products for the Israeli market.

Then it developed a chemical synthesis process to assure a steady supply of the active ingredients in its products and reduce its reliance on outside suppliers of raw materials. This became the cornerstone of Taro's future strength, particularly in the generic drug business.

For two more decades it remained an Israeli operation, developing, making, and selling everything from over-the-counter medications to anti-cancer drugs. And it was in these early years that it developed many of its flagship products—warfarin sodium tablets, carbamazepine tablets, and acetazolamide tablets.

But in 1984 Taro entered the North American market with the purchase of K-Line Pharmaceuticals in Toronto, a company focused on creams and ointments. That foothold saw it expand into the U.S. four years later where it established itself as a manufacturer of generic products. The Taro Research Institute was created in 1991. And in 1992 Taro International was established to take advantage of global opportunities. Taro International sells bulk pharmaceutical chemicals and finished products to 38 countries around the world.

The explosive decade of the '90s saw Taro's sales grow to over $150 million in 2001 from US$12.7 million in 1990. It now sells over a dozen prescription products in 60 different dosages, a dozen different over-the-counter medications, and half a dozen generic active pharmaceutical ingredients (APIs).

Taro International has invested around 14 percent of annual revenues in Research and Development for the last 10 years.

Opportunities and Challenges

Taro completed a new state-of-the-art research and development centre employing 150 in Haifa in 2000. Taro also funds biotech research at Tel Aviv University. Taro's Canadian R&D labs doubled in size in 2000 and in 2001 the Canadian subsidiary created a new division focused on dermatology—OptimaPharma. It hosts the largest topical product R&D team in Canada. And in August 2002, Taro bought a building near its American headquarters in Hawthorne, New York to establish its first U.S. R&D facility.

Twenty percent of the company's employees worldwide work in R&D with much of the focus on its Generic Drug Development Program. Other programs include Proprietary Drugs and Delivery

Systems. Besides controlled release technology, the latter has also developed a novel drug delivery system in NonSpil™. This patented product is, if you can believe it, a liquid that pours but does not spill. You can pour it from a bottle into a spoon, but if you turn the spoon over, the liquid stays put—sort of like a Dairy Queen Blizzard. This is a boon for parents trying to administer cough medicine to a child, for example, or for the elderly who may have shaky hand coordination.

Also in 2001, four generic products were approved by the FDA to compete with drugs from Schering Plough, Wyeth Ayerst, and Merck. Twelve more filings are under review by the FDA, and several more applications are pending in other countries worldwide.

Although much research is done in Canada, the U.S., and Britain, Taro's primary research facilities are in Israel. One of its key challenges down the road could be recruiting and keeping qualified scientists in Israel's climate of continuing terrorist violence.

Financial Highlights

Look at the numbers! Sales for 2001 up 44.6 percent. Earnings per share up 135.7 percent. Wow! And the first-quarter numbers for 2002 were even more impressive, with revenues up 57.0 percent and EPS up—are you ready for it—209.1 percent. Double wow! In fact, as of the first quarter of 2002, Taro's revenues set new records for the 25th consecutive time. Net income hit new highs for the 15th consecutive quarter.

In spite of its stellar growth, Taro's stock has been having a hard time since July 2001. It's P/E shows it's a bargain. By the time this is published that may have changed, but Taro is certainly a company on the move and one to keep your eye on!

Taro Pharmaceutical Industries Ltd. at a Glance
Fiscal Year-end: December
10-Year Return: 18.8%

	1997	1998	1999	2000	2001	10-Year Growth Average (%)	10-Year Growth Total (%)
Revenue (US$ mlns.)	61.0	66.7	83.8	103.8	150.1	21.9	465.5
Net Income (US$ mlns.)	1.4	2.3	5.5	10.0	26.0	227.4	6,497.5
Earnings/ Share (US$)	0.07	0.12	0.26	0.42	0.99	207.5	4,850.0
Dividend/ Share (US$)	–	–	–	–	–	–	–
Price/ Earnings	30.4 - 88.4	15.6 - 30.2	9.4 - 36.5	8.7 - 41.6	11.8 - 50.2	–	–

Table data courtesy of  www.shareowner.com

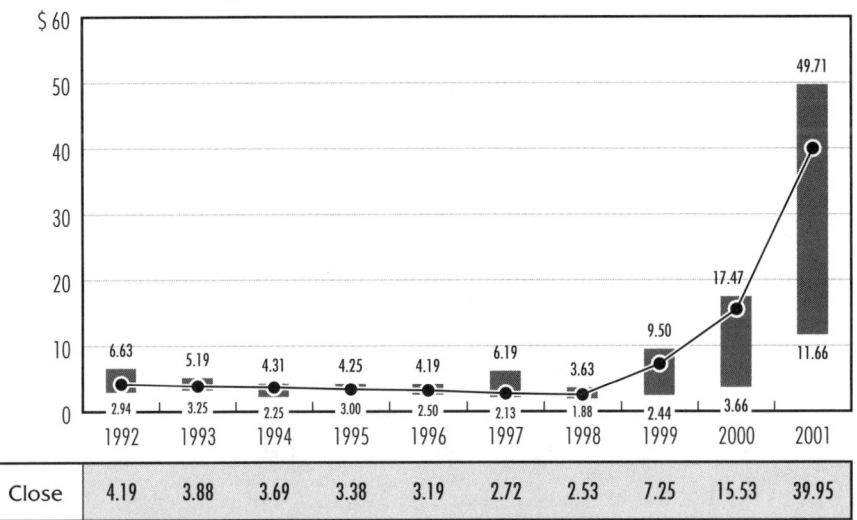

AXCAN PHARMA INC.

597 Laurier Boulevard
Mont St. Hilaire, QC J3H 6C4

Tel: (450) 467-5138
Fax: (450) 464-9979
www.axcan.com
Symbol: AXP (TSX) (Also AXCA-NASDAQ)

Employees: 1,500
Founded: 1982
Listed: 1995

Chairperson, President, and CEO: Léon F. Gosselin

Share Price Growth	★ ★
Revenue Growth	★ ★ ★ ★ ★
EPS Growth	★ ★ ★ ★ ★
AXP	**12**

About the Company

Quebec-based Axcan Pharma is the leading North American pharmaceutical company in the field of gastroenterology. Founded in 1982 as Interfalk by Leon Gosselin and Dr. Herbert Falk, the company launched its first product, Salofalk, a treatment for ulcerative colitis, in 1986.

A year later, the company began a research collaboration with the Mayo Clinic on the treatment of primary biliary cirrhosis with ursodiol. Axcan's drug Urso was approved by the FDA in December 1997, giving Axcan the distinction of being one of only four Canadian companies ever to have received approval for an innovative drug from the FDA.

Over the years, Axcan acquired a number of non-prescription gastrointestinal medications to complement the company's lines. These include several drugs from Wyeth-Ayerst and Jouveinal Inc.

Axcan also adopted a strategy of acquiring gastrointestinal-related products in the late stages of development from other companies. It then completes the clinical trials and brings them to market. One product so acquired is Photofrin, a light-activated treatment for esophageal cancers and Barrett's esophagus purchased from QLT Phototherapeutics. It is now sold in Canada, the U.S., and Britain with approval for 18 other countries.

Today Axcan Pharma markets 25 different product formulations under 12 different brand names, including antacids, laxatives, ulcer medications, and treatments for pancreatitis, cystic fibrosis, and inflammatory bowel diseases, including Crohn's disease. Additional products are in development.

The company was listed as one of the fastest growing in Canada in the 2001 Deloitte & Touche Fast Fifty. Axcan was added to the TSE 300 in 2000 and is dual traded in U.S. dollars on the NASDAQ exchange.

Opportunities and Challenges

Gastroenterology is the second-largest pharmaceutical market in the world, with 60 to 70 million people affected by digestive diseases in North America alone. This represents an American market potential of US$9.5 billion and US$30 billion worldwide.

In 2001, the FDA approved Axcan's Canasa® mesalamine suppositories for the treatment of active ulcerative proctitis. Sales have soared since the U.S. launch in April of that year.

In late October 2001, Axcan signed a definitive agreement to acquire the Paris, France-based Laboratoires Entéris, giving it a solid presence in Europe, the second-largest market for gastroenterology products.

And on April 20, 2002 the company acquired the Laboratoire du Lactéol du Docteur Boucard, a French company specializing in the treatment of diarrhea.

Eighty percent of Axcan's revenues are generated in the U.S., which helps insulate the company from declines in the Canadian dollar, and also gives the stock upside potential from a deteriorating exchange rate. The recent acquisitions should help the company expand in the lucrative European market.

New share offerings in 2001 and 2002 allowed the company to eliminate its long-term debt and to finance these acquisitions. But the downside to new stock issues is the dilution of shares and earnings per share. Tied to the company's strategic growth objectives, this effect should be mitigated by increased earnings.

The company's primary challenge has been to grow its presence in this niche market. The company is still small compared to the giants of the big pharmaseuticals, but it remains a leader in its specialized field.

Financial Highlights

Axcan Pharma was thinly traded prior to January 2000 and its share price fluctuated widely. But since then it has had strong volume and moved up steadily to $24 by mid-May 2002 from $6. Revenues for fiscal 2001 were up 19.2 percent, with earnings per share up 24.0 percent. The first nine months of fiscal 2002 saw revenues up 24.7 percent over the same period the year before. This was the largest revenue increase in the company's history. Earnings per share were up 78.9 percent for the period.

An FDA request to review inspection procedures at one of Axcan's plants sent the stock spiralling back down to $16 in August. Resolution of the issue should see Axcan continue its uptrend. Axcan's solid price appreciation to May has added a star for that category in our ratings system.

Axcan Pharma Inc. at a Glance
Fiscal Year-end: September
6-Year Return: 13.5%

	1997	1998	1999	2000	2001	7-Year Growth Average (%)	7-Year Growth Total (%)
Revenue ($ mlns.)	18.8	42.6	63.3	131.8	165.2	55.7	1,015.0
Net Income ($ mlns.)	-1.33	0.6	2.2	7.4	17.6	–	–
Earnings/ Share ($)	-0.09	0.04	0.14	0.27	0.49	–	–
Dividend/ Share ($)	–	–	–	–	–	–	–
Price/ Earnings	-108.3 - -167.8	250.0 - 362.5	47.1 - 76.4	21.3 - 68.5	25.5 - 37.6	–	–

Table data courtesy of  www.shareowner.com

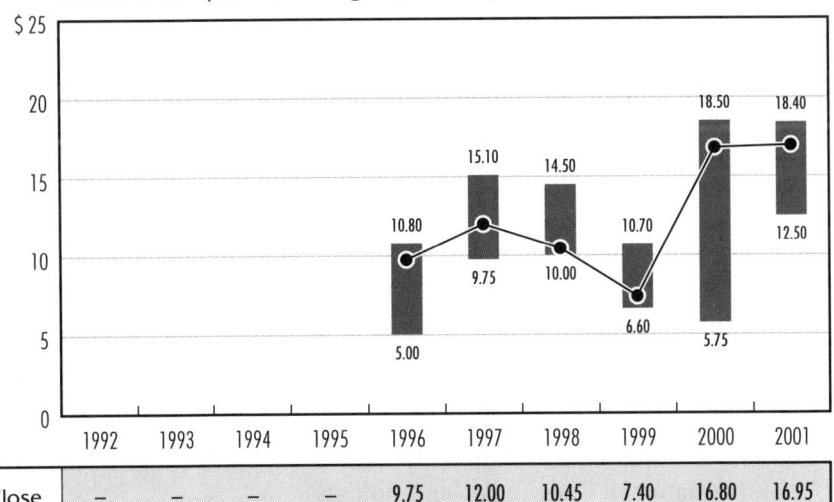

CANGENE CORPORATION

104 Chancellor Matheson Road
Winnipeg, MN R3T 5Y3

Tel: (204) 275-4200
Fax: (204) 269-7003
www.cangene.com
Symbol: CNJ (TSX)

Employees: 400
Founded: 1984
Listed: 1991

Chairperson: Bernard C. Sherman
President and CEO: John Langstaff

Share Price Growth	★ ★ ★ ★
Revenue Growth	★ ★ ★
EPS Growth	★ ★
CNJ	**9**

About the Company

While antibiotics remain a strong tool in the fight against disease, viruses often develop resistance to antibiotics, making the continuous development of ever-newer antibiotics necessary. One alternative to these disease fighters are derivatives of the bodies own immune system—hyperimmunes. This is Cangene's specialty.

The Winnipeg-based company is a world leader in the development and production of hyperimmunes, which are highly purified human antibodies made from specialty plasma for therapeutic use and disease prevention. It also develops recombinant protein drugs using its patented Cangenus™ technology.

Hyperimmunes differ from vaccines in that vaccines stimulate the body's immune system to develop antibodies, whereas a hyperimmune acts directly on the infectious agent.

Its lead product is WhinRho SDF™, a product sold in 30 countries that prevents hemolytic disease of the unborn, and immune thrombocytopenic purpura (ITP). Its other product is VariZIG SDF™, a product approved in January 2001 for the prevention of chicken pox in pregnant women.

Besides the two products being manufactured, the company has several products in its pipeline. Most promising is a treatment for hepatitis B. The company filed for approval of its anti-hepatitis B hyperimmune in the U.S. in September 2001 and in Canada in December the same year.

In fiscal 1997 the company entered the contract manufacturing business and its Winnipeg plant became the first of its kind in Canada to win ISO registration. The company augmented its contract drug manufacturing business with the acquisition of Chesapeake Biological Laboratories of Baltimore, also ISO registered, in January 2001. Both plants are FDA-approved. The acquisition doubled Cangene's manufacturing capability.

It made the Profit 100 list of the fastest growing companies in Canada for the fifth straight year in 2001.

Opportunities and Challenges

Cangene is in the enviable position of being able to finance research and development for its pipeline of new drugs from a steady revenue stream derived from sales of product, contract manufacturing, and an ongoing research and development contract from majority shareholder Apotex Inc.

Because of the focus on hyperimmunes, Cangene's research products result from a common R&D base and usually enter directly into phase two clinical testing, reducing the time and cost of research.

Among the initiatives being undertaken is the development of a new platform technology based on a type of antibody called IgA. This is an immunoglobulin found in such secretions as tears and saliva. Drugs based on these natural secretions would be taken orally, and possible targets include respiratory infections, gastrointestinal diseases, and even sexually transmitted diseases.

The company still derives 95 percent of pharmaceutical sales from one product—WhinRho SDF. But as new drugs come onstream, this dependence should be reduced. The drug used to account for most of the company's revenue, but contract manufacturing now contributes 37 percent of revenues and the acquisition of Chesapeake Labs has contributed to this growth. A major five-year contract with the Center for Disease Control and Prevention in Atlanta to provide Vaccinia immune globulin or VIG should help. The deal is expected to be worth CDN$60 million in 2003 alone, almost the same as the entire revenue for fiscal 2001.

Financial Highlights

The company has had some hard times, losing money in both 1994 and 1995. Its stock price also slumped from 1991 to 1996. So, strictly speaking, Cangene missed our guidelines. But we made an exception because it became profitable in 1996 and hasn't looked back since. Our star ratings are based on performance since 1996.

Fiscal 2001 revenues were up 14.6 percent and earnings per share gained 25.0 percent. This solid performance was improved upon greatly in the first half of fiscal 2002, with revenues up 82.6 percent and EPS up 85.7 percent.

With an increased interest in biologically-based therapies, solid growth in its contract manufacturing business, and new drugs in the pipe, the future looks bright for Cangene.

Cangene Corporation at a Glance

Fiscal Year-end: July
10-Year Return: 19.1%

	1997	1998	1999	2000	2001	8-Year Growth Average (%)	8-Year Growth Total (%)
Revenue ($ mlns.)	23.7	34.7	49.2	58.3	65.8	117.9	4,433.5
Net Income ($ mlns.)	5.3	11.0	15.4	13.9	12.9	–	–
Earnings/ Share ($)	0.09	0.19	0.26	0.24	0.20	–	–
Dividend/ Share ($)	–	–	–	–	–	–	–
Price/ Earnings	20.6 - 27.8	10.5 - 26.1	12.9 - 21.2	17.5 - 50.0	27.0 - 50.0	–	–

Table data courtesy of  www.shareowner.com

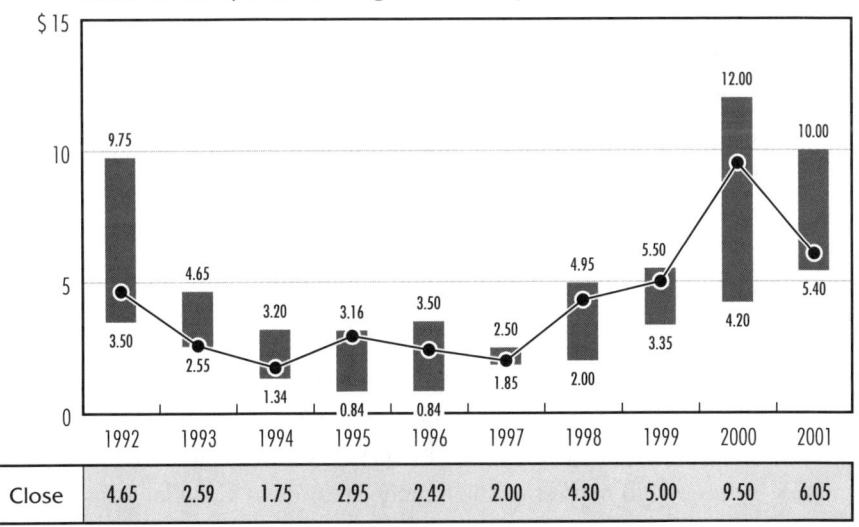

PALADIN LABORATORIES INC.

6111 Royalmount Avenue, Suite 102
Montreal, QC H4P 2T4

Tel: (514) 340-1112
www.paladinlabs.com
Symbol: PLB (TSX)

Employees: 36
Founded: 1995
Listed: 1995

Chairperson: Ted Wise
President and CEO: Jonathan Ross Goodman

Share Price Growth	★ ★ ★
Revenue Growth	★ ★ ★ ★ ★
EPS Growth	★
PLB	**9**

About the Company

Paladin Laboratories is a small but fast-growing pharmaceutical company focused on niche markets that may be underserved by the giant drug companies. Founded in 1996 as a spinoff of Pharmascience Inc., the company became profitable in its third year.

The company's focus is commercialization of specialty products, not research. It acquires or in-licenses late-stage specialty pharmaceuticals from other small- to medium-sized pharmaceutical and biotechnology companies with little or no sales and marketing expertise in Canada. And it acquires products from large multinational pharmaceutical companies that don't want to expend the resources necessary to market to small niche areas or to Canada.

The company's expertise is twofold: shepherding acquired products through the Canadian regulatory process, including conducting any additional clinical trials that may be required, and focused marketing to high-prescribing specialty physicians.

In its annual report for 2001, the company reported 39 products on the market, of which 10 had been launched in 2001 and early 2002. An additional nine were in trials or awaiting approval. These aren't just a mish-mash collection of products either. The company is selective in choosing products that complement existing lines and specialty areas. These include urology, endocrinology, women's health, dermatology, palliative care, and hospital emergency room products.

One of the strengths of Paladin is its background. It was spun off from Pharmascience in 1995 through a reverse takeover of a moribund company. Pharmascience is privately held and Canada's fourth-largest generic drug manufacturer. It has had an astounding 41 percent annual compounded growth in sales.

Paladin Labs is virtually debt free with $22 million in cash and securities in its coffers. It was featured in the 2000 Profit 100 as one of the "hottest startups" in Canada.

Opportunities and Challenges

Paladin Labs serves a valuable niche market—partnering with Big Pharmaceuticals to market niche products it might not want to devote much time or expense to, licensing foreign products from companies who don't want to bother with the small Canadian market, and licensing new late-stage therapies.

In 2001, it acquired six new products and launched eight. New launches included Androderm, a testosterone patch; Muse, a treatment for erectile dysfunction; Valtaxin, a treatment for bladder cancer; and Plan B, an "oops" pill that can be taken to prevent pregnancy if regular contraceptive methods were forgotten or failed. The latter is not an abortion pill like RU-486. It cannot reverse a pregnancy, but if taken within 72 hours, it can prevent pregnancy from occurring.

Paladin is working with the Canadian Pharmacists Association and the Society of Obstetricians and Gynecologists in lobbying the government to make Plan B a non-prescription, over-the-counter drug across Canada. It is already available over-the-counter in British Columbia and Quebec.

Although the company has a sizeable bankroll of cash and securities, the company may need to seek additional financing or issue additional stock as it grows.

Financial Highlights

Paladin Labs had an excellent year in 2001 with revenues up 41.3 percent. Earnings were mitigated by a one-time write-off of intellectual property. With write-offs, earnings were $0.12 per share, down from $0.24 the year before. Without the write-offs, however, earnings were up 25 percent to $0.30. Revenues for the first half of 2002 increased 45.6 percent and EPS jumped 75.0 percent.

The company's stock was flat for its first two years because it suffered losses. That also gives it two years of negative ROI, so Paladin doesn't strictly meet our criteria. But we made an exception because of its solid growth and profitability since then.

The stock soared to over $10 in early 2000 and fell back to the $5 level in the ensuing downturn, as it had become overvalued during the technology boom. From October 2000 on, the stock climbed back to its former highs peaking at an intraday high of $11.25 in January 2002. The big nasty bear took a bite in April with the stock appearing to have bottomed around $6.30 in early September. Watch for a comeback in 2003!

Paladin Laboratories Inc. at a Glance

Fiscal Year-end: December
10-Year Return: 32.5%

	1997	1998	1999	2000	2001	6-Year Growth Average (%)	6-Year Growth Total (%)
Revenue ($ mlns.)	0.8	6.0	11.2	12.6	17.8	537.9	43,302.4
Net Income ($ mlns.)	-1.0	0.8	2.0	2.6	3.7	–	–
Earnings/ Share ($)	-0.25	0.13	0.21	0.21	0.30	–	–
Dividend/ Share ($)	–	–	–	–	–	–	–
Price/ Earnings	9.6 - 33.8	-4.4 - -10.4	16.2 - 35.7	18.6 - 57.1	13.3 - 27.8	–	–

Table data courtesy of  www.shareowner.com

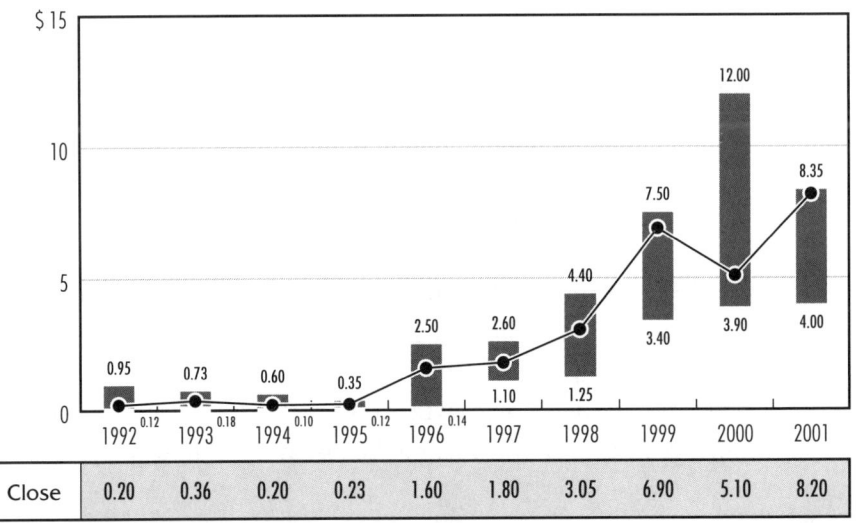

* Data for the years 1996–98 from company reports.

PFIZER INC.

235 East 42nd Street
New York, NY 10017-5755

Tel: (212) 573-2323
Fax: N/A
www.pfizer.com
Symbol: PFE (NYSE)

Employees: 90,000
Founded: 1849
Listed: 1942

Chairperson and CEO: Henry A. McKinnell

Share Price Growth	★ ★ ★
Revenue Growth	★ ★ ★
EPS Growth	★ ★ ★
PFE	**9**

About the Company

Pfizer is the largest and most profitable pharmaceutical company in the world by sales, and the sixth-largest company in the world by market cap. Most people know it as the company that gave us Viagra, but it is much more than that.

Founded in 1849 by two immigrant cousins, Charles Pfizer and Charles Erhart, Pfizer started out as a chemical company. Early products were medicinal: an anti-parasitic, camphor, iodine, and borax, among others. In 1880 it found the product that would become its mainstay and source of growth for over 50 years: citric acid. A lemon shortage in World War I led to the discovery of how to make citric acid artificially by fermenting sugar. This was later refined into a deep-tank fermentation process using molasses. The stage was set for what was to become Pfizer's first major breakthrough in pharmaceuticals: penicillin.

Alexander Fleming's discovery of penicillin in 1928 had gone undeveloped because of the inability to mass-produce it. But 10 years later, scientists at Oxford went to the U.S. to solve the production problem, and Pfizer successfully applied deep-tank fermentation to the task in 1944. Although 19 other companies were authorized to make penicillin, none could match Pfizer's production levels, and it supplied 90 percent of the penicillin used on the front lines for the rest of World War II.

Following the war, Pfizer set out to discover other antibiotics. Terramycin, the first proprietary product developed by Pfizer scientists, hit the market in 1950. This marked the transition from chemical company to drug company, and the rest, as they say, is history.

Today Pfizer manufactures dozens of drugs, eight of which each generate over a billion dollars a year in sales. The company also has a veterinary medicine division and an extensive Global Research and Development Division, which had a budget of US$5.3 billion for 2002, the largest in the industry.

In June 2000, Pfizer acquired Warner Lambert, which has been incorporated into the Pfizer Consumer Group. This subsidiary includes over-the-counter medications such as BenGay, Reactine, Sudafed, and Visine, confectionery products such as Adams brand gums and mints, Certs, Chiclets, and Dentyne, as well as shaving products from Schick.

The decade to the end of 2001 was one of solid growth, with sales tripling, R&D spending quadrupling, and net income up 1,100 percent. Its presence is international, with 22 markets generating over US$100 million a year. It is the fastest growing pharmaceutical company in Germany, France, the U.K., Spain, and Japan.

Opportunities and Challenges

Pfizer is at the forefront of pharmaceutical research, operating three research campuses in the U.S. as well as one each in France, Britain, and Japan. There are also numerous satellite research centres worldwide, in addition to strategic alliances with more than 250 partners in academia and industry. In fact, Pfizer Canada is the 13th largest spender on research and development in Canada.

In the past few years the company has had three of the most successful product launches in the pharmaceutical industry: Lipitor for lowering cholesterol, Viagra for treating erectile disfunction, and Celebrex for treating osteoarthritis and rheumatoid arthritis.

In July 2002, Pfizer announced a $60-billion offer to buy rival Pharmacia Corporation. This deal will mean about $2.5 billion in cost efficiencies, but most importantly, it will add several drugs to its stable that still have a long patent life left. This will mitigate the effects of patent expiry on Pfizer's bottom line.

Financial Highlights

For fiscal 2001, Pfizer's revenues grew 9.1 percent, while undiluted earnings per share soared 111.9 percent. On an adjusted basis for continuing operations and excluding merger-related costs, diluted EPS was up 26.2 percent, more than double the industry average. These figures were reinforced with a strong first half for fiscal 2002—revenues up 8.2 percent and EPS up 16.9 percent (net of the effect of a change in accounting principles). Nevertheless, Pfizer's stock has continued to languish. Continuing growth in revenues and earnings should see the stock advancing in the future. This is a good long-term buy.

Because of its lagging stock price, Pfizer's star rating for that category dropped by two.

Pfizer Inc. at a Glance
Fiscal Year-end: December
10-Year Return: 21.7%

	1997	1998	1999	2000	2001	10-Year Growth Average (%)	10-Year Growth Total (%)
Revenue (US$ mlns.)	12,504.0	13,544.0	16,204.0	29,574.0	32,084.0	19.7	343.7
Net Income (US$ mlns.)	2,213.0	2,439.1	3,372.2	6,575.0	8,257.1	28.1	709.6
Earnings/ Share (US$)	0.57	0.62	0.87	1.03	1.30	20.4	420.0
Dividend/ Share (US$)	0.23	0.25	0.31	0.36	0.44	15.7	266.7
Price/ Earnings	23.6 - 46.8	38.2 - 69.3	36.3 - 57.5	29.1 - 47.8	26.2 - 36.0	–	–

Table data courtesy of  www.shareowner.com

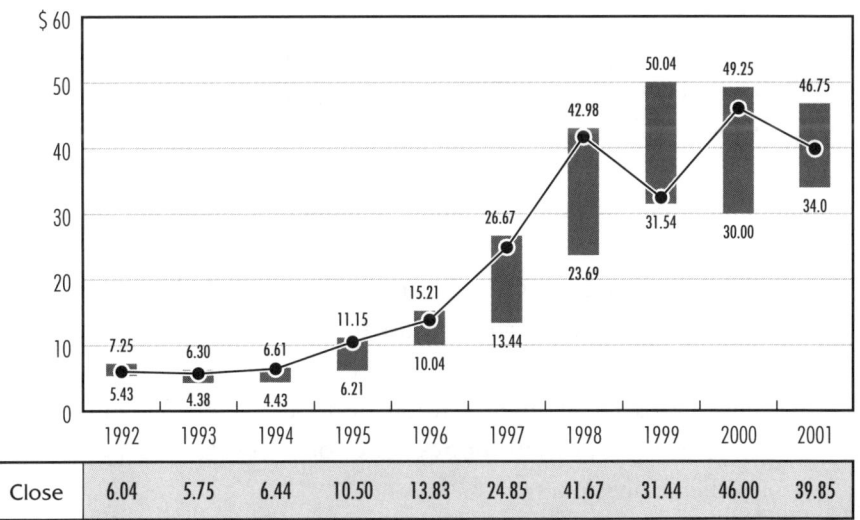

MERCK & COMPANY, INC.

1 Merck Drive, P.O. Box 100
Whitehouse Station, NJ 08889-0100

Tel: (908) 423-1000
www.merck.com
Symbol: MRK (NYSE)

Employees: 78,100
Founded: 1889
Listed: 1946

Chairperson, President, and CEO: Raymond V. Gilmartin

Share Price Growth	★
Revenue Growth	★ ★ ★
EPS Growth	★ ★
MRK	**6**

About the Company

Merck is a global pharmaceutical company with nine research and 30 manufacturing facilities serving people in about 200 countries worldwide. Its Canadian subsidiary, Merck Frosst Canada, operates the world-class Merck Frosst Centre for Therapeutic Research in Montreal. This is the largest private biomedical research facility in Canada, employing over 300 scientists and representing more than 10 percent of the R&D budget for Canada's entire pharmaceutical industry.

With a research budget of close to US$2.5 billion annually, Merck has pioneered many medical advances in a number of fields including atherosclerosis, hypertension, heart failure, anti-inflammatories, osteoporosis, and antibiotics. The company also has a veterinary medicine division.

Products include several billion-dollar annual sellers such as Zocor, Vioxx, Cozaar, Hyzaar, Fosamax, and Singulair. These five drugs accounted for 68 percent of Merck's 2001 health-care product sales and are its key drivers of growth.

Merck's largest revenue generator is Merck-Medco Managed Care, which accounted for half of the company's US$47 billion of sales in 2001. Merck is also a medical information company, publishing some of the largest reference works for doctors: *The Merck Index*, *The Merck Manual of Diagnosis and Therapy*, and *The Merck Manual of Geriatrics*. The Merck Manual is the most widely used medical text in the world, and since 1955, the Merck Veterinary Manual has been the standard reference for vets.

Merck has had growing revenues, earnings, and dividends every year for the last 10 years, except for 1993 when earnings dropped due to the acquisition of Medco and restructuring.

Opportunities and Challenges

With 7,800 employees engaged in research at nine facilities in the U.S., Canada, Britain, Spain, Italy, France, and Japan, Merck is well positioned to continue developing new and profitable medications.

Major new filings made or expected in 2001 and 2002 include Arcoxia™ for arthritis, as well as for menstrual and chronic pain, Zetia™ for cholesterol control, and a new drug for chemotherapy-induced nausea and vomiting.

The R&D pipeline includes treatments for anxiety, depression, asthma, diabetes, infant diarrhea, HIV/AIDS, shingles, and a vaccine for the human papillomavirus, which is indicated in the development of cervical cancer.

Merck-Medco has been an increasingly important source of growth for Merck. In 1998, it accounted for 43.1 percent of sales. That grew to 46.6 percent in 1999, 49.9 percent in 2000, and 55.3 percent in 2001. Sales have grown to US$26 billion from US$2.2 billion in less than

10 years. Because of this growth, Merck plans to spin off Merck-Medco as a separate publicly-traded company, MedcoHealth Solutions.

The IPO registration for MedcoHealth Solutions was filed in April 2002. The company plans to retain 80.1 percent of the stock, which it will distribute to its shareholders within 12 months of the IPO. However, that may be delayed some time after the company restated its books in July 2002. Medco apparently overstated its revenues by US$14.1 billion over the last five years.

The company faced increasing challenges in 2001 as its leading osteoarthritis drug Vioxx achieved lower market penetration than expected even though it is still the fastest-growing treatment for arthritis. This, coupled with patent expirations, meant that the company would not meet expectations. A planned increase in research spending to $2.9 billion, as well as the factors noted, make 2002 a transition year according to chairperson Ray Gilmartin.

Financial Highlights

Merck's revenues grew 18.2 percent in 2001, while earnings climbed 8.3 percent. Although this is certainly respectable, it was less than the company expected and adversely affected share price. Revenues in the first half of 2002 were up 7.5 percent but earnings per share were down 1.3 percent.

The stock rose steadily from mid-1994 through the first quarter of 1999, when it started trading in a wide range between US$60 and US$90 for two years. It hit a new high of US$96 in December 2000 before declining steadily to $50 in May 2002. The fundamentals of the company remain strong and prices below US$65 represent a real bargain for the long-term investor.

Because of the sliding share price, Merck lost three stars in its rating for that category. It continued to slide through September 2002, partly as a result of the Medco accounting scandal. Nevertheless, as the company divests itself of Medco and refocuses on its core competencies, 2003 should be a good year.

Merck & Company, Inc. at a Glance

Fiscal Year-end: December
10-Year Return: 10.8%

	1997	1998	1999	2000	2001	10-Year Growth Average (%)	10-Year Growth Total (%)
Revenue (US$ mlns.)	23,636.9	26,898.2	32,714.0	40,363.2	47,715.7	19.8	393.8
Net Income (US$ mlns.)	4,617.8	5,236.7	5,891.3	6,821.7	7,281.8	12.9	197.6
Earnings/ Share (US$)	1.87	2.15	2.45	2.90	3.14	13.1	199.0
Dividend/ Share (US$)	0.87	0.99	1.12	1.26	1.38	12.5	187.5
Price/ Earnings	20.9 - 28.9	23.6 - 37.6	24.9 - 35.7	17.9 - 33.3	18.1 - 30.3	–	–

Table data courtesy of  www.shareowner.com

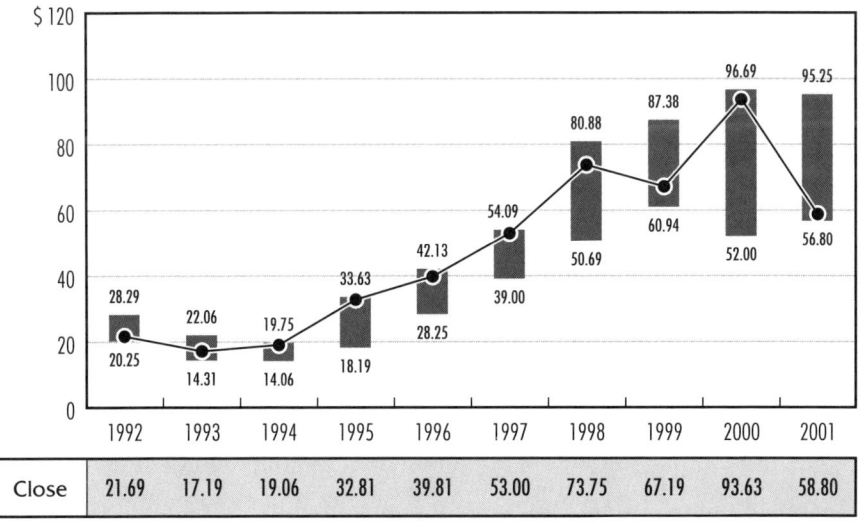

ENERGY & RESOURCES

Energy
Calpine Corporation
Enerchem International Inc.
Pason Systems Inc.
Canadian Hydro Developers, Inc.

Resources
Goldcorp Inc.
Trican Well Service Ltd.

CALPINE CORPORATION

50 West San Fernando Street
San Jose, CA 95113

Tel: (408) 995-5115
Fax: (408) 995-0505
www.calpine.com
Symbol: CPN (NYSE) (Also CF.UN-TSX)

Employees: 3,719
Founded: 1984
Listed: 1996

Chairperson, President, and CEO: Peter Cartwright

Share Price Growth	★ ★ ★
Revenue Growth	★ ★ ★ ★ ★
EPS Growth	★ ★ ★ ★ ★
CPX	**13**

About the Company

Calpine Corp. is the fastest-growing independent producer of electricity in the U.S. and the world's largest provider of power from geothermal sources.

Founded in 1984 by its visionary leader, Pete Cartwright, Calpine focuses on producing electricity using new and environmentally friendly technologies. While the established power companies continue to struggle along with outdated, inefficient coal-fired plants, Calpine is building fuel-efficient natural gas plants as well as developing geothermal energy.

Deregulation has allowed Calpine to enter new markets with efficient new plants and underprice its competitors. It now operates 64 plants in 21 states, three provinces, and the U.K. with an output capacity of 12,200 megawatts (enough to power 12 million homes). By 2005 it plans to have 100 plants in operation with total output capacity of 70,000 megawatts.

The company has been vertically integrating by buying up natural gas companies to assure itself continuous supply. The April 2001 merger with Canada's Encal Energy is a case in point.

To mitigate a volatile energy market, Calpine hedges sales by locking in long-term contracts. Ninety percent of the company's 2001 production had been sold this way, as was 65 percent of production for 2002.

Opportunities and Challenges

The electricity needs of the U.S. are growing at a rate of more than 3 percent a year. Much of that demand is being driven by the communications revolution. Computers already consume 13 percent of the power produced in the U.S. and that is expected to increase to 50 percent in the next decade. The U.S. already has been experiencing periodic power shortages as supply fails to keep pace with demand.

But if you're familiar with the company, you know it faced a series of challenges in 2001 and 2002. The biggest challenge it faced was Enronitis.

When power broker Enron collapsed in the biggest bankruptcy in U.S. history (at the time), people started looking twice at corporate accounting methods. And one of the companies they looked at was Calpine. An article in *The New York Times* in December 2001 likened Calpine to Enron, and the stock took a huge nosedive. The article alleged that, like Enron, Calpine was a high-growth company and had financial statements that were not always clear.

This charge was vigorously denied by Calpine CEO Pete Cartwright, who argued that Calpine's business model is based on ownership of low-cost generating facilities, not on energy brokering.

Nevertheless, Calpine's significant debt load and a changing market environment resulted in a credit downgrade by Moody's a few days later. Standard & Poor's downgraded the company in March 2002. To add to Calpine's woes, a number of law firms filed class action lawsuits on behalf of shareholders.

But the company has aggressively worked to pay down debt by redeeming outstanding debentures and in April 2002 announced the issuing of close to $1 billion of new stock to be used for debt retirement. It also sold off non-core Canadian assets and launched an IPO of its Canadian holdings as the Calpine Power Income Fund in August 2002, raising more cash for debt retirement.

To allay the fears of investors and critics, the company announced in August 2002 that it would expense future stock options, and its president and chief financial officer signed the newly mandated truth-in-accounting disclosure statements a full month before they were legally required.

And though it cancelled a number of pending projects due to to slowing demand in 2002, Calpine brought 11 new plants on-stream in 2001 and made two acquisitions.

Financial Highlights

Fantastic revenue growth! Fantastic earnings growth! Rotten share price performance! What a contradiction, but not in the world of energy stocks in the wake of Enron. Revenues, in fact, increased a whopping 198.0 percent in 2001, with earnings up 54.2 percent. For the first half of 2002, revenue was up 24.6 percent. However, the company lost a penny a share compared to a profit of $0.68 the year before, largely because of project cancellation charges and drastically lower electricity rates.

When Calpine re-establishes its credit and credibility with the public, and when energy prices and the economy recover, the stock should recover as well, perhaps to its former highs again. Meanwhile, we had to knock two stars off its 15-star rating of last year because of its price slump.

Calpine Corporation at a Glance

Fiscal Year-end: December
5-Year Return: 40.2%

	1997	1998	1999	2000	2001	8-Year Growth Average (%)	8-Year Growth Total (%)
Revenue (US$ mlns.)	260.5	530.7	811.1	2,258.2	7,581.2	98.3	7,674.2
Net Income (US$ mlns.)	34.7	46.3	96.2	324.7	728.1	107.4	10,759.7
Earnings/ Share (US$)	0.21	0.27	0.43	1.16	1.96	69.5	2,700.0
Dividend/ Share (US$)	–	–	–	–	–	–	–
Price/ Earnings	7.4 - 13.7	5.9 - 12.8	7.3 - 38.1	13.9 - 45.7	5.1 - 29.6	–	–

Table data courtesy of  www.shareowner.com

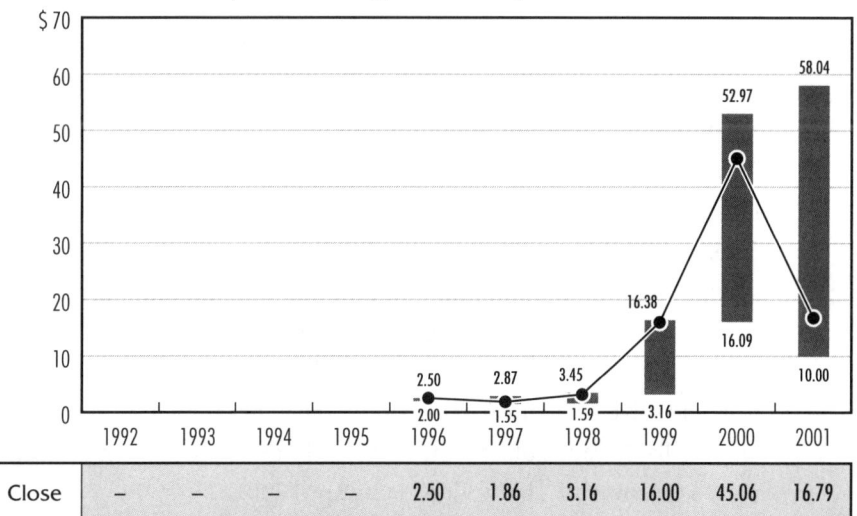

ENERCHEM INTERNATIONAL INC.

1406–8th Street
Nisku, AB T9E 7M1

Tel: (780) 955-3388
Fax: (780) 955-2064
www.enerchem.com
Symbol: ECH (TSX)

Employees: 77
Founded: 1988
Listed: 1989

President and CEO: Larry B. Phillips

Share Price Growth	★ ★ ★ ★ ★
Revenue Growth	★ ★ ★ ★ ★
EPS Growth	★ ★ ★
ECH	**13**

About the Company

The oil industry needs a host of support industries to facilitate exploration and production, and Enerchem International is one of them. It manufactures specialty chemicals and hydrocarbon-based fluids to service conventional and heavy oil production by controlling deposits, demulsifying emulsions, controlling corrosion, and more.

The company, in fact, has 18 product lines with 300 different chemicals and solvents, many of them proprietary. These include the Fracsol and Drillsol brands of frac and drilling fluids acquired with the company's takeover of Trysol Canada in April 2001.

Other lines include proprietary asphaltene dispersants developed in the company's own laboratories. These eliminate asphaltene deposits that can plug pipelines and contaminate gas production. Other products focus on bacteria control, degreasing, foaming and defoaming, and paraffin control.

Enerchem International also produces scale and corrosion inhibitors, oxygen scavengers, well stimulation fluids, surfactants, and clarifiers, along with such conventional products as ammonia, methanol, and glycols used in the industry.

The company operates an extensive research and development laboratory at its head office in Nisku, Alberta. It features a complete oil and water chemistry facility capable of analysis, testing, and development of new products. It also does custom analytical testing of samples from client wells to determine the optimum product selection. Enerchem's Quality Management System is ISO-registered.

Enerchem also maintains the Trysol plant in Sundre, Alberta, and is building a new fractionation plant at Slave Lake, Alberta. This fully automated plant became operational in fiscal 2002.

Besides its Canadian operations, the company also owns an American subsidiary based in Midland, Texas and has a joint venture partnership in Egypt operating as the Egyptian Canadian Company for Chemical Industries (ECC) in the Free Zone at Alexandria. ECC has several long-term contracts with major oil producers in the Middle East. And the company has initiated operations in Mexico as well.

Although Enerchem is a relatively small company, it has been consistently profitable since 1993.

Opportunities and Challenges

With increasing tensions in the Middle East and potential disruptions to oil supply internationally, demand for domestic crude is increasing. Companies like Enerchem International that service the oil industry are well positioned to profit from this increasing energy demand.

In 2001, the company refocused on its core business—specialty chemicals and fluids for the oil industry. It had divested itself of its Decarson Rentals, an oil field equipment rental business, in late 2000, and in April 2001 it bought Trysol Canada, a leader in well servicing and drill fluids. The acquisition marked the first step in Enerchem's strategy of expanding its technologies, services, and product line.

The 6,000-barrels-per-day fractionation plant in Slave Lake complements the Trysol plant and adds further production capacity for its Fracsol and Drillsol lines. As the Enerchem and Trysol operations are integrated, new efficiencies should help control costs and add to the bottom line.

One of the challenges facing Enerchem is that its record performance in 2001 reflects its acquisition more than internal growth. But the synergies produced by the amalgamation of Enerchem and Trysol should spur growth going forward.

And of course, the oil industry and suppliers like Enerchem are subject to fluctuations in the price of oil.

Financial Highlights

Enerchem's revenues increased 107.9 percent in fiscal 2001, with earnings per share up marginally at 4.5 percent. Much of the revenue growth, 95.8 percent actually, was the result of the Trysol acquisition. Trysol provided revenues for the five-month period from acquisition in April to fiscal year-end in August. Full-year production should add to revenues for 2002.

The company's stock price has grown twentyfold since the end of 1993, rising to around $4.50 in April 2002 from $0.20. The chart pattern shows a steady long-term uptrend, albeit somewhat volatile at times with not uncommon drops from peak to valley of 50 percent or more. Since the beginning of 2002 this volatility has been decreasing as the stock continues its upward path.

Enerchem International Inc. at a Glance
Fiscal Year-end: December
10-Year Return: 32.4%

	1997	1998	1999	2000	2001	8-Year Growth Average (%)	8-Year Growth Total (%)
Revenue ($ mlns.)	12.1	16.4	16.0	15.3	31.8	33.8	925.8
Net Income ($ mlns.)	1.2	1.8	0.0	2.0	2.3	29.0	666.7
Earnings/ Share ($)	0.18	0.24	0.00	0.22	0.23	21.0	360.0
Dividend/ Share ($)	0.0	0.0	0.0	0.0	0.0	–	–
Price/ Earnings	4.9 - 12.2	6.8 - 15.2	31.3 - 77.5	8.2 - 18.2	10.0 - 18.5	–	–

Table data courtesy of  www.shareowner.com

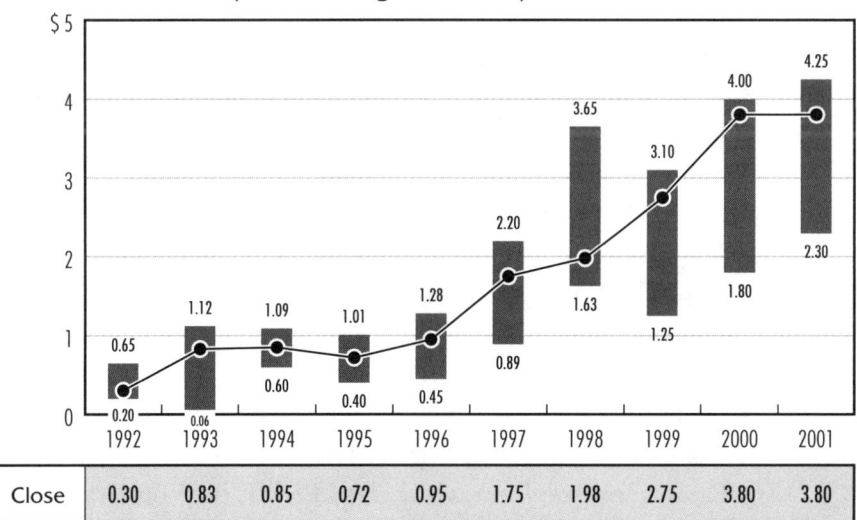

PASON SYSTEMS INC.

6130–3rd Street S.E.
Calgary, AB T2H 1K4

Tel: (403) 301-3400
Fax: (403) 301-3499
www.pason.com
Symbol: PSI (TSX)

Employees: 180
Founded: 1992
Listed: 1996

President and CEO: Jim Hill

Share Price Growth	★ ★ ★
Revenue Growth	★ ★ ★ ★ ★
EPS Growth	★ ★ ★ ★ ★
PSI	**13**

About the Company

Pason Systems is bringing the digital age to the oil patch. The company provides a variety of electronic monitoring services at the wellhead that allow head offices to follow activity at drilling sites.

Pason's Penless Electronic Drilling Recorder (EDR) records, stores, and reports drilling parameters and events to assist drillers in monitoring and planning their activities. Each rig is networked to share drilling data with geology and engineering personnel in real time.

The Pit Bull PVT (Pit Volume Totalizer) enhances drilling safety by giving early warning of high-pressure hydrocarbon inflow "kicks." It's considered functional, reliable, and easy to use.

Pason's technology also includes LPLOT, its proprietary mud-logging software. (Mud is a colloidal suspension of clay and chemical additives in water that is circulated through a wellbore during drilling.) And Pason's Internet Data Hub lets home office management monitor drilling remotely.

All this stuff used to be done with pen and paper, and oral reports by telephone. But, as Dundee Securities put it in a May 2001 research report, "Pason is quietly and quickly bringing the management of drilling rigs into the 21st century."

Pason has grown to annual revenues of $63 million in 2001 from just $500,000 in 1992. It has captured 90 percent of the Canadian market for EDRs, outfitting 500 or so rigs. The big opportunity for the company is south of the border where Pason EDRs are used on just 20 percent of rigs.

Because Pason's products are leased, they provide a constant revenue stream, rather than just a one-shot sale.

President and CEO Jim Hill owns 32 percent of the company, with insiders holding a further 15 percent. That spells a strong commitment to the success of the company.

Opportunities and Challenges

Pason is constantly adding new products to its line, including the Electronic Choke System, designed to replace hydraulically operated wellhead valves, and the Total Gas System, which monitors natural gases entering the borehole. These products have barely dented Pason's revenues so far, but could contribute up to 20 percent in the future. The company is also working on an electronic oilfield accounting and payment system called WebPay—another potential strong revenue generator.

Two challenges face Pason going forward. First is market saturation, as its products are already used on over 90 percent of Canadian rigs. New product development and increased inroads into the U.S. market are keys to future growth. This potential is huge considering that its 20 percent share of the U.S. market for EDRs already contributes 45 percent of the company's revenues. The international arena offers further opportunities that the company has just begun to explore. The company has developed franchise operations in Mexico that should start generating good revenues in 2003.

The second challenge is the oil industry itself. Pason's performance is tied to the industry, and while the industry is in expansion mode, this spells extremely good fortune for Pason. But when oil prices fall and exploration and development tail off, Pason's growth could be affected. The company's strategy of continuous development of additional services has mitigated this problem so far. Even though the active rig count in Canada for the fourth quarter of 2001 dropped from to 341 from 541 the year before, quarterly revenues and earnings were up substantially.

Financial Highlights

Revenues were up 44.8 percent for 2001, with earnings per share up a solid 87.2 percent. And the share price kept pace, with Pason hitting new highs in April 2002.

Pason's stock fluctuates to a certain extent with the oil industry. But since February 1999, Pason has been in a long upward trend with occasional flat or moderately declining periods.

Because of its continuing growth in revenues, earnings, and share price, Pason gained two stars in its rating this year, one for share price and one for EPS.

Pason Systems Inc. at a Glance
Fiscal Year-end: December
5-Year Return: 37.4%

	1997	1998	1999	2000	2001	6-Year Growth Average (%)	6-Year Growth Total (%)
Revenue ($ mlns.)	14.5	23.8	24.7	43.5	63.0	82.3	1,301.3
Net Income ($ mlns.)	4.1	4.9	4.1	8.1	15.4	108.6	1,598.2
Earnings/ Share ($)	0.26	0.28	0.23	0.47	0.88	90.6	1,157.1
Dividend/ Share ($)	–	–	–	–	–	–	–
Price/ Earnings	7.9 - 30.8	8.9 - 30.4	9.8 - 30.0	11.7 - 20.7	6.8 - 11.8	–	–

Table data courtesy of  www.shareowner.com

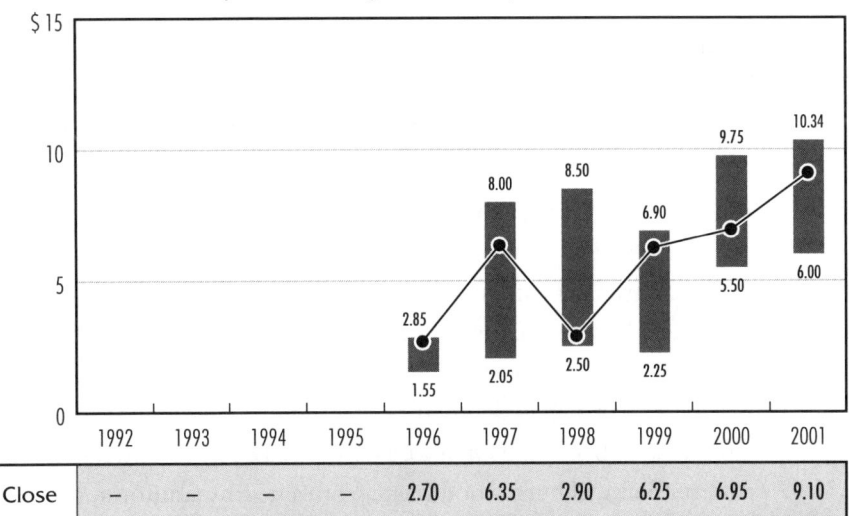

CANADIAN HYDRO DEVELOPERS, INC.

1324–17th Avenue S.W., Suite 500
Calgary, AB T2T 5S8

Tel: (403) 269-9379
Fax: (403) 244-7388
www.canhydro.com
Symbol: KHD (TSX)

Employees: 18
Founded: 1990
Listed: 1995

Chairperson: Dennis M. Erker
President and COO: J. Ross Keating
CEO: John D. Keating

Share Price Growth	★ ★ ★ ★
Revenue Growth	★ ★ ★ ★ ★
EPS Growth	★ ★
KHD	**11**

About the Company

Founded in 1990, Canadian Hydro Developers' objective is to generate electricity in an environmentally friendly way. The company operates 13 power plants in Ontario, Alberta, and British Columbia: nine "run-of-river" hydro plants, one natural gas plant, and three wind plants. Five more hydro plants are under development in British Columbia, Alberta, and Ontario, as is a biomass plant in Grande Prairie, Alberta that will burn wood waste from a nearby Canfor mill.

Canadian Hydro has experienced a 35 percent annual growth in electricity generating capacity for the last five years, a figure it expects to ramp up to 50 percent over the next three. Its production capacity of 88.9 megawatts (as of March 2002) is expected to grow significantly over the next few years. The Pingston project under construction in British Columbia will add another 15 megawatts and a further 223 megawatts are in the permit stage. The goal is 300 megawatts on-stream by 2006.

In November 2000, the company offered power directly to the general public for the first time—previously it had fed power into the provincial grid or to business clients. Consumers in parts of Ontario and Alberta now have the choice of buying electricity certified as Ecologo emissions-free energy under Environment Canada's Environmental Choice program.

Canadian Hydro Developers was the seventh best performing stock on the Toronto Stock Exchange in 2000.

Opportunities and Challenges

It's estimated that demand for electricity in the U.S. is growing at 3 percent a year, yet supply is not keeping up. We've already seen rolling blackouts in California, while other jurisdictions are also feeling the pinch. California even asked the U.S. navy to hook up a few nuclear submarines to the grid to get it through the summer of 2001—the Navy declined. In Canada, the situation is similar. Low reservoir levels and the decommissioning of nuclear power plants have added to the strain.

With increasing deregulation of electricity generation, private companies like Canadian Hydro Developers are filling the breach.

Can it compete with the big utilities? You bet! All of Canadian Hydro's power plants are less than 12 years old—new by industry standards. Half of them are less than five years old. All are state-of-the-art technology, requiring no staffing and low maintenance.

However, low snowpacks have affected the generating capacity of some of Canadian Hydro's plants in the past and may do so again in the future.

The huge challenge for Canadian Hydro is the declining price for spot electricity, which was $131 per megawatt hour (Mwh) in January 2001 and had declined to just $28/Mwh in January 2002. A forward-hedging program has 75 percent of current production sold ahead for the next 12 years; this has helped mitigate the effect of sliding prices to some extent, but not completely.

The company was also affected by low snowpacks cutting production on its run-of-river plants, but made up for that with two new wind plants coming onstream and windier-than-normal conditions boosting production.

Financial Highlights

Revenues for Canadian Hydro Developers declined by 12.8 percent in 2001, primarily because of lower spot electricity prices. Power generation actually increased to 245,113 Mwh from 235,160 Mwh during the year. Diluted earnings per share slipped a penny to $0.09, but net earnings were up 33.6 percent due to cost efficiencies. Per-share earnings were adversely affected by the issuance of approximately 13 million new shares.

The stock price soared in 2000, making Canadian Hydro Developers one of the top 10 performing stocks on the Toronto Stock Exchange that year, with a gain of 298.7 percent. An improving economy and strengthening energy prices should give the stock impetus throughout the next few years.

Canadian Hydro Developers, Inc. at a Glance

Fiscal Year-end: December
10-Year Return: 22.1%

	1997	1998	1999	2000	2001	8-Year Growth Average (%)	8-Year Growth Total (%)
Revenue ($ mlns.)	5.3	6.1	9.3	17.2	15.0	47.5	888.8
Net Income ($ mlns.)	0.5	0.4	1.3	2.8	3.7	–	–
Earnings/ Share ($)	0.03	0.01	0.05	0.10	0.09	–	–
Dividend/ Share ($)	0.00	0.00	0.00	0.00	0.00	–	–
Price/ Earnings	18.3 - 41.7	90.0 - 160.0	13.0 - 22.0	7.2 - 32.0	19.4 - 38.3	–	–

Table data courtesy of  www.shareowner.com

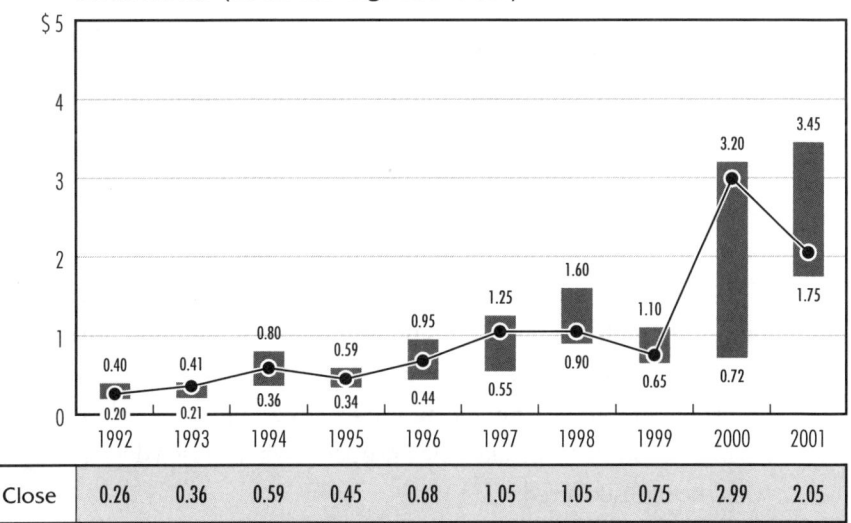

GOLDCORP INC.

145 King Street West, Suite 2700
Toronto, ON M5H 1J8

Tel: (416) 865-0326
Fax: (416) 361-5741
www.goldcorp.com
Symbol: G- (TSX) (Also GG-NYSE)

Employees: 523
Founded: 1994
Listed: 1994

Chairperson and CEO: Robert R. McEwen

Share Price Growth	★ ★ ★ ★ ★
Revenue Growth	★ ★
EPS Growth	★ ★ ★ ★ ★
G	12

About the Company

Goldcorp was listed in the March 2002 issue of *Fast Company* as number two in its Fast 50 Champions of Innovation. The innovation? Virtual exploration of mining properties. Tapping into the brainpower of the world through the Internet to generate the ideas that would help create the world's most cost-effective gold mine.

The Goldcorp Challenge, as it was called, was an exploration contest that made the company's proprietary geological database as well as the company's analytical software available over the Internet. People were invited to be online explorers and geologists to help the company exploit its Red Lake Mine property, where a rich deposit of gold had been discovered.

The Red Lake Mine in northwestern Ontario was long thought to have been tapped out, but chairperson and CEO Robert McEwen thought differently and started a $7-million exploration program in 1995. And he hit the motherlode, so to speak. Rich core samples were pulled from shafts 200 to 1,000 feet from the original mine.

That high-grade find grew to be 2.3 million ounces of reserves, but the surface barely had been scratched. That is where the Goldcorp Challenge came in. Find us our next six million ounces of reserves, the company said. And 475,000 web page hits and 1,400 actual online prospectors from 51 countries later, the company has increased reserves to 4.3 million ounces. Some US$575,000 in prize money was paid out.

Not only did an innovative use of the Internet help to explore the mine, the mine itself has been revamped as a high tech operation. An extensive fibre optic network provides mine-to-surface video, voice, and data communications. This gives the company huge benefits in costs, safety, and time.

The Red Lake Mine only started tapping these new reserves in August 2000, but managed to produce 85,115 ounces by year-end. This almost matched the production for the entire year at the company's other property, the Wharf Mine in South Dakota. In 2001, production at Red Lake was ramped up to an incredible 503,385 million ounces.

Opportunities and Challenges

Goldcorp has continued the novel virtual explorer concept with its new Global Search Challenge. Exploration, as the company puts it, is R&D for the mining industry. And with the Challenge concept, it "taps into the ingenuity and intellectual capital of the world's explorers."

Just as a string of Internet incubator companies popped up to foster development of Internet properties and concepts, so too has Goldcorp's Challenge become "an incubator for new exploration ideas and proposals." Its aim is to identify "the most promising exploration properties in the world."

A key challenge to any mining company is reserves. Mined material must be replaced with new reserves or the mine will eventually run out and close. Goldcorp's innovative strategies have seen reserves growing every year.

Of course the biggest challenge for Goldcorp is the price of gold itself. But with production costs of $92 an ounce in 2001 and expected to fall, the company will be profitable even if prices stay flat.

Financial Highlights

With an up and down earnings history, Goldcorp does not strictly meet our criteria. But look at these numbers! Revenues soared in 2001 for Goldcorp—up 170.3 percent with earnings per share jumping to a profit of $0.64 in 2001 from a loss of $0.24 in 2000. In the first quarter of 2002, the company reported earnings per share up 11.1 percent, but this was understated as the company added gold bullion to its reserves in the belief that the price of gold will go higher. The company is now socking away 10% of its production into bullion reserves and holds more gold than 25% of gold holding countries including Luxemburg and Hong Kong!

Goldcorp is debt free and does not hedge its sales, so any increase in the price of gold goes straight to the bottom line. If gold does, as some people think, move substantially higher, Goldcorp shareholders will be sitting on, well…a goldmine!

Goldcorp Inc. at a Glance
Fiscal Year-end: December
10-Year Return: 40.7%

	1997	1998	1999	2000	2001	10-Year Growth Average (%)	10-Year Growth Total (%)
Revenue ($ mlns.)	88.7	86.5	74.7	91.9	263.9	19.8	141.7
Net Income ($ mlns.)	-140.66	-2.76	6.79	-18.98	84.1	–	–
Earnings/ Share ($)	-1.92	-0.05	0.09	-0.24	1.00	–	–
Dividend/ Share ($)	–	–	–	–	0.28	–	–
Price/ Earnings	-2.0 - -6.4	-80.0 - -184.0	67.2 - 138.9	-26.0 - -46.9	8.4 - 19.8	–	–

Table data courtesy of  www.shareowner.com

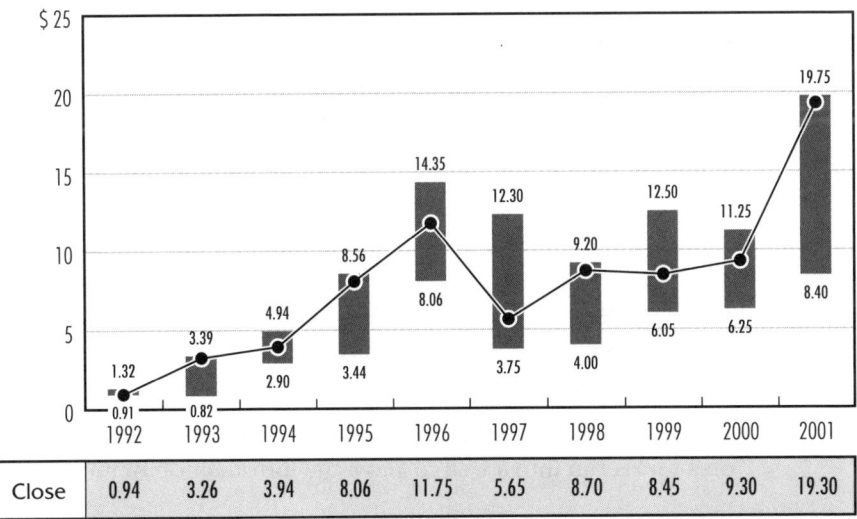

Stock Growth (Fiscal Year High-Low-Close)

TRICAN WELL SERVICE LTD.

645–7th Avenue S.W., Suite 2900
Calgary, AB T2P 4G8

Tel: (403) 266-0202
Fax: (403) 237-7716
www.trican.ca
Symbol: TCW (TSX)

Employees: 626
Founded: 1979
Listed: 1996

President and CEO: Muray L. Cobbe

Share Price Growth	★ ★ ★
Revenue Growth	★ ★ ★ ★
EPS Growth	★ ★ ★
TCW	**10**

About the Company

You may think that an oil services business is out of place in a book on science and technology stocks. And indeed, many of the services provided by Trican seem elementary—pumping, pouring cement, sticking tubing down a well. But the business demands the application of specialized technology to attain results. For example:

- **Cementing:** Oil and gas wells need cementing treatments from a highly specialized apparatus during the drilling phase to support the production casing inside the wellbore.
- **Coiled tubing:** Thousands of feet of jointless steel pipe coiled on a reel is run into a well to allow the introduction of nitrogen,

acids, and other materials to remove unwanted fluids or solids. This allows a well to remain in production while impurities are removed.

- **Fracturing:** Sometimes geological formations do not allow a smooth steady flow of oil, so fluid is pumped into the cased well at high pressure to fracture the formation. A "proppant" is then injected into the fracture to prop it open.

Trican had a modest beginning in 1979—two pumping units and a bulk truck—and it continued its modest ways until going public in 1996. Then, with new management, the company proceeded to expand. First it entered the cementing, coiled tubing, and nitrogen markets, followed by the acquisition of Superior Cementers. It continued to add new gear, including fracturing equipment, spending $61 million on equipment in its first three years as a public company.

In the fall of 2000, Trican opened a 6,000-square-foot research facility in Red Deer, Alberta, the second-largest lab of its type in Western Canada. The company has a number of patents pending on proprietary systems, including four for fracturing fluids. It also has developed new lightweight "titanium" cements and a variety of specialized equipment. A redesigned liquid CO_2 blender and Canada's first "one-truck" fracturing unit give the company significant competitive advantages.

Today the pumping business makes up only half of the company's revenue. The rest comes from fracturing, nitrogen, and coiled tubing. Trican's revenues have grown more than 550 percent since going public. Trican Well Services was added to the TSE 300 index in December 2000.

Opportunities and Challenges

The company has benefited greatly from the oil boom and grown steadily. In December 2000, it completed its acquisition of Canadian

Oilfield Stimulation Services. Also in December 2000, Trican obtained the Canadian rights to the patented Polybore system. This process facilitates the repair of a wellbore, thereby extending its life.

The company's primary business has been oil well services, but it is also pursuing new technology for the gas market. And Trican's technology has been exported to Russia, South America, the U.S., and the Middle East.

Trican is another one of the stocks that bucked the technology downturn, no doubt because it served a booming industry—oil. To some extent, its stock price is affected by the price of oil, as was the case in 2001. But Trican is diversifying, and the coiled tubing business is less prone to market fluctuations since it is used as much for well enhancement and life extension as for new drilling.

Financial Highlights

Despite moderating oil prices throughout 2001, Trican's revenues gained an impressive 39.2 percent, while earnings per share jumped 42.7 percent. The share price, however, did not fare as well, nose-diving to $12 in December 2001 after hitting a peak of $23 in June that year. But you can't keep a good stock down. Its excellent financial picture spurred the stock on again in late December. Nevertheless, investors should keep a finger on the pulse of the oil market while holding industry stocks.

Trican gained a star in our ratings because of its outstanding revenue gain.

Trican Well Service Ltd. at a Glance

Fiscal Year-end: December
5-Year Return: 42.6%

	1997	1998	1999	2000	2001	5-Year Growth Average (%)	5-Year Growth Total (%)
Revenue ($ mlns.)	28.1	39.5	61.8	130.9	182.2	62.0	548.7
Net Income ($ mlns.)	2.2	1.8	4.9	14.8	21.9	100.0	881.3
Earnings/ Share ($)	0.23	0.15	0.34	0.88	1.27	73.8	452.2
Dividend/ Share ($)	–	–	–	–	–	–	–
Price/ Earnings	11.5 - 37.0	15.0 - 43.3	5.0 - 21.9	7.2 - 19.3	9.4 - 18.1	–	–

Table data courtesy of  www.shareowner.com

Stock Growth (Fiscal Year High-Low-Close)

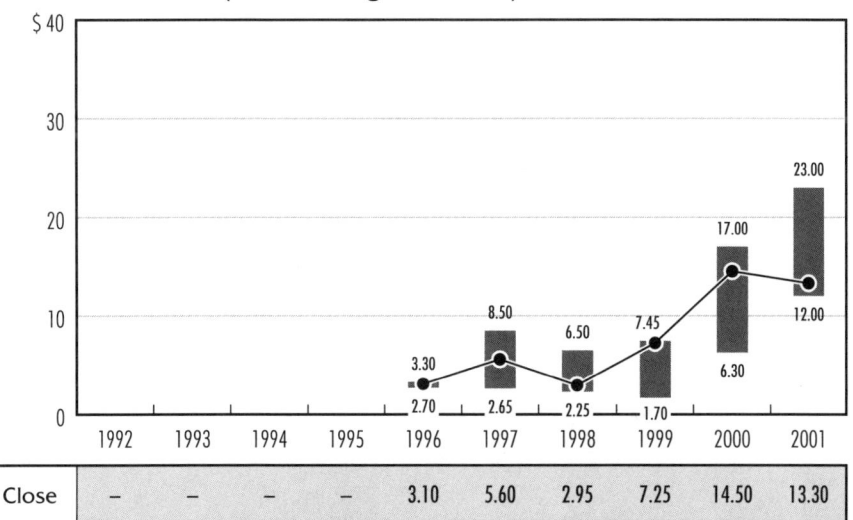

| Close | – | – | – | – | 3.10 | 5.60 | 2.95 | 7.25 | 14.50 | 13.30 |

INDUSTRY

Magna International Inc.
Silent Witness Enterprises Ltd.
ADF Group Inc.
Bombardier Inc.
BW Technologies Ltd.
SNC-Lavalin Group Inc.
Gennum Corporation
Groupe Laperrière & Verreault
Stantec Inc.
Winpak Ltd.
DuPont Canada Inc.
ATS Automation Tooling Systems Inc.
CAE Inc.
Tesma International Inc.
Magellan Aerospace Corporation

MAGNA INTERNATIONAL INC.

337 Magna Drive
Aurora, ON L4G 7K1

Tel: (905) 726-2462 Employees: 67,000
Fax: (905) 726-7164 Founded: 1957
www.magna.ca Listed: 1962
Symbol: MG.A (TSX) (Also MGA-NYSE)

Chairperson: Frank Stronach
President and CEO: Belinda Stronach

Share Price Growth	★ ★ ★ ★ ★
Revenue Growth	★ ★ ★ ★
EPS Growth	★ ★ ★ ★ ★
MG.A	**14**

About the Company

Three years after immigrating from Austria in 1954, Frank Stronach started a one-man tool-and-die shop, Multimatic. By the end of the year he had 10 employees and $13,000 in sales. From that humble beginning evolved a global industrial empire with 67,000 employees working in 173 factories and 43 research and development centres in 19 countries. Magna is one of the largest diversified auto parts suppliers in the world and designs, engineers, and manufactures just about anything and everything that goes into making a car.

The company got sidetracked with non-core investments as it grew, and restructured in 1990–91, selling off most of its non-strategic divisions. It went on to expand its core business through the acquisition of a number of European auto systems suppliers including Steyr-Daimler-Puch, now Magna Steyr. The company's growth strategy has been to add to the number of different auto parts it makes. So even during the auto industry's periodic slumps, Magna has enhanced or maintained sales by increasing component contributions to various makes of car. Revenues have grown from just over $2 billion in 1991 to more than $17.5 billion in 2001.

Magna International is Canada's fourth-largest spender on research and development in dollar terms—$359.2 million in 2001. However, because of its huge sales, R&D as a percentage of sales is actually quite low—2.1 percent. Among Magna's interesting R&D developments is hydroforming technology, a manufacturing process that uses water pressure to bend and form metal, and the built-in child safety seat, co-developed by Magna, which was named one of the great innovations of the 1980s by the Smithsonian Institute.

Frank Stronach groomed his daughter Belinda to take over the company some day, and that day came in February 2001 when she assumed the role of vice-chairperson and CEO. A short while later she was made president of the company. Dad continues on as chairperson of the board.

Mr. Stronach was honoured with the Order of Canada in 1999 and received the Ontario Lifetime Achievement Award from the Ernst & Young Entrepreneur of the Year program in 2000.

Opportunities and Challenges

In 2001, 75 percent of Magna's sales were to the big three U.S. automakers. The balance was divided among Volkswagen, BMW, and other manufacturers. Magna has been actively expanding its European presence. One of Magna's new contracts in 2001, in fact, was a $1 billion-deal with BMW to commence in 2004. BMW currently makes up 6 percent of Magna's business. Although Magna has a modest presence in Asia, that continent represents huge untapped potential for future growth.

The company has consistently managed to increase sales and profits even during lean years for the automotive industry, by constantly developing new products and parts, thereby increasing the company's contribution to each car. The October 2002 acquisition of Donnelly Corporation, the second largest supplier of auto mirrors, will further the company's goal of doubling sales in the next four years as auto makers continue to increase outsourced components.

Magna has successfully created shareholder value in the past by spinning off its Tesma and Decoma divisions as new public companies. Last year this "spinco" strategy, as Magna calls it, was applied to the Intier division. A plan to merge Magna Steyr with Tesma was scuttled after Magna Steyr acquired the Eurostar assembly facility in Graz, Austria from Daimler-Chrysler in mid-2002. An IPO spinoff of Magna Steyr is now expected to be launched in March of 2003.

Financial Highlights

Despite a slowdown in auto sales and a slump in the industry, Magna managed to increase sales by 4 percent in 2001. Earnings per share were down slightly by 3.7 percent. The company's added value strategy continues to work effectively; Magna saw a 9-percent increase in North American per vehicle content for the year and a 27-percent increase in European per vehicle content. The first six months of 2002 were even better as revenues climbed 12.6 percent and EPS from operations jumped 7.5 percent.

The fortunes of Magna's stock have been on a long-term uptrend for more than 10 years. But the road is not always a straight line. Investors should look at the company's stock chart and note its cyclical pattern of higher highs and higher lows.

Magna International Inc. at a Glance

Fiscal Year-end: December
10-Year Return: 16.8%

	1997	1998	1999	2000	2001	10-Year Growth Average (%)	10-Year Growth Total (%)
Revenue ($ mlns.)	7,691.8	9,190.8	13,514.8	15,764.0	17,560.1	25.5	644.5
Net Income ($ mlns.)	427.4	461.1	620.9	744.4	822.8	28.1	739.6
Earnings/ Share ($)	5.39	5.51	6.86	7.97	9.00	18.6	332.7
Dividend/ Share ($)	1.14	1.28	1.32	1.86	2.11	36.8	955.0
Price/ Earnings	11.4 - 17.4	15.0 - 20.5	8.6 - 14.0	6.9 - 10.0	6.7 - 11.8	–	–

Table data courtesy of  www.shareowner.com

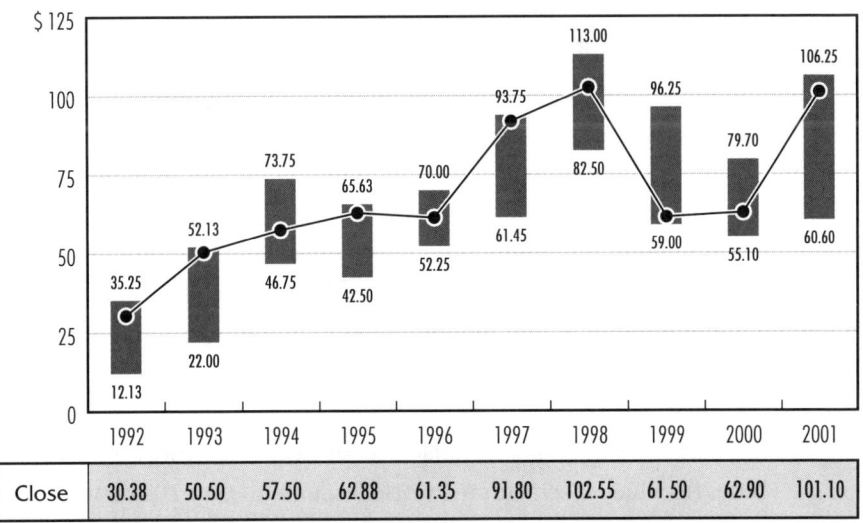

* As of fiscal 1999, the company's fiscal year-end changed from July to December. The months from August through December 1998 are not included in these data.

SILENT WITNESS ENTERPRISES LTD.

6554–176th Street
Surrey, BC V3S 4G5

Tel: (604) 574-1526   Employees: 160
Fax: (604) 574-7736   Founded: 1986
www.silentwitness.com   Listed: 1987
Symbol: SWE (TSX) (Also SILW-NASDAQ)

Chairperson, President, and CEO: Rajeev (Rob) Bakshi

Share Price Growth	★ ★ ★ ★ ★
Revenue Growth	★ ★ ★ ★
EPS Growth	★ ★ ★
SWE	**12**

About the Company

You've probably seen this scenario in the movies: robbers enter a bank, notice the security camera, and blow it away. But not if the bank was using one of the high tech, super-durable V-100 Bullet Resistant cameras from Silent Witness. This baby can withstand an attack from a 9-mm handgun or even a shotgun blast! The V-100 is just one of many award-winning, closed-circuit television security systems made by Silent Witness.

Founded in 1986 as a manufacturer of video-monitoring systems for buses (in which it remains the world leader with over 100,000 installed systems), the company expanded its product line over the years to provide security solutions for commercial businesses, security firms, casinos, prisons, schools, universities, warehouses, loading docks, emergency vehicles, transit, and taxicabs.

Products include The Puck (because it vaguely looks like one), an infrared illumination unit that enables pictures in complete darkness at up to 40 feet. The company also makes mini-cams, including a pinhole camera for covert operations.

Silent Witness underwent tremendous growth from 1995 through 2000 with a compound average sales growth of 57 percent and earnings growth of 158 percent. It was featured as one of the fastest-growing companies in Canada in the Profit 100 list released in the spring of 2001. More than 80 percent of sales are to the U.S., and the company was one of several honoured at the Canada Export Awards in October 2000.

In 2000, the company positioned itself for a new wave of growth by embracing both digital and wireless technologies. Seven percent of revenues goes into research, and the company foresees tremendous opportunities in real-time video surveillance over the Internet, among other things.

The company also opened an OEM (original equipment manufacturing) division in 2000 to leverage its video expertise beyond the security business.

In April 2001, the company acquired Gyyr's Pan/Tilt/Zoom (PTZ) product line along with associated intellectual property. The PTZ market is expected to hit $134 million by 2004.

Opportunities and Challenges

With the terrorist attacks on America in September 2001, there has been an increased emphasis on domestic security and security systems. With Silent Witness's high tech expertise in this area, it should grow well into the future.

Meanwhile the low-end video surveillance market is huge, with over $3 billion in annual sales. Major players like Sony, Panasonic, and JVC have most of this market. Silent Witness moved to enter the budget market in June 2001 with the release of the Sigma M12 surveillance unit, suited for small business, residential, and daycare applications.

And OEM manufacturing led to a joint venture with Stanley Works to develop a Digital Video Sensor for automatic doors at commercial sites. The first order for the new OEM manufacturing division was placed in November 2001.

Silent Witness scored a major coup in June 2002 with a US$1.6 million order to supply its DVMS 1600 Digital Video Management System to the Fifth Third Bank of Cincinnati. The DVMS system is part of its Gyyr acquisition and the sale is the largest in Silent Witness's history.

Financial Highlights

Revenues for fiscal 2001 grew marginally at 2.9 percent while earnings per share rose 7.5 percent. But revenues for the first and second quarters of fiscal 2002 were up 26.4 percent and 38.8 percent, respectively. As impressive as that is, it was lower than expected because of the slowing economy and a delay in bringing a new product to market. One-time integration costs for the Gyyr takeover cut into earnings and produced a loss in the second quarter.

Silent Witness fell precipitously from a high of $14.50 to a low of $7 during the technology downturn, but resumed a long-term uptrend in 2001, rising 50.3 percent for the year. The first half of 2002 saw a retracement and consolidation with the bear taking a big bite in August and September.

Silent Witness gained a star in our ratings this year for share price growth in 2001.

Silent Witness Enterprises Ltd. at a Glance

Fiscal Year-end: July
5-Year Return: 48.2%

	1997	1998	1999	2000	2001	6-Year Growth Average (%)	6-Year Growth Total (%)
Revenue ($ mlns.)	13.4	21.7	33.8	39.9	40.0	39.5	382.4
Net Income ($ mlns.)	1.0	2.2	4.4	5.1	4.5	53.9	334.8
Earnings/ Share ($)	0.18	0.37	0.65	0.75	0.69	–	–
Dividend/ Share ($)	–	–	–	–	–	–	–
Price/ Earnings	4.4 - 10.8	5.0 - 17.2	6.5 - 22.8	9.7 - 19.3	10.1 - 16.3	–	–

Table data courtesy of ✓Canadian Shareowner   www.shareowner.com

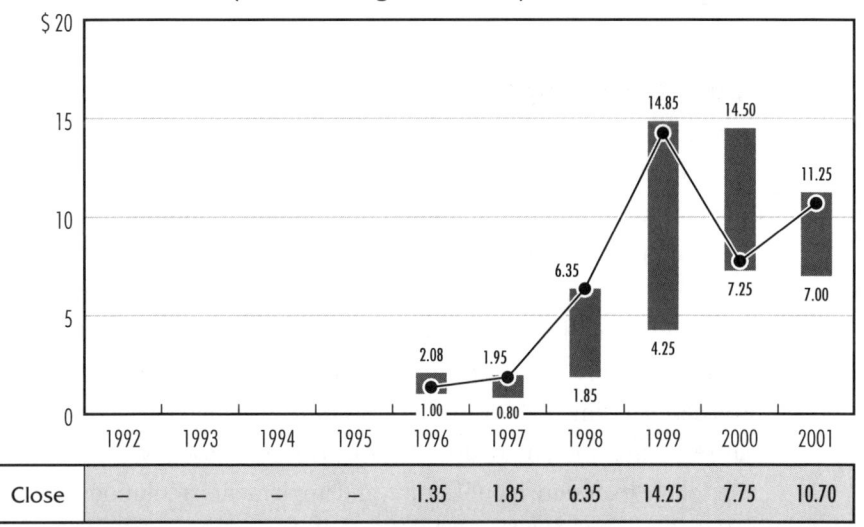

Stock Growth (Fiscal Year High-Low-Close)

Close	1992	1993	1994	1995	1996	1997	1998	1999	2000	2001
	–	–	–	–	1.35	1.85	6.35	14.25	7.75	10.70

* Net income growth based on five years. Data for 1996 from company reports.

ADF GROUP INC.

300 Henry-Bessemer
Terrebonne, QC J6Y 1T3

Tel: (450) 965-1911
Fax: (450) 965-8558
www.adfgroup.com
Symbol: DRX (TSX)

Employees: 1,200
Founded: 1956
Listed: 1999

Chairperson and CEO: Jean Paschini
President and COO: Pierre Paschini

Share Price Growth	★
Revenue Growth	★ ★ ★ ★ ★
EPS Growth	★ ★ ★ ★ ★
DRX	**11**

About the Company

Founded as a blacksmith shop specializing in complex forged iron works in 1956, ADF Group has since grown to become an international player in the structural steel business. ADF stands for Au Dragon Forgé, literally "forged by a dragon." The company was incorporated in 1979 and went public in 1999. In 1992, the company launched a branch office in Florida to offset the seasonality of business in Canada.

The company specializes in large-scale structural steel for megaprojects including high-rise office towers, bridges, airports, convention centres, museums, and hydro-electric projects. It uses state-of-the-art technology to design, manufacture, and implement its solutions. In fact, ADF has been ISO 9001 certified since 1994.

The company has recently expanded beyond Canada and the U.S. and built a maintenance hangar for Air Algeria, a casino in the Bahamas, and industrial complexes in the Sudan and Madagascar.

ADF Group aims to have 55 percent of its business in the U.S. and 20 percent international within five years. In 2000, it garnered a Canada Export Award from the Canadian federal government. It has numerous other awards, including being named as one of the 50 Best Managed Companies in Canada for 1996, 1997, and 1998.

Opportunities and Challenges

One of ADF's key strengths, and indeed, the foundation of its success, is its engineering department employing 250 top engineers and designers. Computer-assisted design and management, as well as automated fabrication equipment, have made ADF a leading-edge company.

One of its novel offerings is the OSD, or Optimal Structural Design Solution. This involves early pre-construction analysis of a project to see where design modifications can create a more efficient and cost-effective solution. As ADF puts it, "The OSD Solution is ingenuity working for you."

Projects landed in 2001 and 2002 include Phase 1 of the Smithsonian's National Air and Space Museum in Washington, D.C.; the Performing Arts Center in Miami, Florida; a 54-story office tower at 731 Lexington Place in New York City, which will house Bloomberg Financial, among other tenants; and a new building for the King's County Hospital in Brooklyn, New York.

Out of the ashes of the World Trade Center in New York, new structures will arise. ADF Group is likely to be a major player in the reconstruction. Bovis Lend Lease LMB Inc., a major general contractor in New York, is the lead manager in the cleanup of the WTC site and one of four prime contractors assigned to rebuild the business district. The new buildings likely will be more complex for security reasons, and complex projects are ADF's forté. Bovis has subcontracted structural design and construction to ADF on previous occasions, including the above noted 731 Lexington building and Columbus Center. ADF Group, in fact, is becoming one of the preferred steel structure subcontractors in the Big Apple.

In April 2002, ADF Group completed the acquisition of SMI-Owen Steel Company of Columbia, South Carolina, one of its competitors in the New York market. ADF Group had a project backlog of $450 million near the end of 2001.

Financial Highlights

ADF Group has grown wildly in the last four years, with revenues exploding to $510.2 million in fiscal 2002 from $108.9 million in fiscal 1999. Growth for fiscal 2002 alone was 52.6 percent. Earnings per share, however, were down 16.1 percent because of negotiations on payments for cost overruns due to design changes. The company expects to recover these profits in the future. The slow-down in the economy, however, began to take its toll in 2002. Revenues in the first half of 2002 dropped 12.8 percent and EPS fell 74.2 percent.

ADF Group only went public in 1999, just barely squeaking in on our three-year listing requirement. Our star ratings are based on available data going back to 1997. Since inception, ADF's stock had been on a decided long-term uptrend with intervening corrections along the way until the stock plunged from $15.50 in March 2002 to $6.25 in early September. Watch for the stock to make ground once the economy recovers.

ADF Group Inc. at a Glance

Fiscal Year-end: January
2-Year Return: 15.1%

	1998	1999	2000	2001	2002	4-Year Growth Average (%)	4-Year Growth Total (%)
Revenue ($ mlns.)	–	108.9	218.2	334.4	510.2	68.7	368.5
Net Income ($ mlns.)	–	11.8	15.5	24.2	24.2	29.2	105.1
Earnings/ Share ($)	–	0.56	0.73	1.11	0.89	20.9	58.9
Dividend/ Share ($)	–	–	–	–	–	–	–
Price/ Earnings	–	–	10.3 - 17.8	6.4 - 10.8	9.0 - 17.1	–	–

Table data courtesy of  www.shareowner.com

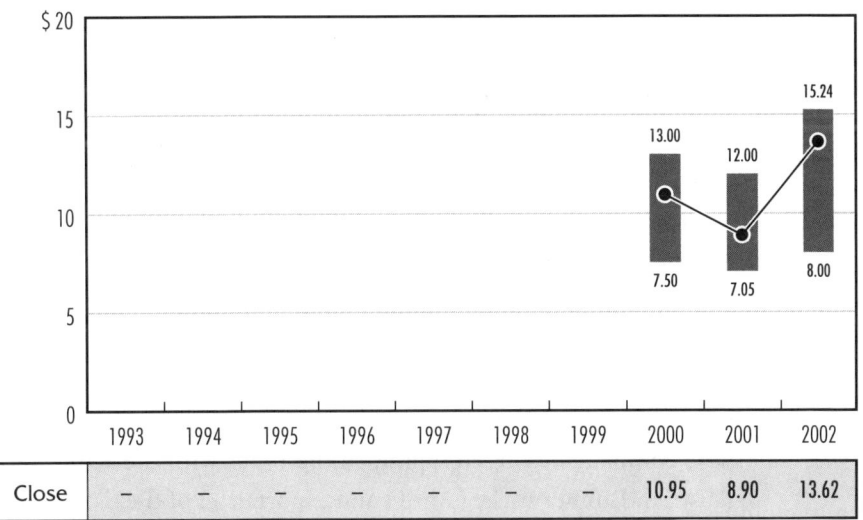

BOMBARDIER INC.

800 René Lévesque Boulevard. W., 29th Floor
Montreal, QC H3B 1Y8

Tel: (514) 861-9481
Fax: (514) 861-7053
www.bombardier.com
Symbol: BBD.B (TSX)

Employees: 79,000
Founded: 1942
Listed: 1946

Chairperson: Laurent Beaudoin
President and CEO: Robert L. Brown

Share Price Growth	★ ★ ★ ★
Revenue Growth	★ ★ ★ ★
EPS Growth	★ ★
BBD.B	**10**

About the Company

When J.-Armande Bombardier invented the snowmobile in 1937, he had no idea that it was the genesis of a multi-billion dollar business. Commercialization of this invention with the formation of his company in 1942 proved a boon for the forestry, mining, and petroleum industries, which often operate in remote and difficult terrain. But the company really made strides with the invention of the personal snowmobile-—the Ski-Doo—which debuted in 1959 and created a whole new winter sport.

The company expanded rapidly in the 1970s with the acquisition of Austrian Lohnerwerke GmbH and exportation of the Ski-Doo to the U.S. In 1974, Bombardier diversified into mass transit with a contract to build rolling stock for Montreal's metro. This was followed by the acquisition of several railcar design and manufacturing operations in the U.S. and Europe in the 1980s.

The 1980s also saw the company move into the aerospace business with the takeover of Canadair as well as the acquisition of Short Brothers PLC. In the 1990s, Bombardier bought out Learjet and de Havilland.

Today the company has five operating divisions: Bombardier Aerospace, Bombardier Transportation, Bombardier Recreational Products, Bombardier Capital, and Bombardier International, with plants in 12 countries. The company also owns and operates the J.-Armande Bombardier Museum in Valcourt, Quebec, the largest privately owned science and technology museum in Canada.

Bombardier had the 16th-largest R&D expenditure in Canada in 2001 at $123.4 million, which was only 0.8 percent of its sales.

Opportunities and Challenges

The company's operations are concentrated in Europe and North America, and it hasn't even begun to tap the huge Asian market. The function of its International division is just that—to expand the company with specific interest in Asia, Eastern and Central Europe, Russia, and Latin America. Bombardier maintains an office in Beijing as well as in Montreal.

The year 2001 saw the acquisition of Adtranz, the rail division of DaimlerChrysler in Europe, making Bombardier the leading supplier of rail equipment in the world. Rail equipment now accounts for 40 percent of revenues.

Like all companies involved in the airline industry, Bombardier was affected by the terrorist attacks of September 11, 2001, as well as the economic slowdown worldwide. Two weeks later the company adjusted its earnings growth target from 30 percent for fiscal 2001–2002 to 15 percent. That may be optimistic. August 2002 saw a flood of bad publicity for the company including disclosure by Amtrak of problems with Bombardier's Acela trains, a major contract with the New York Metropolitan Transportation Authority going to a French rival, cutbacks by major airlines trying to stem the flow of red ink, a slowdown in business jet sales, concern over Bombardier's debt levels and accounting practices, and the company' first ever profit warning.

Financial Highlights

Despite an earnings expectations downgrade, Bombardier grew revenues 34.9 percent for fiscal 2002, but earnings per share suffered, sliding 61.4 percent due to special charges relating to the company's withdrawal from the retail financing business as well as write-offs in the Aerospace Division.

Bombardier stock had been on a steady upward trend from 1993 to October 2000 when it started to falter. Post 9/11, it recovered somewhat and traded flat for the first half of 2002. Then the problems noted above precipitated a plunge from $14 to $5. A general economic recovery is vital for the company's future prospects.

While Bombardier gained a star for revenue growth, it lost one for share price growth and two for EPS growth this year.

Bombardier Inc. at a Glance

Fiscal Year-end: January
10-Year Return: 24.7%

	1998	1999	2000	2001	2002	10-Year Growth Average (%)	10-Year Growth Total (%)
Revenue ($ mlns.)	8,508.9	11,500.1	13,618.5	16,100.6	21,633.8	19.6	386.4
Net Income ($ mlns.)	407.8	517.1	711.3	944.6	1,126.1	27.6	764.9
Earnings/ Share ($)	0.29	0.38	0.52	0.69	0.81	26.7	710.0
Dividend/ Share ($)	0.08	0.09	0.11	0.14	0.19	24.0	533.3
Price/ Earnings	21.4 - 29.3	18.5 - 31.3	18.2 - 31.0	20.1 - 38.7	11.3 - 30.4	–	–

Table data courtesy of  www.shareowner.com

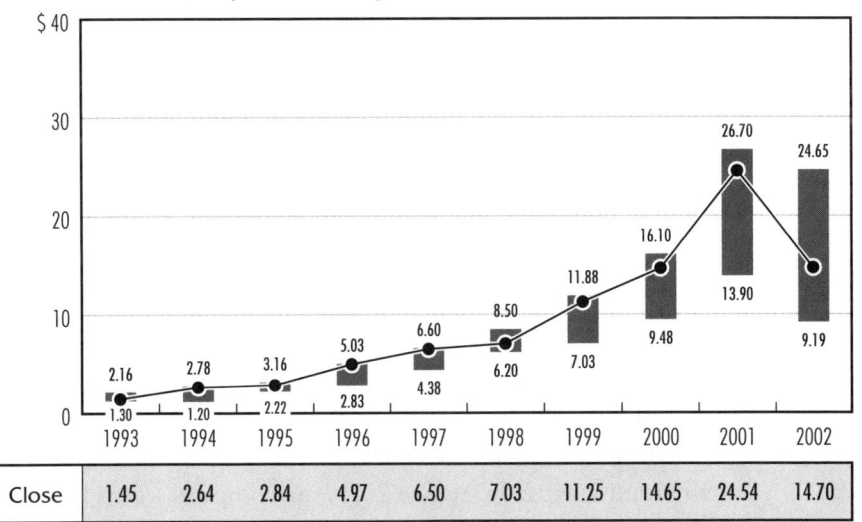

BW TECHNOLOGIES LTD.

2840–2nd Avenue S.E.
Calgary, AB T2A 7X9

Tel: (403) 248-9226
Fax: (403) 273-3708
www.bwtnet.com
Symbol: BWT (TSX)

Employees: 159
Founded: 1987
Listed: 1997

Chairperson: Dr. John Finbow
President and CEO: Cody Z. Slater

Share Price Growth	★ ★ ★ ★
Revenue Growth	★ ★ ★
EPS Growth	★ ★ ★
BWT	**10**

About the Company

Calgary-based BW Technologies was founded in 1987 when president and CEO Cody Slater took a term off from university to design a wireless gas detection unit. One term turned into 15 years, as BW has grown into a world leader in gas-detection technologies. Its products are used primarily by the oil industry and other industrial customers to detect noxious gases that might endanger employees or create a hazardous situation. Products include portable units the size of a cellphone as well as fixed units and stand-alone wireless units.

BW is also involved in other markets including heating, ventilation, and air conditioning. In August 2000, the company won a lucrative contract to design and manufacture custom systems for the Eurotunnel, the rail link between England and France.

In 2001, the company expanded beyond the industrial market into the commercial arena with a product that detects carbon monoxide and other gases in underground parking garages. Current systems require frequent and expensive manual calibration, but BW's detectors are maintenance-free and can be connected to the standard control systems manufactured by Honeywell, Siemens, and Johnson Controls. After three years the detectors are replaced like a light bulb. This promises to be a lucrative and growing market with repeat business built-in.

The company also incorporated multimedia cards (used in MP3 players and digital cameras) into its GasAlert Max monitors so that data can be logged continuously. These units record data more frequently, can store more data, and are 30 percent cheaper than their competitors. By allowing the recording of real-time details, this technology allows BW to pursue the telecom and utilities market it was previously unable to serve.

The company has offices in Texas and the U.K. as well as in Calgary and a network of authorized dealers with more than 400 offices in over 50 countries. A regional office was opened in Dubai in the Middle East in December 2001. Seventy-five percent of sales are exported out of Canada. In January 2002, BW Technologies was named as one of the 30 fastest-growing companies in Alberta by *Alberta Venture Magazine* for the fourth consecutive year.

Opportunities and Challenges

The global market for gas detection equipment is estimated to be around US$1 billion annually. The industry is fragmented, with no company controlling more than 15 percent. And for most suppliers, gas detection equipment is a small fraction of their total operations.

With its focus on gas detectors and nothing else, BW Technologies has developed an edge in research and development, and in marketing.

Its units' compact size and competitive pricing have seen sales growing at an annual compounded rate of 44 percent a year from 1997 to 2001. With sales for 2002 of $38.9 million, BW Technologies obviously still has tremendous room for growth. Sales are expected to hit $51.5 million in fiscal 2003.

In November 2001, the company purchased an additional warehouse in Texas to expand its service capabilities five-fold.

Gas detection equipment is in high demand in the oil industry and the ongoing boom in the oil patch drives 35 percent of BW's revenues. However, a drop in oil prices, coupled with a fall-off in exploration, could impact BW's sales. Diversification into the home heating and air conditioning field as well as underground parking should mitigate this possibility.

Financial Highlights

Fiscal 2002 to April 30 saw revenues jump 40.3 percent, with earnings up a whopping 70.6 percent. BW Technologies was one of the few technology companies that gained in price during the NASDAQ bear market, hitting new highs through April 2002. BW Technologies may still represent a good investment for 2003.

We've given BW Technologies two additional stars this year, one for share price growth and one for EPS growth.

BW Technologies Ltd. at a Glance

Fiscal Year-end: April
5-Year Return: 52.4%

	1998	1999	2000	2001	2002	5-Year Growth Average (%)	5-Year Growth Total (%)
Revenue ($ mlns.)	12.3	17.3	18.4	27.8	39.0	34.6	217.1
Net Income ($ mlns.)	0.6	1.2	1.2	2.8	4.9	77.4	722.2
Earnings/ Share ($)	0.15	0.28	0.25	0.49	0.82	59.8	446.7
Dividend/ Share ($)	–	–	–	–	–	–	–
Price/ Earnings	13.0 - 30.0	8.9 - 17.3	18.0 - 34.0	10.2 - 21.2	10.1 - 27.0	–	–

Table data courtesy of *Canadian Shareowner* www.shareowner.com

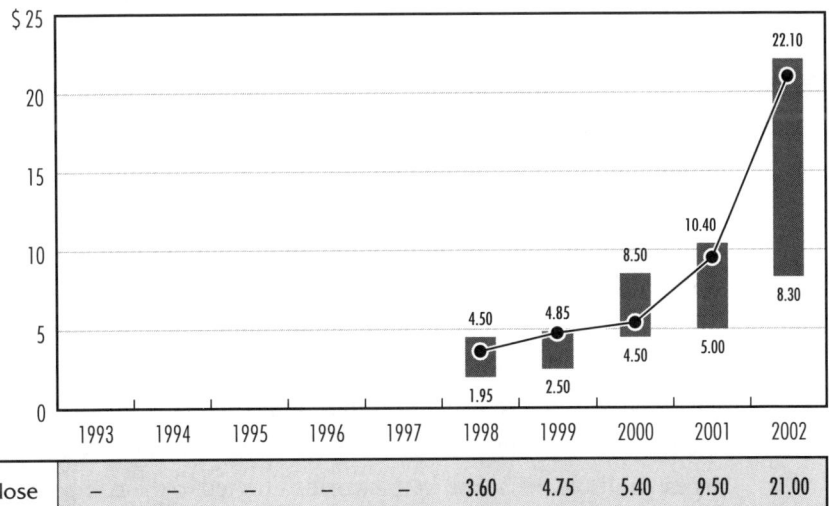

Stock Growth (Fiscal Year High-Low-Close)

SNC-LAVALIN GROUP INC.

455 René Lévesque Boulevard W.
Montreal, QC H2Z 1Z3

Tel: (514) 393-1000
Fax: (514) 866-0795
www.snc-lavalin.com
Symbol: SNC (TSX)

Employees: 8,819
Founded: 1911
Listed: 1992

Chairperson: Guy Saint-Pierre
President and CEO: Jacques Lamarre

Share Price Growth	★ ★ ★ ★
Revenue Growth	★ ★ ★
EPS Growth	★ ★ ★
SNC	**10**

About the Company

The origins of SNC-Lavalin go back to 1911 when Arthur Surveyor started a small engineering consulting firm. It developed a growing reputation and in 1937, Surveyor was joined by Emil Nenniger and Georges Chênevert, the partnership whose initials gave the company its new name—SNC—10 years later.

The company continued to grow its reputation for excellence in civil engineering, power, and industrial plants, and in the early 1960s became part of the consortium that built the giant Manic 5 hydro-electric power project in Northern Quebec. The Manic 5 dam is the largest multiple-arch dam in the world. This led to the company's first international project—the Idukki Power Station in India.

The company went public in 1986 and in 1991, SNC and Lavalin, the two largest engineering companies in Canada, merged to form the present company—SNC-Lavalin.

Today it is one of the leading engineering firms in the world, with over 8,800 employees in 30 countries and engaged in projects in 100 countries worldwide.

SNC-Lavalin's expertise covers such diverse fields as industry, power, transportation, telecommunications, aerospace, infrastructure, and the environment. It offers complete design, construction, and management of projects and even provides project financing.

Past projects the company has been involved in include the Daniel Johnson Dam in Quebec; the Chamera Dam in India; the Alusaf Aluminum Smelter in South Africa; the Ankara Metro in Turkey; the Skytrain light rail transit system in Vancouver; a light rail transit system in Kuala Lumpur, Malaysia; offshore platforms for the Hibernia oil project; electric power plants in Indonesia, Korea, and Tanzania; the International Airport in Eldoret, Kenya; the European Parliament Buildings in Brussels, Belgium; and even the Radarsat Satellite for the Canadian Space Agency.

The latter project was a feasibility study for the privatization of Radarsat; privatization of public projects is one of SNC-Lavalin's areas of expertise.

In the decade since SNC and Lavalin merged, revenues have grown to $2,326.8 million from $580.8 million.

Opportunities and Challenges

SNC-Lavalin saw another record year in 2001, with the Murraylink power transmission grid project in Australia, a waste water treatment project in Venezuela, a gas storage project in New York state, a sulfuric acid plant in Turkey, an aluminum smelter in Mozambique and another in Russia, a water supply project in Libya, and more.

The company also formed a number of partnerships to increase its presence in selected fields. One was a partnership with an American company to construct electricity-generating stations in the U.S., another a partnership with Cogeco Cable to pursue opportunities in broadband networks internationally. And the company has also pursued complementary acquisitions.

One of SNC's biggest challenges in the last few years has been its co-ownership of the Highway 407 toll road in Toronto. A major extension of this $4-billion project produced in partnership with Grupo Ferrovial/Cintra and Capital d'Amerique, was completed in August 2001. It is the world's first all-electronic, barrier free, open access toll highway in the world. Unfortunately, it has been losing money and eating into SNC's profits. Although revenues have been increasing and the project would eventually reach profitability, SNC sold off 26 percent of its interest to Cintra in March 2002, leaving it with a 16.8 percent interest. The shares were sold at a hefty profit—four times SNC's investment on a per share basis.

In May 2002 SNC-Lavalin made news and saw its shares rise when it took over construction of eight gas-fired electricity-generating plants from bankrupt Enron Corporation.

Financial Highlights

SNC-Lavalin's revenues increased by 33.7 percent in 2001, with earnings up marginally at 7.8 percent. Not bad for a "bad" year in the economy! The first half of 2002 saw revenues rise 31.5 percent and earnings up 23.2 percent (excluding Highway 401). The windfall gain from the 401 sale would have made the earnings growth 199.0 percent.

SNC's share price has also done well, recently soaring. This pace could slow and the stock could face a correction, but the company's solid growth in spite of a poor economic environment bodes well for the future.

SNC-Lavalin Group Inc. at a Glance

Fiscal Year-end: December
10-Year Return: 24.4%

	1997	1998	1999	2000	2001	10-Year Growth Average (%)	10-Year Growth Total (%)
Revenue ($ mlns.)	1,412.9	1,507.5	1,270.8	1,740.4	2,326.8	14.7	211.4
Net Income ($ mlns.)	40.2	45.6	36.3	23.9	26.4	17.1	184.1
Earnings/ Share ($)	0.80	0.93	0.78	0.51	0.54	15.3	157.1
Dividend/ Share ($)	0.20	0.20	0.24	0.24	0.28	20.0	366.7
Price/ Earnings	13.4 - 23.8	9.1 - 16.0	13.5 - 17.6	19.9 - 29.0	24.5 - 53.5	–	–

Table data courtesy of  www.shareowner.com

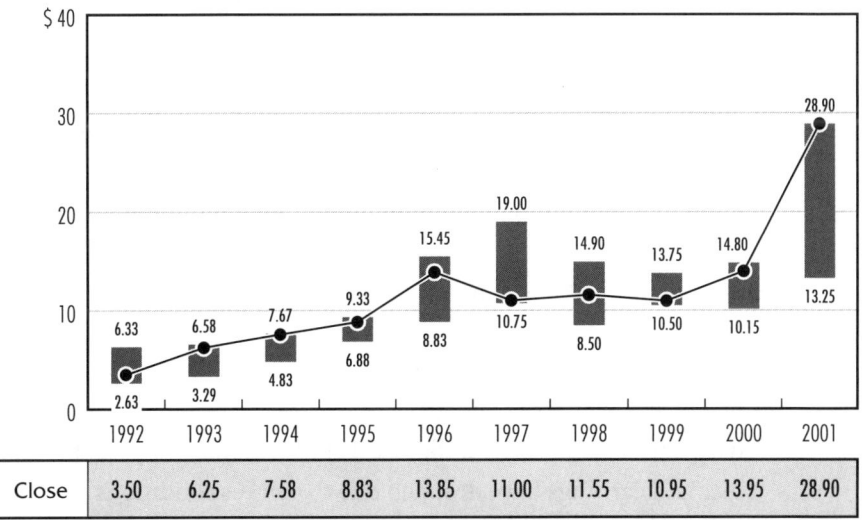

GENNUM CORPORATION

P.O. Box 489, Station A
Burlington, ON L7R 3Y3

Tel: (905) 632-2996
Fax: (905) 632-2055
www.gennum.com
Symbol: GND (TSX)

Employees: 507
Founded: 1973
Listed: 1982

Chairperson: H. Patrick Thode
President and CEO: Dr. Ian L. McWalter

Share Price Growth	★ ★ ★ ★ ★
Revenue Growth	★ ★
EPS Growth	★ ★
GND	**9**

About the Company

Gennum is a high technology company focused on three separate areas: technology for the hearing impaired, video processing and distribution for the television broadcasting industry, and data communications. More specifically, the company designs and manufactures electronic components—silicon integrated circuits and thick-film hybrid circuits—for these systems.

The company was founded in 1973 and since then has grown revenues at an average of over 20 percent a year through 2000. Earnings have grown every year as well. Fiscal 2001 was the first year that revenues and earnings have dropped due to market conditions.

The company's strength comes from high-speed signal transmission, miniaturization of components, and low power usage. And it maintains its edge through focused research and development. The company has increased R&D spending every year including 2001, when sales declined. In fact, because of this, R&D was 24.2 percent of sales for fiscal 2001, significantly above its average R&D spending of 15 percent to 20 percent of revenues.

The company's core markets—hearing aids and video processors—made up 98.6 percent of revenues in 2001 with data contributing 1.4 percent. A two-year agreement with Tyco International signed in April 2001 to market Gennum's data solutions should see additional growth in this area.

Gennum has two production facilities in Burlington, Ontario, and opened a new design centre in Ottawa in the first quarter of 2001. The company also has purchased a 12-acre parcel in Burlington for a new 68,000-square-foot facility, originally slated for completion by the first quarter of 2002. This will house 300 employees and accommodate the company's expansion for the next three to five years.

Opportunities and Challenges

As baby boomers start to lose their hearing after years of abusing their ears with loud rock concerts, boom boxes, and blaring Walkmans, Gennum is there to fill the need for hearing equipment. The company released Paragon Digital, its first line of digital signal processing components for hearing instruments, in April 2001. The patent-pending technology delivers superior-quality sound with low power consumption. These components are among the smallest on the market, allowing for complete "in-the-canal" hearing aids. Digital hearing aids are the fastest growing segment of the hearing instrument market.

The company's sales mix shifted considerably in fiscal 2001, with hearing aid components up to 52 percent from 46.7 percent in 2000.

Video components did the reverse, slipping to 46.6 percent from 51.9 percent. The shift represents a 21.6 percent decline in video component sales due to reduced capital expenditures by broadcasters.

Nevertheless, despite the drop in revenues, Gennum maintained or increased its market share in the areas it serves.

The continuing shift to digital and high definition television and digital hearing aids should spell continued growth, as the company is a leader in both fields.

Financial Highlights

Fiscal 2001 was the first year in over a decade that revenues and earnings have fallen for Gennum, reflecting weakness in the economy. But its second quarter to May 31, 2002 showed revenues up 13.3 percent and earnings up 14.3 percent for the quarter. Gennum's stock moved in a broad trading range between $14 and $20 throughout 1999 and most of 2000 before slumping to a $12.50 to $13.50 trading range in October 2000. After a move up to the $16 level followed by a slump to $11, the stock once more entered a trading range between $12 and $14.

Gennum lost a star for revenues and two stars for earnings because of its slump.

Gennum Corporation at a Glance

Fiscal Year-end: November
10-Year Return: 30.4%

	1997	1998	1999	2000	2001	9-Year Growth Average (%)	9-Year Growth Total (%)
Revenue ($ mlns.)	61.5	83.5	93.6	106.5	93.1	17.3	238.6
Net Income ($ mlns.)	11.9	16.2	17.5	18.8	10.5	15.8	147.5
Earnings/ Share ($)	0.33	0.45	0.49	0.53	0.30	15.8	150.0
Dividend/ Share ($)	0.06	0.08	0.09	0.12	0.12	12.4	9.1
Price/ Earnings	23.9 - 35.8	18.7 - 32.6	27.3 - 42.2	22.2 - 36.8	33.3 - 56.7	–	–

Table data courtesy of  www.shareowner.com

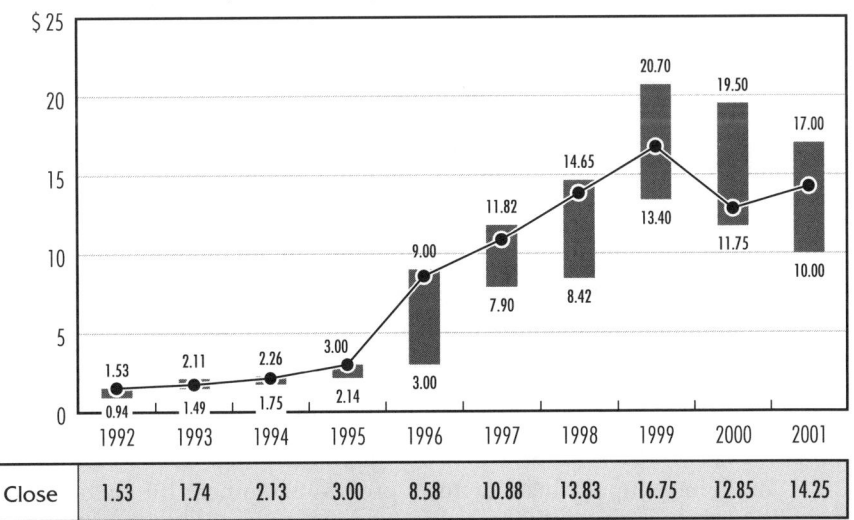

GROUPE LAPERRIÈRE & VERREAULT INC.

25 des Forges Street, Suite 420
Le Bourg de Fleuve Building
Trois-Rivières, QC G9A 6A7

Tel: (819) 371-8265
Fax: (819) 373-4439
www.glv.com
Symbol: GLV.A (TSX)

Employees: 1,400
Founded: 1975
Listed: 1986

Chairperson, President, and CEO: Laurent Verreault

Share Price Growth	★★
Revenue Growth	★★
EPS Growth	★★★★★
GLV.A	**9**

About the Company

Groupe Laperrière & Verreault (GL&V as it's usually called) is a Quebec-based industrial engineering company with an international presence. Its primary focus since inception in 1975 has been the pulp and paper industry, which still accounts for 73 percent of its business. But it has also diversified, with 18 percent of revenues coming from the chemical, food, and mineral industries and the balance split among environment, energy, and other fields.

The company manufactures process equipment for clients using, in many cases, proprietary technology. This includes such things as pulping equipment, scrubbers, filtration systems, pumps, effluent clarifiers, combustion systems, chemical treatment equipment, underground mining equipment, and so on.

The company has grown through internal expansion and through acquisition, expanding beyond Quebec into the rest of Canada with the purchase of Dorr-Oliver Canada in 1990.

The year 1996 saw the acquisition of Black Clawson-Kennedy Ltd. and its formidable stable of intellectual property, as well as a second American company, LaValley Industries of Washington state. This marked the beginning of the company's expansion into the U.S. market.

Its most important acquisition took place in 1998—the Swedish company Alfa Laval Celleco, a leader in filtration and pulp-cleaning technologies for the pulp and paper industry. In 1999, GL&V took over the Connecticut-based Dorr-Oliver group of companies, a world leader in liquid-solid separation processes with branches in a half-dozen countries worldwide. These acquisitions gave GL&V a solid international presence.

And in February 2000, the company bought pulp industry giant Beloit of New Hampshire, further solidifying GL&V's American presence.

The company's GL&V Manufacturing subsidiary was acquired in 1993 and is one of Canada's largest industrial manufacturing facilities. It was originally founded in 1908 by Canada Iron and has been involved in projects as varied as the St. Lawrence Seaway, the Toronto subway, the Trans-Canada Pipeline, and the James Bay hydroelectric project.

Today the company has subsidiaries in Sweden, Finland, Australia, Brazil, Chile, France, Germany, and South Africa, as well as in Canada and the U.S.

GL&V went public in 1986. The company's revenues quadrupled from 1997 to 2001, and like other industrial engineering firms such as SNC-Lavalin and Stantec, the company's profits are growing. In December 2001 the company was recognized as one of the 50 Best Managed Companies in Canada.

Opportunities and Challenges

GL&V is the North American leader in technology for the pulp and paper industry with research and development centres in Watertown, New York and Pittsfield, Massachusetts. Its international presence is substantial.

The company's focus on technological superiority and the optimization of equipment through custom-engineered upgrades have placed its products in high demand.

Although electronic documents are increasingly used in today's world, the demand for newsprint and paper continues strong. Demand for GL&V's technology will continue as long as people use paper.

The company's biggest opportunities for growth lie with its marginal activities such as the energy sector, heavy industry manufacturing, and the environment. It took a major step in this direction with the announcement of the acquisition of the Eimco process equipment division of U.S.-based Baker, Hughes Inc., in August 2002. It's the largest acquisition in the company's history and positions it as a major player in the market for equipment to separate industrial solids and liquids.

Financial Highlights

The slumping economy affected GL&V as it did many other businesses. Revenues were off for fiscal 2002 by 13.5 percent and earnings dropped 8.8 percent. But in spite of the drop, earnings were still a healthy $1.34 a share.

Groupe Laperrière & Verreault was recommended in the October 2000 edition of *FutureStock Review* with the recommendation reiterated in the June 2001 edition. The stock was flat from July 1998 to January 2000, hanging around the $4 mark. But throughout 2000, 2001, and into the first half of 2002, the stock has appreciated steadily with occasional minor corrections. Yet even with a tripling in share price over this period, the stock still traded at a low 7.8 P/E multiple as of the end of June 2002.

Groupe Laperrièrre & Verreault Inc. at a Glance

Fiscal Year-end: March
10-Year Return: 18.7%

	1998	1999	2000	2001	2002	9-Year Growth Average (%)	9-Year Growth Total (%)
Revenue ($ mlns.)	156.2	175.9	235.4	407.5	352.6	19.9	262.5
Net Income ($ mlns.)	2.4	4.1	6.8	15.2	16.0	136.5	5,043.9
Earnings/ Share ($)	0.32	0.42	0.69	1.47	1.66	118.6	4,050.0
Dividend/ Share ($)	0.10	0.00	0.00	0.10	0.20	–	–
Price/ Earnings	13.1 - 20.3	8.0 - 14.3	4.9 - 9.0	3.5 - 5.8	4.0 - 7.7	–	–

Table data courtesy of  www.shareowner.com

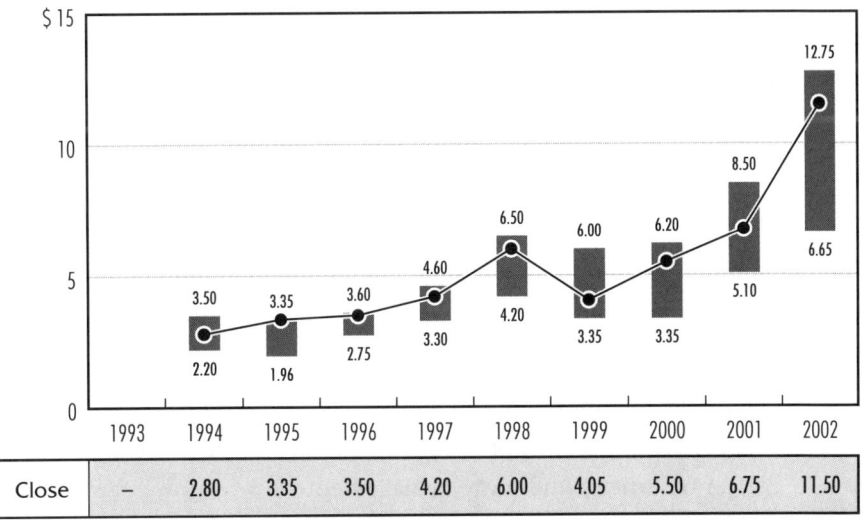

STANTEC INC.

10160–112 Street, Suite 200
Edmonton, AB T5K 2L6

Tel: (780) 917-7000
Fax: (780) 917-7330
www.stantec.com
Symbol: STN (TSX)

Employees: 3,500
Founded: 1954
Listed: 1994

Chairperson: Ronald P. Triffo
President and CEO: Anthony P. Franceschini

Share Price Growth	★ ★ ★
Revenue Growth	★ ★ ★
EPS Growth	★ ★
STN	**8**

About the Company

In 1954, Dr. Don Stanley, a Ph.D. in environmental engineering, launched a one-man consulting firm in Alberta. Humble beginnings. Today, Stantec (an abbreviation of Stanley Technology Group) is an international company with 40 offices and 3,500 employees primarily in Canada and the U.S.

Stantec calls itself a knowledge company with a focus on professional consulting in project design and management of infrastructure and large facilities. This includes such things as bridges, highways, schools, hospitals, airports, commercial and residential construction, water treatment, and waste management.

The company has five divisions specializing in Urban Land, Environment, Buildings, Transportation, and Industrial. It offers cradle-to-grave service, so to speak, from the initial planning of a project to construction, management, and eventually decommissioning as well.

The company has acquired some proprietary technologies over the last few years including Goodfellow EFSOP™, an emissions control system for electric arc furnaces used in the steel industry; Biological Nutrient Removal, a system for treating waste water without chemicals; Integrated Infrastructure Management Systems (IIMS), data management and analysis software used by local governments; and Datria, specialized speech-to-database software.

Stantec's clients include municipal and regional governments, as well as private industry. Industrial projects have included fields such as pharmaceuticals, mining, energy, manufacturing, and forestry. Notable projects have included the Confederation Bridge connecting Prince Edward Island and the mainland, and the $1.3-billion Alberta-Pacific Athabasca Pulp Mill, but the company's focus is generally on smaller projects under $100 million.

Stantec has grown both internally and through acquisition. It has been profitable for every one of its almost 50 years in business. The company went public in 1994 and has grown revenues and earnings at an annual compounded rate of better than 20 percent since. Its stated goal is to become one of the top 10 global design firms in the world. Stantec was added to the TSE 300 in 2001.

Opportunities and Challenges

The market for infrastructure and facilities design services in North America is over US$50 billion a year. Stantec has just one percent of this market, offering excellent opportunity for continued growth. Its competent execution on projects and growing reputation have seen it grow to become the 55th-largest firm in 2001 according to the *Engineering News Record*, up from 75th-largest the year before. The company is closing in on its goal of joining the top 10.

Acquisitions continued apace with the takeovers of The Spink Corporation and English Harper Reta Architects in California, Site Consultants Inc. in South Carolina, Pentacore Inc. in Nevada, Tipton & Kalmbach and Taggart Engineering, both in Colorado, the Ellard Croft Design Group in Saskatchewan, and Associated Consulting Engineers in Barbados. Additional acquisitions augmented existing operations in Saskatchewan, Ontario, and Alberta.

Stantec is clearly a company on the move. Its main challenge will be the successful integration of recent acquisitions into a clearly branded whole. The company, in fact, moved toward unified branding in 1998 with the change from Stanley Technology Group to Stantec and the integration of its varied branches.

Financial Highlights

Stantec grew revenues by 34.4 percent in 2001, with diluted earnings per share up 17.2 percent. It marked the 48th consecutive year of profitability for the company—a record hard to match anywhere. In 2001 it was recognized as the second-fastest growing company in the U.S. between 1997 and 2000 by the prestigious Zweig Letter.

The company's stock traded flat around the $5 range for several years before gaining 50 percent in 2000, and then soaring to over $20 by May 2002 before undergoing a correction to $15. Despite this meteoric rise, the company traded at a conservative 15.3 P/E ratio at mid-September 2002. Long-term growth is a good possibility.

Stantec Inc. at a Glance

Fiscal Year-end: December
8-Year Return: 18.6%

	1997	1998	1999	2000	2001	9-Year Growth Average (%)	9-Year Growth Total (%)
Revenue ($ mlns.)	131.5	185.5	211.9	265.6	356.9	20.3	320.5
Net Income ($ mlns.)	5.3	7.2	8.6	11.2	15.4	49.4	1,355.2
Earnings/ Share ($)	0.82	0.93	1.11	1.51	1.77	3.5	-61.8
Dividend/ Share ($)	–	–	–	–	–	–	–
Price/ Earnings	7.7 - 14.9	10.2 - 15.9	8.7 - 10.4	7.0 - 10.6	8.2 - 16.1	–	–

Table data courtesy of  www.shareowner.com

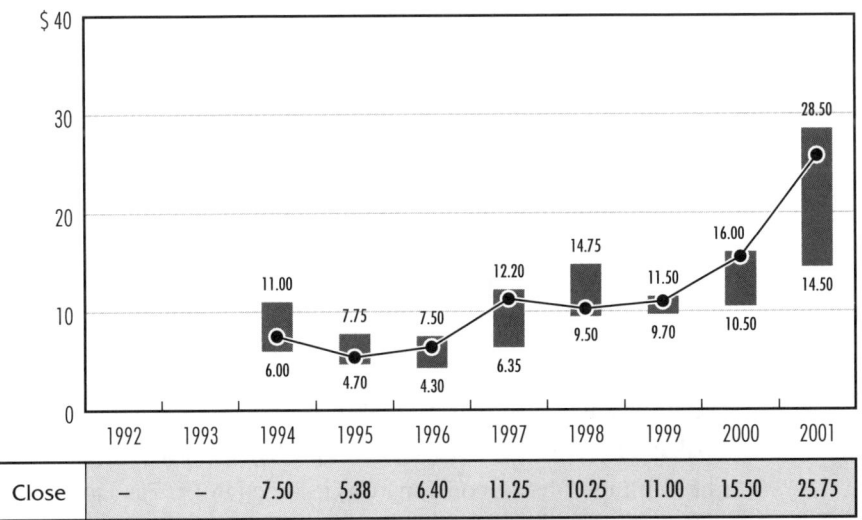

WINPAK LTD.

100 Salteaux Crescent
Winnipeg, MB R3J 3T3

Tel: (204) 889-1015
Fax: (204) 888-7806
www.winpak.com
Symbol: WPK (TSX)

Employees: 1,671
Founded: 1975
Listed: 1986

Chairperson: Antti Aarnio-Wihuri
President and CEO: J. Robert Lavery

Share Price Growth	★ ★ ★ ★
Revenue Growth	★ ★
EPS Growth	★ ★
WPK	**8**

About the Company

When you open up a Mister Big chocolate bar or pop open one of those dairy creamers in a restaurant to add to your coffee, you probably do *not* think to yourself, "Wow! This is high tech stuff!" You probably throw away the candy wrapper or empty creamer without thinking about it at all. But high tech it is.

From soup to nuts, packaged foods meet stringent standards of quality control designed to provide a clean and sanitary product. Many are vacuum-packed to seal in freshness and extend shelf life. And Winpak is a North American leader in packaging technology.

The Winnipeg-based company was founded in 1975 as a joint venture with Finnish packaging conglomerate Wihuri Oy. It operates nine production plants in Canada and the U.S., producing for markets across North and South America and the Caribbean.

The company operates in five divisions. Modified Atmosphere Packaging uses proprietary technology to vacuum seal or gas flush packaging to extend the shelf life of perishable foods. This includes such things as milk pouches. Specialty Films manufactures flexible films using polyethylene, nylon, and ethylene vinyl alcohol at two state-of-the-art facilities in Georgia. Sixty percent of monolayer film production is sold to other packaging companies.

The Rigid Plastic Packaging and Lidding division is the largest North American supplier of rigid portion control packaging. This includes the creamers we mentioned earlier, as well as pharmaceuticals. And the Technical Printing and Laminating division specializes in flexible packaging with high-end printing. Yes! That's the Mister Big wrapper! Not to mention Knorr soups, Chips Ahoy cookies, and many, many other products.

The company's fifth division makes packaging machinery, providing turnkey solutions for manufacturers who want a total solution to packaging including film, machines, and operations support. Winpak custom designs machinery to suit client needs and will even create custom packaging designs. Winpak packaging systems produce 80 percent of the world's single-serving condiment pouches, yogurt packages, juices, salad dressings, creamers, soaps, medical, and hair care products. Chances are, the little shampoo bottle at the last hotel you stayed at was manufactured on Winpak machinery.

Winpak was added to the TSX Composite Index in March 2001.

Opportunities and Challenges

Winpak is a giant in the packaging industry and has grown revenues at an average compounded rate of 19 percent a year since 1986. Earnings have grown at 15.8 percent over the last 10. The key to this success is the company's focus on flexible and innovative custom designing of solutions for its clients.

The company has an extensive in-house R&D facility to work closely with customers to develop economical packaging or equipment for their needs. This includes product testing labs, engineering consultancy, and a state-of-the-art CAD/CAM-enabled machine shop. Finished machinery is quality inspected and given a test run before shipment to the customer. All Winpak's facilities are ISO 9001 certified (ISO is an acronym for International Organization for Standardization).

Winpak invests heavily in technology and plant upgrades to stay on the cutting edge. Capital expenditures from 1996 to 2000 ran to $145 million or 10 percent of revenues. One such development in 2000, was specialized equipment to package dry snack foods, such as peanuts for airlines.

A challenge for Winpak in the last year has been the slowing economy. But only the second quarter of 2001 suffered declining revenues and earnings. It has proved remarkably resilient over the years.

Financial Highlights

Revenues were up 7.4 percent and earnings per share were up 9.7 percent for that "awful" year of 2001. The first half of 2002 saw revenues down slightly by 0.3 percent, with earnings per share soaring due to operational efficiencies by 46.1 percent. Staying on the cutting edge of technology pays off for this company.

The stock maintains a decidedly upwards long-term trend. It increased its dividend 50 percent in August 2002.

Winpak Ltd. at a Glance

Fiscal Year-end: December
10-Year Return: 24.5%

	1997	1998	1999	2000	2001	10-Year Growth Average (%)	10-Year Growth Total (%)
Revenue ($ mlns.)	300.1	336.4	374.0	422.6	453.8	19.1	292.5
Net Income ($ mlns.)	11.9	16.1	22.0	22.7	24.9	18.5	318.6
Earnings/ Share ($)	1.84	2.48	3.38	3.49	3.83	15.8	245.0
Dividend/ Share ($)	0.40	0.40	0.40	0.40	0.40	0.0	0.0
Price/ Earnings	17.9 - 23.9	14.1 - 20.6	13.6 - 20.7	11.2 - 18.3	11.9 - 20.1	–	–

Table data courtesy of Canadian Shareowner www.shareowner.com

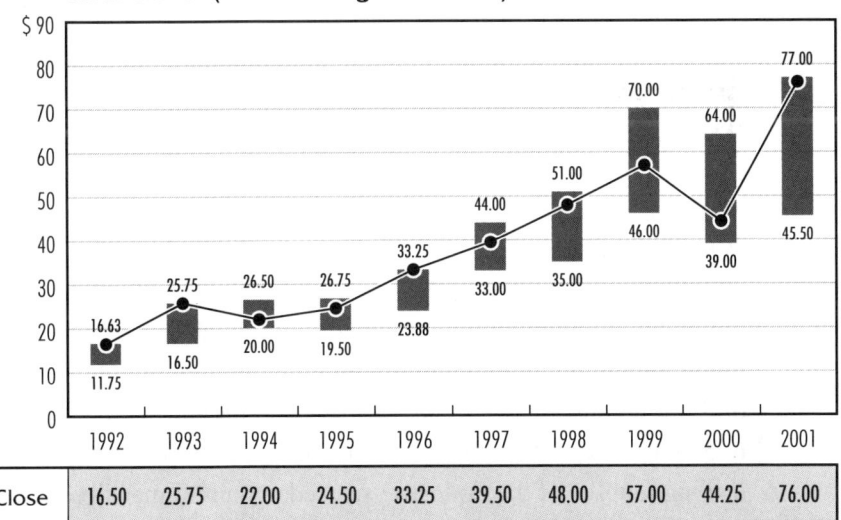

Stock Growth (Fiscal Year High-Low-Close)

| Close | 16.50 | 25.75 | 22.00 | 24.50 | 33.25 | 39.50 | 48.00 | 57.00 | 44.25 | 76.00 |

DUPONT CANADA INC.

7070 Mississauga Road, Box 2200
Mississauga, ON L5M 2H3

Tel: (905) 821-3300
Fax: (905) 821-5110
www.dupont.ca
Symbol: DUP.A (TSX)

Employees: 3,400
Founded: 1862
Listed: 1961

Chairperson, President, and CEO: David W. Colcleugh
President and CEO (effective Jan. 1, 2003): Doug Muzyka

Share Price Growth	★ ★ ★
Revenue Growth	★
EPS Growth	★ ★ ★
DUP.A	**7**

About the Company

If the term "venerable" can be applied to a science and technology company, it describes DuPont. Some of its innovative chemical and petroleum products have even become part of the English language. Who hasn't heard of nylon, Lycra, or Teflon? The American giant is one of the world's great businesses.

But what of DuPont Canada? The company traces its history back to the Hamilton Powder Company, founded in 1862. In 1867, Lammot du Pont bought shares in the company and became a director. This injection of capital and expertise enabled the company to become a leading supplier of the explosives needed to build Canada's emerging railways.

The company amalgamated with several others as Canadian Explosives Ltd. in 1910 and supplied a large portion of the munitions for Canada's war effort in World War I. After the war it acquired three Canadian subsidiaries of E.I. du Pont de Nemours and became Canadian Industries Ltd. (CIL). In 1954, a U.S. antitrust settlement split the company into two: CIL and DuPont Canada. DuPont Canada debuted on the Toronto Stock Exchange in December 1961.

Today, the company manufactures products for the Canadian market and for export in six manufacturing plants. It operates five divisions that make products as diverse as nylon yarn (such brands as Antron and Stainmaster), paints for the automotive industry, Kevlar (used in bulletproof vests), herbicides, and plastic films such as Mylar.

The Canadian subsidiary runs one of the few materials science R&D centres in Canada at its Kingston plant, employing 200 people with an annual budget of $45 million. Among its inventions and developments are specialty air bag yarns, aseptic pouch packaging, and the nylon heat exchanger. DuPont's Kingston plant, in fact, is the largest manufacturer of air bag yarns in the world.

Opportunities and Challenges

The nylon heat exchanger invented at DuPont's Kingston plant has a number of interesting commercial possibilities, including nylon radiators for cars. Such a radiator could be moulded to fit where convenient in a car rather than sitting as a bulky up-front unit.

One of the more interesting developments at DuPont is the creation of a new Fuel Cells unit to supply materials and components to this emerging market. Twenty-seven engineers, scientists, and skilled technicians are working on fuel cell development, with staffing expected to increase to 80 over the next four years. Proton exchange membrane fuel cells are expected to be a $10-billion-a-year business by 2010. DuPont has been providing advanced materials for the fuel cells used in space travel for over 35 years, so it is no stranger to the business. The company is also active in the development of direct methanol fuel cell technology.

In the late spring of 2002, DuPont Canada acquired Liqui-Box Corporation, merging it with wholly owned subsidiary Enhance Packaging Technologies. The acquisition makes DuPont Canada a world leader in aseptic and refrigerated liquid food packaging systems. Aseptic packaging preserves the freshness of food and beverages for up to a year without refrigeration and is used primarily for syrups, bulk condiments such as ketchup and mustard, and other food packaging for restaurants and institutional clients.

Financial Highlights

Revenues declined 4.3 percent for 2001 while earnings per share declined 18.6 percent. For the first half of 2002, revenues increased 6.8 percent with EPS up 9.3 percent. The stock has climbed steadily from October 2000 through May 2002. DuPont managed to weather the tech downturn and has been hitting new highs regularly throughout this period. In May it started a modest and meandering correction.

Despite its advance, we deducted a star for share price growth because the differential over 10 years narrowed. While there have been some wide fluctuations, the general trend for the stock has been upwards since 1982. An excellent long-term stock to buy and hang on to.

DuPont Canada Inc. at a Glance
Fiscal Year-end: December
10-Year Return: 21.1%

	1997	1998	1999	2000	2001	10-Year Growth Average (%)	10-Year Growth Total (%)
Revenue ($ mlns.)	1,997.8	2,025.1	2,211.4	2,288.9	2,191.1	5.0	53.1
Net Income ($ mlns.)	212.1	219.9	252.7	269.5	221.6	14.9	207.0
Earnings/ Share ($)	0.76	0.79	0.91	0.97	0.79	14.8	203.8
Dividend/ Share ($)	1.18	0.21	0.23	0.28	0.57	81.5	612.5
Price/ Earnings	12.7 - 15.8	13.3 - 20.0	14.7 - 22.0	12.0 - 21.3	18.6 - 34.8	–	–

Table data courtesy of  www.shareowner.com

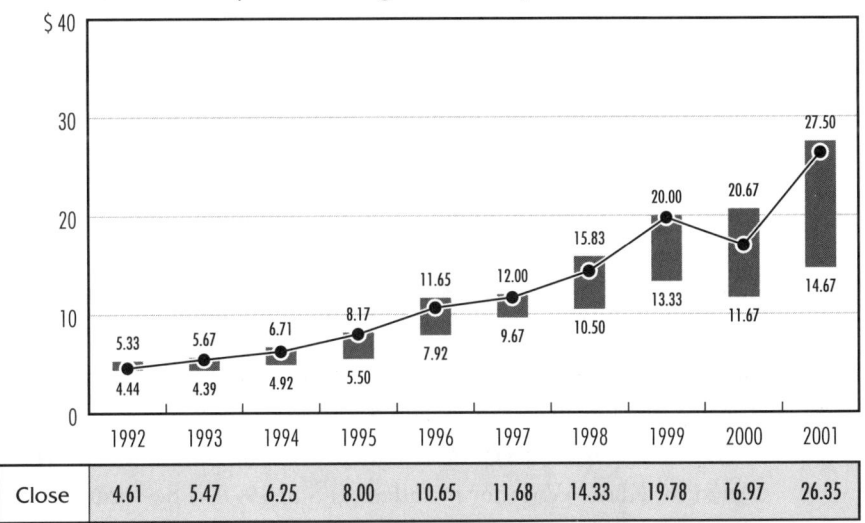

ATS AUTOMATION TOOLING SYSTEMS INC.

250 Royal Oak Road
Box 32100, Preston Centre
Cambridge, ON N3H 5M2

Tel: (519) 653-6500
Fax: (519) 653-6533
www.atsautomation.com
Symbol: ATA (TSX)

Employees: 3,400
Founded: 1978
Listed: 1993

Chairperson: Lawrence G. Tapp
President and CEO: Klaus D. Woerner

Share Price Growth	★ ★ ★ ★
Revenue Growth	★ ★ ★
EPS Growth	0
ATA	**7**

About the Company

What country do you associate with the following: clean, efficient factories? Robotics? Automation? Chances are you answered Japan, the country we usually associate with technically advanced, automated factory assembly lines. But a Canadian company, ATS Automation Tooling, is a key player in this field.

After working for several years as a process engineer at Ford's Truck Division, Klaus Woerner founded ATS in 1978. The company designs and builds turnkey automated manufacturing systems, as well as manufacturing precision components for industry. It has, in fact, built more than 10,000 automation systems for its customers, many of which are large multinational corporations.

ATS employs 3,400 people in 26 facilities across Canada, the U.S., Europe, and the Pacific Rim. This workforce is highly skilled: 45 percent are engineers and technical specialists, 20 percent are skilled tradesman, and the remaining 35 percent are semi-skilled operators and administrative personnel.

Among other things, the company has developed manufacturing solutions for the auto industry (it has been a preferred vendor for Ford since 1992), including assembly facilities for steering, suspension, drivetrain, braking, fuel, seating, windows, wipers, instrumentation, locks, and lighting systems. ATS is also one of the top developers of high-accuracy automated manufacturing systems for the fibre optics and wireless telecommunications industries, and does contract manufacturing for this sector. And it is one of the largest integrators of automated micromanufacturing systems in the semiconductor and computer fields.

Another huge field is the electrical sector, developing systems for making motors, switches, transformers, and circuit breakers. The company also develops systems for packaging and manufacturing pharmaceuticals and consumer goods.

Opportunities and Challenges

As manufacturers continue to look for ways to cut costs and improve efficiency, more and more will look to automation and outsourcing solutions. ATS Automation Tooling is there on both fronts, which gives it solid long-term potential.

Its market is global, with 63 percent of sales south of the border. Forty-five percent of revenues come from the automotive sector, 36 percent from computers and electronics, 13 percent from health care, and 6 percent from other areas.

This mix has changed over the last year, with the company increasing the European market to 20 percent of the mix from 13 percent the year before. There was also a client shift from computers and electronics to the automotive industry, not surprising considering the meltdown in the computer sector. This included a five-year deal with a major American automaker to provide power seat adjustment subsystems, and an $8 million deal in biotech.

The company is dedicated to after-service and support, and 75 percent of its customers are repeat buyers. Twenty-three percent of revenues in 2000 came from just three customers, but this concentration is down from 30 percent in 1999. The company's major challenge is to continue expanding its reach into its newest markets—the fields of fibre optics, semiconductors, and health care. To that end, the company forged a strategic alliance with EXFO Electro-Optical Engineering in December 2001 to better meet the needs of optical component and systems manufacturers. And it signed a deal to produce private label heat sinks (cooling agents for computer chips) for Tyco Electronics in March 2002.

Nevertheless, a cooling market for manufacturing infrastructure has hurt ATS in the last two years even though it had $168.3 million in backlogged orders at the end of fiscal 2002 (March 31, 2002).

Financial Highlights

The general economic malaise produced a slow year for ATS in the fiscal year ended March 31, 2002. Revenues were down 19.1 percent, with earnings per share off 72.4 percent. But the company did report its order book starting to fill up again, good news in today's economy. The stock has been on a steady downtrend punctuated by occasional rallies since September 2000. A general economic recovery should help ATS regain its footing and continue its growth path.

The poor numbers for fiscal 2002 wiped out half of ATS's star ratings—one star in share price growth, two in revenues growth, and all four stars in EPS growth. We view this as a temporary setback and expect to see the company regain its form in the years ahead.

ATS Automation Tooling Systems Inc. at a Glance

Fiscal Year-end: March
8-Year Return: 28.4%

	1998	1999	2000	2001	2002	9-Year Growth Average (%)	9-Year Growth Total (%)
Revenue ($ mlns.)	402.9	515.3	530.0	679.0	549.5	27.3	488.4
Net Income ($ mlns.)	27.4	40.2	37.1	46.2	12.6	26.2	158.2
Earnings/ Share ($)	0.50	0.70	0.64	0.76	0.21	13.4	23.5
Dividend/ Share ($)	–	–	–	–	–	–	–
Price/ Earnings	20.4 - 60.3	13.6 - 37.1	16.4 - 51.6	24.9 - 53.3	60.0 - 138.3	–	–

Table data courtesy of  www.shareowner.com

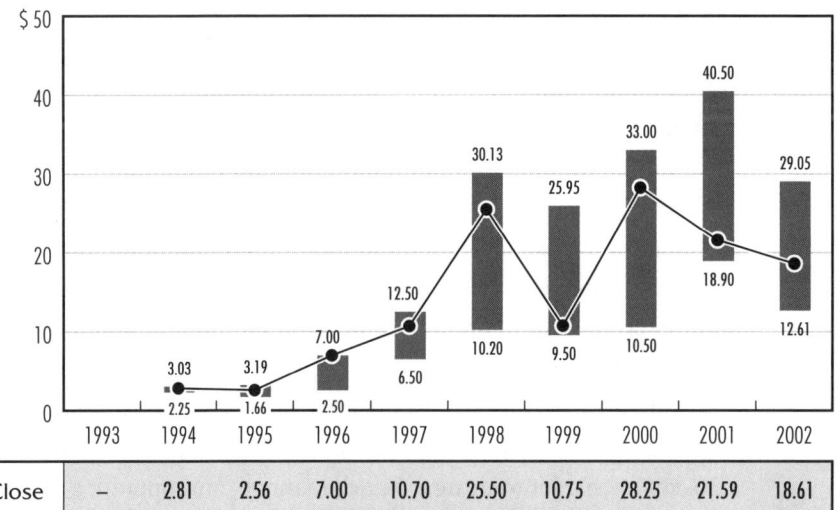

CAE INC.

P.O. Box 30, Suite 3060
Royal Bank Plaza
Toronto, ON M5J 2J1

Tel: (416) 865-0070
Fax: (416) 865-0337
www.cae.com
Symbol: CAE (TSX) (Also CGT-NYSE)

Employees: 6,375
Founded: 1947
Listed: 1961

Chairperson: Lynton R. Wilson
President and CEO: Derek H. Burney

Share Price Growth	★ ★
Revenue Growth	★
EPS Growth	★ ★ ★
CAE	**6**

About the Company

CAE Inc. is the world's major manufacturer of state-of-the-art flight simulators for pilot training. Its simulators not only reproduce the controls used on various aircraft, but also create as realistic a setting as possible in a complete immersion environment with a wraparound motion picture screen. The MAXVUE visual system uses computer-generated graphics that pilots see as an "out of the window" experience.

Simulators are built to duplicate a variety of aircraft, including Boeing, Airbus, and military helicopters. In 1997, the company won a 20-year contract to design, build, manage, and operate a training facility for Royal Air Force helicopter crews.

In April 2001 CAE opened a six-simulator training facility in São Paulo, the first independently owned and operated flight training centre in South America. Latin American airlines used to have to train pilots abroad, but can now train them close to home.

The company also manufactures marine control systems and is building the controls and instrumentation for the British Royal Navy's new Astute Class nuclear submarines.

In March 2002, the company sold off its forestry systems business to focus on the aviation, defence, and marine sectors. Increasingly the emphasis has shifted from being a supplier of training equipment to offering total training solutions in these three fields.

CAE has the 17th largest R&D budget in Canada according to RE$EARCH Infosource, earmarking around 10 percent of revenues to research.

Opportunities and Challenges

In October 1999, president and CEO Derek Burney joined the company with a mandate to enhance shareholder value. This he did in spades as he streamlined the business, discarding non-core operations and focusing on three distinct high-margin areas: aviation simulation and training, military simulation and training, and marine controls.

The fiscal year to March 31, 2002 saw a number of significant moves at CAE, including three acquisitions to beef up its aviation training business. In April 2001, it acquired BAE Systems Flight Simulation and Training in Tampa, Florida. This was followed by the acquisition of Dutch-based Schreiner Aviation Training and the takeover of SimuFlite Training International of Dallas in December 2001. The company also opened a state-of-the-art training facility at Toronto in December 2001.

CAE acquired the Norwegian company Valmarine in August 2001 to augment its marine controls business. Within days, CAE Valmarine was chosen to supply the complete systems control package for the Queen Mary 2 cruise liner. Although the events of September 11th affected CAE as it did most aviation-related businesses, CAE has managed to focus and expand its business. It is making great strides in the military simulation and training fields with new contracts. Among these are a $170-million contract to supply visual systems for Eurofighter Simulation Systems, a US$3-billion deal with the U.S. Air Force for simulators and training over 15 years, a $30-million contract with the Royal Netherlands Air Force, a $370-million contract with the U.K. Royal Navy for nuclear submarine training, and deals with the Korean, Norwegian, Indian, Singaporean, Australian, Malaysian, Omani, and German military.

CAE is also forging a military strategy with the appointment of two retired U.S. generals and an admiral to its board in August 2002.

Financial Highlights

CAE increased revenues on continuing operations (reflecting the divestiture of the forestry business) by 26.4 percent for fiscal 2002, with earnings per share up 40.8 percent. Revenue from continuing operations for the first quarter of fiscal 2003 was up 13.9 percent and EPS rose 13.3 percent.

CAE did not meet our minimum requirements in the revenue category. Revenues dropped sharply to $657.6 million in 1995 from $1,027.3 million in 1994 due to restructuring. Revenues and earnings have grown steadily since then, however, so we are making an allowance in this case and have also given the company one star for revenue growth. Its star rating remains unchanged at six.

A chart of CAE's stock shows steady, almost straight-line growth from November 1999 to July 2001, when information technology, telecommunications, and Internet stocks were experiencing wild fluctuations. The stock has fluctuated wildly since. The war on terrorism should continue to fuel military sales, while a recovering economy should boost CAE's sales in civil aviation. Nevertheless, weakness in commercial aviation created enough fear to send the stock plummeting 39 percent in one week in August.

CAE Inc. at a Glance

Fiscal Year-end: March
10-Year Return: 16.6%

	1998	1999	2000	2001	2002	10-Year Growth Average (%)	10-Year Growth Total (%)
Revenue ($ mlns.)	922.4	1,070.1	1,164.3	1,191.4	1,126.5	2.8	12.5
Net Income ($ mlns.)	70.6	77.3	90.7	134.7	149.3	19.3	363.0
Earnings/Share ($)	0.32	0.35	0.42	0.63	0.69	19.3	360.0
Dividend/Share ($)	0.08	0.08	0.09	0.10	0.12	4.8	50.0
Price/Earnings	15.9 - 20.4	11.1 - 19.5	8.7 - 20.2	10.1 - 20.6	10.7 - 22.4	–	–

Table data courtesy of  www.shareowner.com

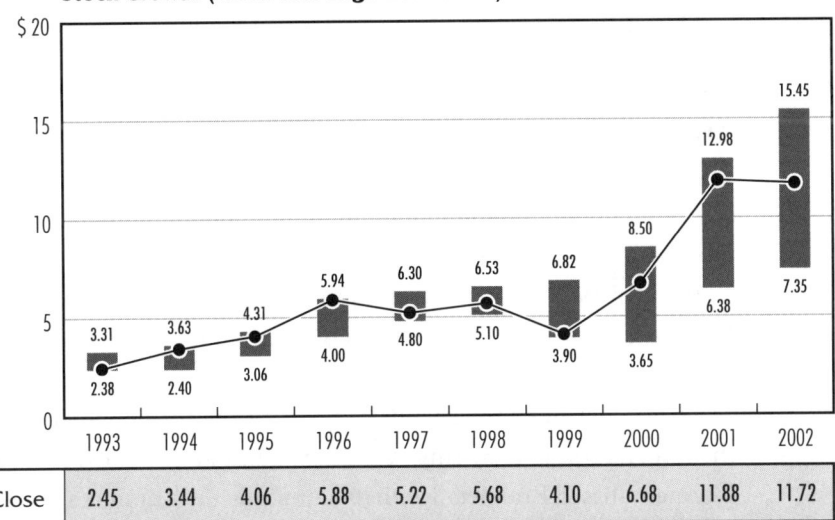

Stock Growth (Fiscal Year High-Low-Close)

TESMA INTERNATIONAL INC.

1000 Tesma Way
Concord, ON L4K 5R8

Tel: (905) 417-2100
Fax: (905) 417-2101
www.tesma.com
Symbol: TSM.A (TSX) (Also TSMA-NASDAQ)

Employees: 4,600
Founded: 1983
Listed: 1995

Chairperson: Donald J. Walker
Vice-Chairperson and CEO: Manfred Gingl
President and CFO: Anthony E. Dobranowski

Share Price Growth	★ ★
Revenue Growth	★ ★ ★
EPS Growth	★
TSM.A	**6**

About the Company

Tesma originated in 1983 when auto parts giant Magna International combined five of its divisions involved in engines and transmissions into one unit, the Maple Group, renamed the Tesma International Group in 1988. In 1993, Tesma acquired its first manufacturing facility in Europe, and in 1995, Magna spun off this wholly owned subsidiary in an initial public offering.

Tesma continued to expand, taking over the Blau companies and their operations in Germany, Austria, Spain, and Canada in 1995, and Germany-based Eralmetall with its aluminum die-casting capabilities in 1997. Further acquisitions in Detroit strengthened its North American operations and the takeover of HAC Corporation of South Korea in 1999 gave it a toehold in Asia.

Tesma is focused on three areas—engines, transmissions, and fuel systems. It has an Advanced Product Development team associated with each. Tesma's research labs are state-of-the-art and have developed several proprietary technologies, including a thin gauge sheet metal pulley that remains the industry standard and the first production application automotive belt tensioner for a single-belt drive system. This allowed the company to gain significant market share in accessory drive belt tensioners. Other innovations include camshaft phasers, balance shafts, and alternator decouplers.

Tesma is the leading supplier of water pumps for the automotive industry in North America and is a world leader in front-end accessory drive systems.

The company operates 22 manufacturing facilities and two research centres, shipping in excess of a billion dollars of product annually to OEMs on six continents.

Opportunities and Challenges

Outsourcing is gaining popularity in many industries from electronics to pharmaceuticals to the automotive field. Tesma is well positioned to meet this growing demand in the global automotive market. Its client list includes DaimlerChrysler, Ford, General Motors, VW, Nissan, Audi, BMW, Daewoo, Fiat, Honda, Mazda, Toyota, and SAAB.

Tesma's fortunes are tied to those of the automotive industry, although a diversified clientele makes it immune from troubles plaguing any one particular manufacturer.

In July 2002, Tesma signed a contract with Preventive Technologies for the use of Preventive's revolutionary Integral Strain Gauges technology. This is a method of high-precision, computerized testing of material fatigue to assess durability of components in manufacture and improve the time to market. It has applications in manufacturing, aerospace and the automotive industry.

A possible challenge in the future could be a large-scale shift to fuel-cell driven cars. Major auto manufacturers like Ford and DaimlerChrysler are pouring lots of money into alternative fuel research and development. But Tesma should be more than up to such challenges as they materialize. Its R&D team is well experienced at developing fuel-efficient engines and low emissions fuel systems.

Financial Highlights

Despite a 12 percent decline in North American auto production, Tesma increased revenues by 6.6 percent for the fiscal year ended July 31, 2001. Earnings per share were up by 3.4 percent. This came about from Tesma's development of new products and an increased share of product per vehicle produced. This has long been a strategy of Magna International and its related companies, and it continues to be a successful one.

After the stock traded in a wide range between $15 and $23 from 1997 through the first quarter of 2000, investors finally clued in to the company's steadily growing revenues and earnings and the stock advanced steadily from April to October of that year. A sharp correction late in the year was followed by a strong advance to new highs in the first half of 2001. This was followed by another sharp correction and another strong advance to new highs. The stock has been in a long-term uptrend since March 2000, but there has been some volatility and strong retracements along the way.

Our star rating is unchanged from last year.

Tesma International Inc. at a Glance

Fiscal Year-end: July
6-Year Return: 26.1%

	1997	1998	1999	2000	2001	8-Year Growth Average (%)	8-Year Growth Total (%)
Revenue ($ mlns.)	551.5	645.9	893.7	1,127.8	1,202.1	23.5	328.8
Net Income ($ mlns.)	24.6	38.4	52.3	84.9	81.1	26.2	315.9
Earnings/ Share ($)	1.13	1.28	1.76	2.83	2.74	13.7	100.0
Dividend/ Share ($)	0.20	0.22	0.31	0.54	0.64	35.4	326.7
Price/ Earnings	8.0 - 20.1	13.3 - 18.8	8.2 - 12.8	5.8 - 11.0	7.7 - 12.4	–	–

Table data courtesy of  www.shareowner.com

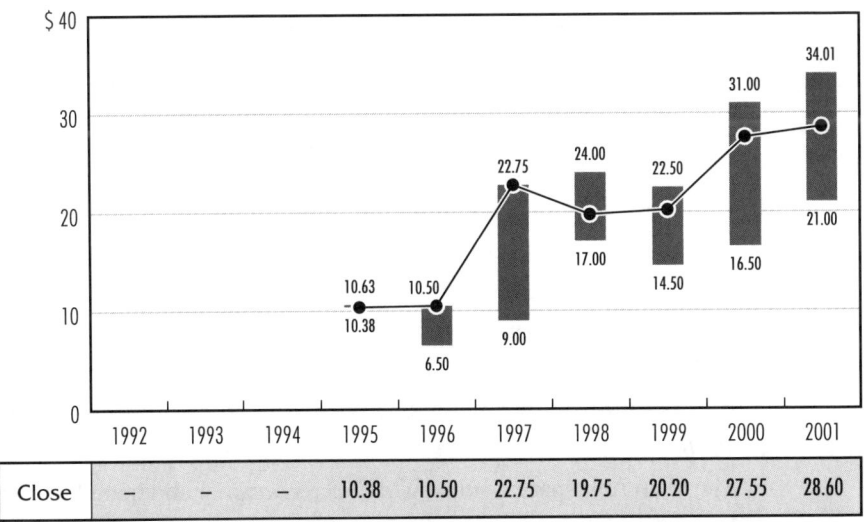

* Dividend growth figures based on six years.

MAGELLAN AEROSPACE CORPORATION

3160 Derry Road E.
Mississauga, ON L4T 1A9

Tel: (905) 677-1889
Fax: (905) 677-5658
www.malaero.com
Symbol: MAL (TSX)

Employees: 3,200
Founded: 1930
Listed: 1996

Chairperson and CEO: N. Murray Edwards
President and COO: Richard A. Neill

Share Price Growth	0
Revenue Growth	★ ★ ★
EPS Growth	★
MAL	**4**

About the Company

Founded in 1930 as Fleet Aerospace, the company underwent restructuring in 1995 as the commercial aviation industry started to recover from its longest slump ever. Retirement of debt, new equity financing, and new contracts from Southwest, Boeing, Bombardier, and McDonnell Douglas breathed new life into the veteran company. This was followed by a name change as the company went public in 1996.

Magellan Aerospace is now a world-class designer and manufacturer of high tech aerospace components and systems for the commercial and military aviation industries. The company maintains strong relationships with such aircraft manufacturers as Boeing, Airbus, Lockheed Martin, Bell Helicopter, and Northrop Grumman, and engine manufacturers such as Pratt & Whitney and Rolls Royce.

Magellan grew throughout the latter half of the 1990s, partly through the acquisition of a number of smaller aerospace companies. It now has 10 divisions throughout Canada and the U.S., operating under the Magellan umbrella but carrying their own corporate names. These include Fleet Industries (the original company), which specializes in bonded and sheet metal components and makes aircraft structures and sub-assemblies; Bristol Aerospace, which makes rockets and weapons systems (NASA has launched more than 800 Bristol-built rockets); Orenda, which specializes in gas turbine engine technology; and Langley Aerospace, which manufactures precision machined parts including cryogenic seals and thrust gimbals for the space shuttle.

Magellan's proprietary products include exhaust systems, weapons systems, advanced materials, and a wire strike protection system to reduce helicopter accidents. Besides manufacturing, the company does overhaul and repair work for the Canadian and American military.

A potentially lucrative new field for Magellan is power turbines. Its Orenda Aerospace division commissioned its first 2.5 megawatt gas turbine in June 2001, marking the company's re-entry into this field. Deregulation of the power industry and the continuing power shortage in America should fuel growth, especially as the economy recovers.

Opportunities and Challenges

Nearly every business involved in aviation took a serious downturn as the economy slowed in 2001 and was further hit by the aftermath of 9/11. Magellan Aerospace was no exception. But things began to turn around for the company in the months after the market hit bottom on September 21.

The reason? Thirty-five percent to 40 percent of Magellan's business is military related. And the war on terrorism has seen a number of significant contracts go Magellan's way, including ones with the U.S. army, navy, and air force, and the Canadian air force.

The company also landed a $49-million contract with General Electric in April 2002 to build fan frames for the CF34 jet engine, the engine of choice for regional jets like the Bombardier Challenger and the Embraer ERJ170.

One-third of the company's sales are to Boeing, so the health of Boeing affects Magellan. The commercial airline business has been in a bit of a slump post 9/11, but should be well recovered in 2003.

In August 2002, Magellan moved to take over Haley Industries, a maker of magnesium and aluminum castings for the aerospace industry which should provide synergies going forward.

Financial Highlights

Magellan suffered a slight loss of revenue for fiscal 2001—down 1.7 percent, but earnings per share increased by 5.1 percent due to cost-cutting efficiencies. A recovering economy and the continuing demand for military equipment should see revenues pick up again through 2002 and 2003. At September 2002, the company had a backlog of $750 million, more than a year's worth of work.

Magellan Aerospace did not meet all of our selection criteria, as it experienced losses from 1991 to 1995. But those losing years are far behind it, with the company turning a profit every year since reorganization in 1996. Given an up-and-down stock history, investors should monitor performance carefully and be prepared to sell if circumstances warrant.

There is no change in star rating.

Magellan Aerospace Corporation at a Glance
Fiscal Year-end: December
10-Year Return: 2.5%

	1997	1998	1999	2000	2001	8-Year Growth Average (%)	8-Year Growth Total (%)
Revenue ($ mlns.)	256.3	426.9	561.8	625.4	614.5	34.0	729.0
Net Income ($ mlns.)	15.5	32.3	42.8	37.9	40.6	–	–
Earnings/ Share ($)	0.30	0.54	0.68	0.59	0.61	–	–
Dividend/ Share ($)	0.00	0.00	0.00	0.00	0.00	–	–
Price/ Earnings	10.3 - 37.3	9.7 - 20.2	8.8 - 15.1	8.1 - 12.7	6.2 - 14.3	–	–

Table data courtesy of  www.shareowner.com

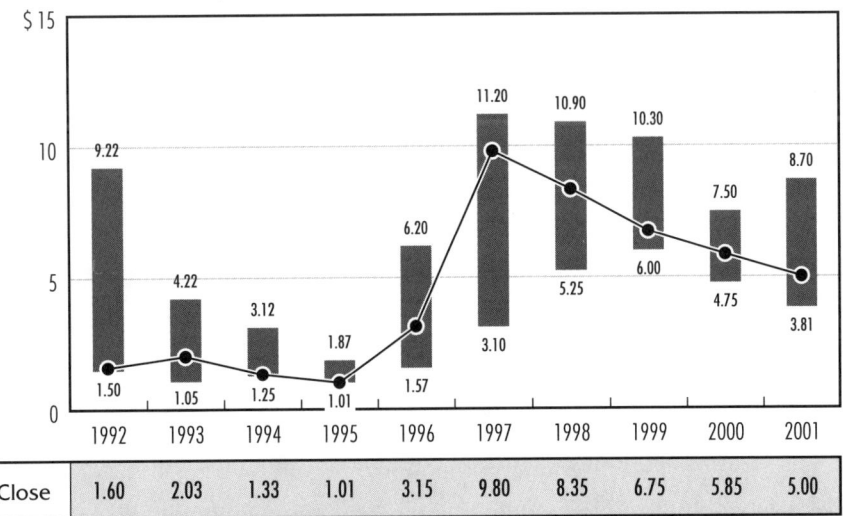

INFORMATION TECHNOLOGY

CGI Group Inc.
Microsoft Corporation
Siebel Systems, Inc.
THQ Inc.
Mercury Interactive Corporation
Check Point Software Technologies Ltd.
Cognos Inc.
Network Appliance, Inc.
Intel Corporation

CGI GROUP INC.

1130 Sherbrooke Street W., 5th Floor
Montreal, QC H3A 2M8

Tel: (514) 841-3200   Employees: 13,700
Fax: (514) 841-3299   Founded: 1976
www.cgi.ca   Listed: 1986
Symbol: GIB.A (TSX) (Also GIB-NYSE)

Chairperson and CEO: Serge Godin
President and COO: Michael Roach

Share Price Growth	★ ★ ★ ★ ★
Revenue Growth	★ ★ ★ ★ ★
EPS Growth	★ ★ ★ ★ ★
GIB.A	**15**

About the Company

Founded in 1976 by Serge Godin and André Imbeau, CGI Group Inc. started as a modest Quebec City consulting firm with six employees and revenues of $138,000. From there it has grown to become the fourth-largest IT services provider in North America and the largest in Canada, with annual revenues of $1.58 billion in 2001. Acquisitions have given it a global presence, with over 60 project offices in 20 countries as well as Canada, the U.S., and the U.K.

The company offers complete end-to-end IT services and business solutions with a focus on large-scale, multi-year renewable contracts. Services include implementing computer infrastructure on site or through CGI's data centre, installation of custom-designed programming solutions, systems integration, and service and maintenance of on-site computer networks.

CGI's IT solutions include proprietary products such as its Global Insurance Open Solution software, co-developed with the Allianz financial services company.

The company focuses on servicing six economic sectors: financial services, telecommunications, manufacturing/retail/distribution, governments, utilities and energy, and health care. In 2001, the company reorganized into three business units: Canada and Europe, U.S. and Asia, and Business Process Services. Each unit has its own president reporting to the CEO.

In 1994, CGI became the first IT services company in North America to get ISO 9001 certification for its project management framework. The company was recognized as Services Provider of the Year by Microsoft in 2000.

Opportunities and Challenges

CGI Group is positioned to do well in both good and bad economic climates. When the economy is booming, companies spend money to upgrade their IT services and the company benefits from the business. When the economy is on the ropes, companies look to cut costs by outsourcing—again they look to CGI for solutions.

The company continues to make strategic acquisitions. Fiscal 2001 saw CGI acquire eight niche companies, one major acquisition, and one strategic outsourcing alliance. These included IT consulting firms in Detroit, Montreal, Toronto, California, and Portugal. The major acquisition, IMRglobal, added high-end consultancy capabilities in the U.S. and U.K., as well as a presence in France, India, Japan, and Australia. The outsourcing alliance was with Quebec's Desjardins Credit Union. This 10-year alliance is worth an estimated $1.2 billion and involves the acquisition by CGI of certain assets, intellectual property, and liabilities from Desjardins, as well as the transfer of 450 employees and two Montreal data centres under the CGI umbrella.

CGI's main challenge is the integration of new acquisitions into a unified organization. The company takes a widely decentralized approach with local accountability within the context of CGI's best practices and support functions. Integrations are managed on a strict timetable with well-defined goals.

Major contracts signed include Sun Life Financial, Interac Association, Allianz Insurance, Laurentian Bank, California's Fireman's Fund Insurance Company, League Data, Domtar, and the Credit Union Alliance.

Financial Highlights

CGI Group had a stellar year in 1999 as a result of Y2K remediation work. This business dried up somewhat in 2000, with revenues showing little growth and earnings off 32 percent.

Fiscal 2001 saw the company rebound strongly despite a weak economy, with revenues up 10.1 percent with significant growth in the third and fourth quarters of 22.2 percent and 46.5 percent, respectively. Earnings stayed even for the year but showed growth in the later quarters as well.

CGI stock took a nosedive in the tech wreck, dropping to $6 from $34. The stock regained its footing from April 2001 through January 2002, doubling to over $12 before correcting back to less than $6 by August. But with rising revenues and profits, the next few years may be good ones for CGI.

CGI Group Inc. at a Glance

Fiscal Year-end: September
6-Year Return: 61.6%

	1997	1998	1999	2000	2001	9-Year Growth Average (%)	9-Year Growth Total (%)
Revenue ($ mlns.)	231.9	741.0	1,409.5	1,436.0	1,581.3	58.0	1,974.3
Net Income ($ mlns.)	7.8	34.8	83.8	55.7	62.8	125.9	15,558.1
Earnings/ Share ($)	0.05	0.15	0.32	0.21	0.21	75.6	2,000.0
Dividend/ Share ($)	0.00	0.00	0.00	0.00	0.00	–	–
Price/ Earnings	8.1 - 97.5	28.0 - 115.3	25.4 - 59.5	41.9 - 164.0	23.9 - 58.1	–	–

Table data courtesy of ✓*Canadian Shareowner* www.shareowner.com

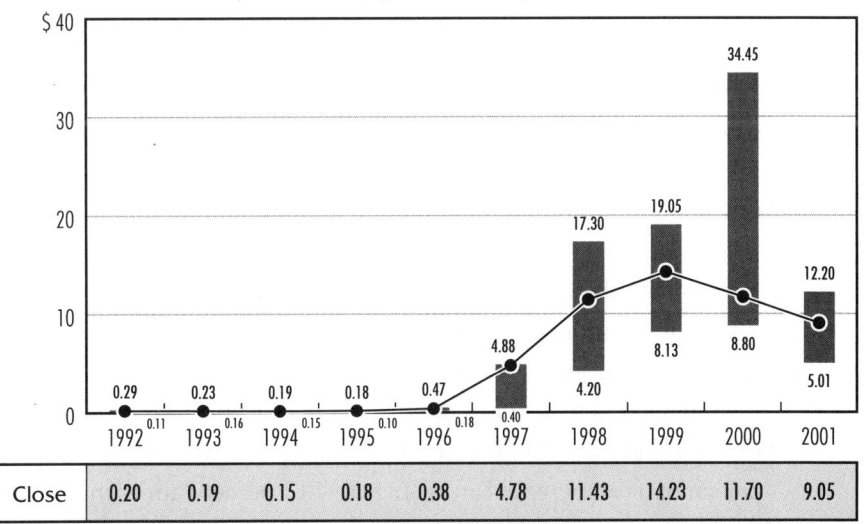

* EPS growth figures based on eight years.

MICROSOFT CORPORATION

1 Microsoft Way
Redmond, WA 98052-6399

Tel: (425) 936-4400
Fax: (425) 936-8000
www.microsoft.com
Symbol: MSFT (NASDAQ)

Employees: 48,030
Founded: 1975
Listed: 1986

Chairperson: William H. Gates III
CEO: Steven A. Ballmer

Share Price Growth	★ ★ ★ ★ ★
Revenue Growth	★ ★ ★ ★ ★
EPS Growth	★ ★ ★ ★ ★
MSFT	**15**

About the Company

Microsoft is the largest and most successful computer software company in the world and the second-largest company in America by market capitalization (after General Electric).

Founded in 1975 by Bill Gates and Paul Allen, Microsoft has come to dominate the computer software industry. Its Windows operating system is on almost every non-Apple personal computer. Its Office software is the software of choice for business.

How successful is it? For the 10 fiscal years from 1991 through 2000, revenues have increased an average of 32.7 percent annually. Earnings per share have increased an average of 40.3 percent annually—an incredible record matched by few.

In March 2001, Microsoft launched its .NET initiative. Basically, .NET is a user-centric set of services based on the XML language that allows people to integrate functions across different computing platforms. Instead of cluttering up your hard drive with files and programs, you'll be able to access them over the Internet. It also allows businesses to share data and work together to provide customers a "more dynamic, personalized and productive experience."

In October 2001, Microsoft released Windows XP, the next generation of its operating system, with enhanced multimedia features. It is also considerably more stable than its predecessors.

And in fall of 2001, the company launched Xbox, its entry into the video game business. The company is the new kid on the block here, going toe-to-toe with Nintendo, Sega, and Sony PlayStation.

Opportunities and Challenges

Although launched in 2001, .NET is still in its infancy and Microsoft is spurring its development with the release in February 2002 of Visual Studio .NET and .NET Framework, two development tools for the creation of XML Web services on the .NET platform. Mr. Gates calls them "among the most important products ever released by Microsoft."

Over 3.5 million copies were released in beta-testing, and pre-release sales of the final version topped 350,000. Over 1,000 businesses deployed on the .NET platform during this time, including L'Oreal, Merrill Lynch, and Autodesk.

The first half of 2002 also saw Xbox released in Japan, Australia, and Europe after a successful launch in the U.S. In April 2002, just four months after launch, Xbox had captured the number two spot in the video game console market, outselling PlayStation 2 by 25 percent. The Xbox game "Halo: Combat Evolved" became the fastest million-unit seller of next-generation video games as well.

Meanwhile, other Microsoft products are making inroads against competitors. MSN is the fastest growing Web portal according to Media Metrix in February 2002. Internet Explorer is taking share away from Netscape, pushing Netscape usership down to just 7 percent of browsers. And SQL Server became the number one database program on the Windows and Windows NT platform in May 2002 with 40 percent of the market.

Mr. Gates expressed the prime challenge for all businesses in the fast-changing world of computers and electronics well: "One day an eager upstart will put Microsoft out of business."

The other challenge for Microsoft is the U.S. government. The antitrust hurdle could well crop up again and again for the company. Microsoft's stock took a big hit in 2000, not from the bursting tech bubble, but from the adverse antitrust ruling. However, in June 2001, an appeals court overturned the ruling that Microsoft should be split in two, though it sustained the verdict that Microsoft was guilty of monopoly practice. Microsoft has pledged to fight for total vindication.

Financial Highlights

Microsoft increased revenues modestly in 2001, with sales up 10.2 percent, but earnings plunged 18.3 percent. This was the first year of earnings decline for Microsoft in the last 10 years. Fiscal 2002 saw revenues climb 12.1 percent with EPS climbing again, up a modest 2.2 percent. Microsoft stock has traded in a wide range between $50 and $70 since September 2000. In July 2002 it dipped below the $50 threshold and may have established a new trading range between $40 and $50. But don't count it out yet! With its new initiatives and .NET starting to take off in a big way, the company could well vault back to its previous highs and beyond.

Microsoft Corporation at a Glance

Fiscal Year-end: June
10-Year Return: 27.5%

	1997	1998	1999	2000	2001	10-Year Growth Average (%)	10-Year Growth Total (%)
Revenue (US$ mlns.)	11,358.0	14,484.0	19,747.0	22,956.0	25,296.0	28.3	816.9
Net Income (US$ mlns.)	3,439.0	4,795.3	7,582.2	9,359.2	7,721.0	32.5	990.4
Earnings/ Share (US$)	0.66	0.89	1.38	1.69	1.38	29.9	820.0
Dividend/ Share (US$)	–	–	–	–	–	–	–
Price/ Earnings	20.8 - 51.1	33.1 - 61.0	31.8 - 69.3	35.7 - 71.0	29.2 - 60.1	–	–

Table data courtesy of  www.shareowner.com

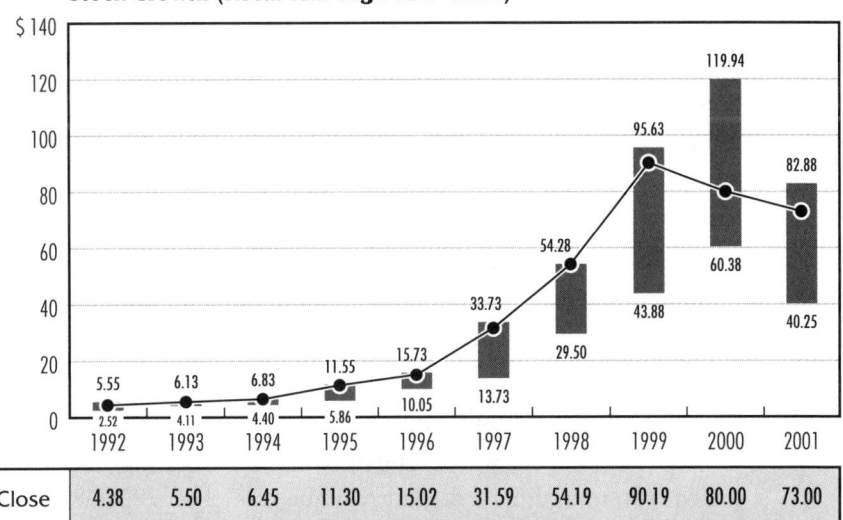

SIEBEL SYSTEMS, INC.

2207 Bridgepointe Parkway
San Mateo, CA 94404

Tel: (650) 295-5000
Fax: (650) 295-5111
www.siebel.com
Symbol: SEBL (NASDAQ) (Also SBL-TSX)

Employees: 8,000
Founded: 1993
Listed: 1996

Chairperson and CEO: Thomas M. Siebel
President and COO: Paul Wahl

Share Price Growth	★ ★ ★ ★ ★
Revenue Growth	★ ★ ★ ★ ★
EPS Growth	★ ★ ★ ★ ★
SEBL	**15**

About the Company

Taking advantage of the increasing popularity of the Internet as a business application, Siebel Systems has become the world's leading provider of e-business applications software, sometimes called customer relations management software (CRM).

Siebel's software enables multi-channel sales, marketing, and customer services to be applied over the Internet as well as private networks. It also supports end-user education through Siebel University, its comprehensive training program.

In 1999, Siebel Systems topped the Deloitte & Touche Fast 500 list with an incredible five-year revenue growth of 782,978 percent.

That's no misprint. Siebel also topped the *Fortune* list of the fastest-growing companies that year. In 2000, it came in third on the *Fortune* list and was named the most influential software company by *Business Week*, beating out Microsoft. And in that terrible economic year of 2001, it moved up a notch on *Fortune*'s list to second. In August 2002, it made the list again, dropping to 19th. It's the only company to have made the top 20, four years in a row.

Siebel was not, however, the only CRM company in the market. Canada's Janna Systems made Deloitte and Touche's Canadian Fast 50 from 1998 to 2000 and was one of Canada's best-performing stocks. Janna merged with Siebel in November 2000, resulting in exchangeable shares of Siebel becoming available on the Toronto Stock Exchange.

In April 2001, the company announced a new line of software—employee relationship management (ERM)—expanding its market reach beyond its CRM offerings. CIBC World Markets says that U.S. companies spend US$160 billion annually on hiring, training, managing, and retaining employees.

Siebel has offices in 37 countries worldwide. Its client list includes such notables as Hewlett Packard, Ford Motor Company, Cisco Systems, GTE, Intuit, Nordstrom, Boeing, Bank of America, Compaq, AT&T, Citibank, Nokia, and Charles Schwab.

Opportunities and Challenges

Siebel Systems keeps adding to its roster of products and boasts the most comprehensive family of multichannel eBusiness applications and services. These now include an extensive set of sales tools such as sales analytics, forecasting, wireless mobile sales tools, and incentive compensation software. Other tools include a suite of marketing tools, call centre management, interactive selling, partner relationship management, and a variety of products geared to specific industries.

Furthermore, Siebel has developed partnerships with over 750 companies worldwide to integrate the companies' software solutions. This lets companies deploy Siebel's software solutions without jeopardizing their existing software investments.

However, Siebel is not without competition. Oracle, the second-largest software company in the world, after Microsoft, has taken aim at the CRM market with its own Oracle11i suite. And in 1999, PeopleSoft acquired Vantive, the number two CRM company, as a basis for the creation of its PeopleSoft 8 CRM software. German software giant SAP has also entered the market with its mySAP CRM line. Those are strong competitors and Siebel faces a real challenge in staying top dog in this field.

The market for CRM is expected to jump to US$16 billion in 2005 from US$5.6 billion in 2001.

Financial Highlights

Sales for 2001 grew 14.1 percent, while earnings per share more than doubled, up 104.2 percent. Not bad for an eBusiness company in the aftermath of the Internet rout and slowing economy. Nevertheless, Siebel's share price had soared to the stratosphere along with other Internet and e-commerce companies in 1999 and the first quarter of 2000. And it also crashed—dropping to a low of $12 in September 2001 from $120 in October 2000. Post 9/11, it climbed steadily to $37 in January 2002 and sank back below $10 by August the same year as tech stocks continued to show weakness. But with Siebel's solid and continuing growth, debt-free position, and US$1.5 billion in its coffers, not to mention a visionary leader, Siebel Systems should see continued growth into the future.

Siebel Systems Inc. at a Glance
Fiscal Year-end: December
5-Year Return: 60.6%

	1997	1998	1999	2000	2001	7-Year Growth Average (%)	7-Year Growth Total (%)
Revenue (US$ mlns.)	118.8	391.5	790.9	1,795.4	2,048.4	177.2	25,384.0
Net Income (US$ mlns.)	20.3	56.1	122.1	164.3	256.3	366.6	80,737.5
Earnings/ Share (US$)	0.07	0.14	0.27	0.31	0.49	103.1	2,350.0
Dividend/ Share (US$)	–	–	–	–	–	–	–
Price/ Earnings	23.7 - 88.2	27.0 - 66.1	29.2 - 170.4	105.6 - 386.7	25.0 - 172.4	–	–

Table data courtesy of ✓Canadian Shareowner   www.shareowner.com

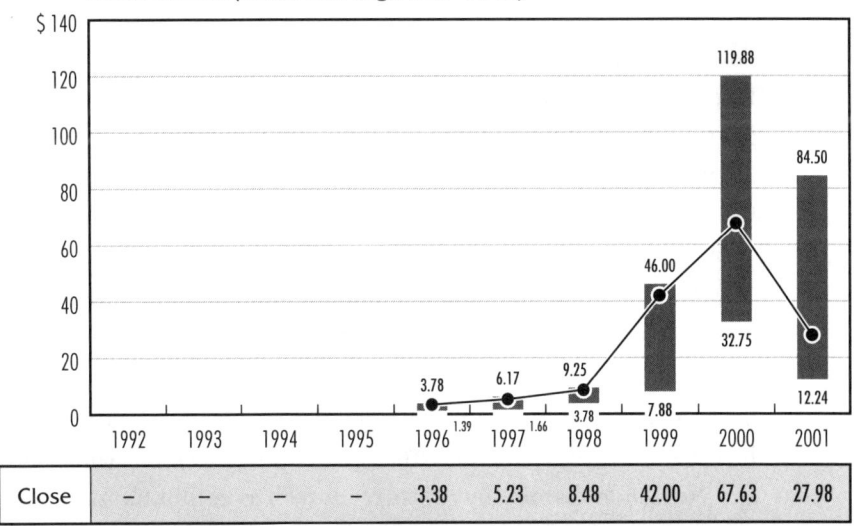

Stock Growth (Fiscal Year High-Low-Close)

| Close | – | – | – | – | 3.38 | 5.23 | 8.48 | 42.00 | 67.63 | 27.98 |

* EPS growth figures based on six years.

THQ INC.

27001 Agoura Road, Suite 325
Calabasas Hills, CA 91301

Tel: (818) 871-5000
Fax: (818) 871-7400
www.thq.com
Symbol: THQI (NASDAQ)

Employees: 410
Founded: 1989
Listed: 1991

Chairperson, President, and CEO: Brian J. Farrell

Share Price Growth	★ ★ ★ ★
Revenue Growth	★ ★ ★ ★ ★
EPS Growth	★ ★ ★ ★ ★
THQI	**14**

About the Company

Is there a North American home with kids that doesn't have a video game system? I don't know of any, and moreover, everyone wants the latest thing. When the PlayStation 2 came out in October 2000, people lined up for 26 hours outside one store in San Francisco.

Whatever game system a kid may have, the slot in the game console is like a hungry mouth demanding more and better games. Enter THQ, the fourth-largest publisher of electronic games.

The company covers all platforms, including the ones launched in the fall of 2001: Game Boy, Game Boy Color, Nintendo 64, PlayStation, PlayStation 2, Sega Dreamcast, Microsoft's Xbox, Nintendo GameCube, and Nintendo Game Boy Advance, as well as computer games for Windows and Macintosh.

THQ makes dozens of games—some developed in-house and many licensed. Its licences include the extremely popular WWF series, which had brought in over US$190 million as of March 2001. WWF SmackDown 2 was the number-one seller for 11 out of 12 weeks in the first quarter of 2001. WWF No Mercy topped the charts in its first week.

Other licensces include popular series for younger children: Rugrats, Scooby-Doo, Hot Wheels, Power Rangers, Star Wars, and Disney Interactive, as well as several properties from Nickelodeon. THQ dominates this juvenile market with a 37 percent market share, more than double that of the next publisher.

THQ has the highest operating margin in the gaming industry at 14.3 percent. It was ranked 20th on the *Forbes* list of the 200 Best Small Companies for 2001 in October 2001.

Opportunities and Challenges

Video gaming is a huge industry. Bigger than the movie industry. Industry-wide revenues of US$20 billion a year in 2002 are expected to reach US$36 billion by 2005. It's not surprising that THQ was one tech company that managed to increase both revenues and earnings in a weaker economy.

Credit Suisse/First Boston initiated coverage of three game makers, including THQ, on May 1, 2001. Analyst Heath Terry said, "We believe that the interactive entertainment industry is just beginning what will be the largest and most significant growth phase in its history."

Wireless and online technology present new opportunities. THQ is working with Siemens to develop games for mobile devices. One of the first games for mobile devices, WWF Mobile Madness, was released commercially in January 2002.

THQ continues to make strategic acquisitions of independent studios, including Phoenix-based Rainbow Studios in January 2002. And it continues to negotiate exclusive licensing deals. May 2002 saw it clinch a deal with Disney for exclusive rights to the next three Disney/Pixar animated flicks: Finding Nemo, The Incredibles, and Cars.

But most exciting is the deal signed with Marvel Comics in April 2002. It gives THQ exclusive rights to Captain America, Nick Fury, and The Punisher. Following hot on the heels of the smashing success of Marvel's Spiderman movie, these other properties should also make it to the movie screen and the gaming console in a big way.

THQ's 10-year history did not meet our criteria for inclusion, as the company lost money in 1993 and 1994 before undergoing a dramatic reorganization in 1995 when it switched from being a toy company (THQ stands for Toy Head-Quarters) to a video gaming company. Our analysis (including star ratings) is based on the company's fortunes after a one-for-15 share consolidation in February that year. This explains why the star rating may seem out of whack with the data as tabulated.

Financial Highlights

THQ increased revenues by 9.2 percent in 2001 in a soft economic environment. Earnings per share (fully diluted) were up 34.7 percent. And the stock did not fare too badly throughout, soaring to a peak in July 2001 while other tech stocks were crashing and burning. The stock has been trading in a wide range from $20 to $40 from then until September 2002 and could consolidate for another rise in 2003.

THQ Inc. at a Glance

Fiscal Year-end: December
10-Year Return: 3.2%

	1997	1998	1999	2000	2001	10-Year Growth Average (%)	10-Year Growth Total (%)
Revenue (US$ mlns.)	89.4	215.1	302.4	347.0	379.0	42.9	571.0
Net Income (US$ mlns.)	9.3	23.3	32.9	24.3	36.0	–	790.1
Earnings/ Share (US$)	0.40	0.89	1.09	0.75	1.01	–	18.8
Dividend/ Share (US$)	0.00	0.00	0.00	0.00	0.00	–	–
Price/ Earnings	4.3 - 17.5	4.7 - 15.7	6.7 - 24.0	6.8 - 26.7	14.2 - 43.0	–	–

Table data courtesy of  www.shareowner.com

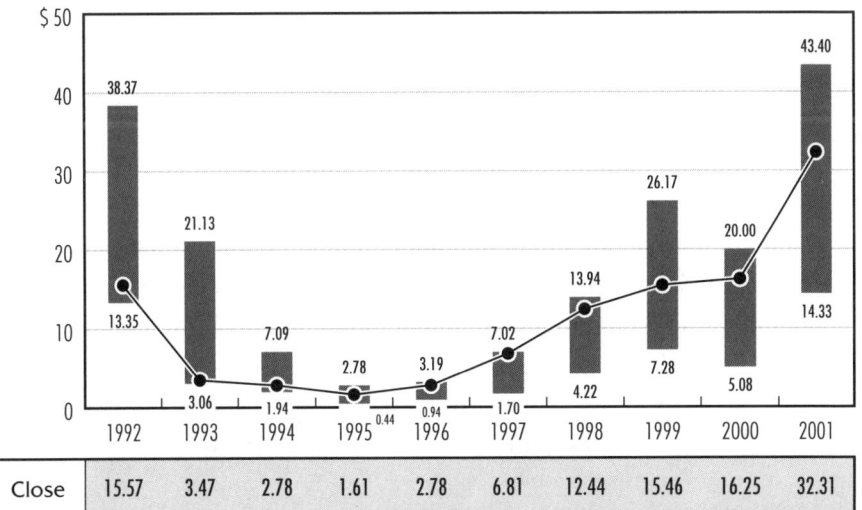

MERCURY INTERACTIVE CORPORATION

1325 Borregas Avenue
Sunnyvale, CA 94089

Tel: (408) 822-5200
Fax: (408) 822-5300
www.svca.mercuryinteractive.com
Symbol: MERQ (NASDAQ)

Employees: 1,600+
Founded: 1989
Listed: 1993

Chairperson, President, and CEO: Amnon Landan

Share Price Growth	★ ★ ★ ★
Revenue Growth	★ ★ ★ ★ ★
EPS Growth	★ ★ ★ ★
MERQ	**13**

About the Company

Mercury Interactive began as a company testing Windows and Unix software for corporate clients. In the late 1990s, it made a splash testing for the Y2K bug. Today Mercury tests website performance and interactive business applications for over 10,000 companies including ABN Amro Bank, Bank of America, Bear Stearns, Cadbury Schweppes, Citibank, Deutsche Bank, E*Trade, Ford Motor Company, Gap Inc., Hewlett-Packard, Merck, Merrill Lynch, Microsoft, Nokia, Qwest, Siemens, SunLife of Canada, Supervalu, and much of the

U.S. government, including three branches of the military, the U.S. Mint, and the Patent and Trademark Office. Even the NASDAQ uses Mercury's software to test the reliability of its trading systems and the additions of new member firms.

When Stephen King decided to go digital and offer his newest book online, he hired Mercury Interactive to make sure his website could manage the expected traffic. Mercury has monitored the websites of Superbowl advertisers. In fact, the company has 53 percent of the worldwide load-testing market and a remarkable 63 percent of the load-testing market for web-based applications—more than seven times its nearest competitor.

Testing is a pretty broad term. What does Mercury do, exactly, that makes it so in demand? As one analyst put it, Mercury provides the equivalent of an insurance policy for a company's software systems. Mercury's service solutions can test load capabilities on a website by simulating two million simultaneous users. Enterprise testing solutions include test management, load testing, scalability, and functional/regression testing. Clients can optimize their software and know it is working properly before it is deployed, and then monitor it 24/7 so they can quickly correct problems as they develop. And Mercury's software can fine-tune the applications as upgrades and modifications occur.

Mercury Interactive has partnered with numerous companies to make sure it can support ERP/CRM software applications from Oracle, Peoplesoft, Siebel, and SAP, application servers from BEA, IBM and Sun, and databases from Microsoft, Oracle, and Sybase. Other alliances include Nokia, RealNetworks, Deloitte Consulting, PriceWaterhouseCoopers, Qwest, and AT&T.

The company was listed as number one in the Software Elite Category of Forbes ASAP's Dynamic 100 for 2001. It was number nine on *Fortune*'s list of Fastest Growing Companies for 2001.

Opportunities and Challenges

Mercury Interactive's clientele is diversified, with only about 15 percent of its business from dot-coms. The rest are, shall we say, more stable companies.

Increasingly the company's services are being used to test software for financial companies, including banks and brokerage houses. The year 2001 saw the company provide performance testing for companies like H&R Block, Intuit, and the U.S. Internal Revenue Service as online filing of tax returns was launched.

In April 2002, the company added Charles G. Schwab as Chief Information Officer. He brings with him a wealth of experience with major brokers such as Lehman Brothers, Paine Webber, JP Morgan, and Charles Schwab company (he's not *that* Charles Schwab, by the way).

Mercury Interactive faced some challenges in 2001 as a slowing economy considerably dampened the company's revenue growth. But an improving economy should see it pick up the pace again.

Financial Highlights

Mercury Interactive's revenue growth rate dropped from 63.6 percent in 2000 to 17.6 percent in 2001. Earnings suffered even more as they dropped from $0.70 a share to $0.25—a 64.3 percent drop. Needless to say, the stock price was also affected by this, plummeting by 75 percent in the technology stock debacle of 2000–2001. It rallied in mid-2001 only to finally hit bottom in September, as did many stocks. It rose steadily from September 2001 through March 2002 when it started trading sideways and then dropped to the $25 level again as the bear reasserted itself. A recovering economy should put the company back on track again.

Mercury Interactive lost two of its 15 stars in our ratings this year, one for share price growth and one for earnings per share growth.

Mercury Interactive Corporation at a Glance

Fiscal Year-end: December
8-Year Return: 33.7%

	1997	1998	1999	2000	2001	10-Year Growth Average (%)	10-Year Growth Total (%)
Revenue (US$ mlns.)	76.7	121.0	187.7	307.0	361.0	69.1	8,233.3
Net Income (US$ mlns.)	10.3	21.8	34.4	64.7	22.2	77.9	1,531.3
Earnings/ Share (US$)	0.15	0.28	0.40	0.70	0.25	59.2	733.3
Dividend/ Share (US$)	–	–	–	–	–	–	–
Price/ Earnings	15.8 - 46.9	18.9 - 56.5	26.3 - 137.8	57.3 - 232.1	72.0 - 401.8	–	–

Table data courtesy of Canadian Shareowner   www.shareowner.com

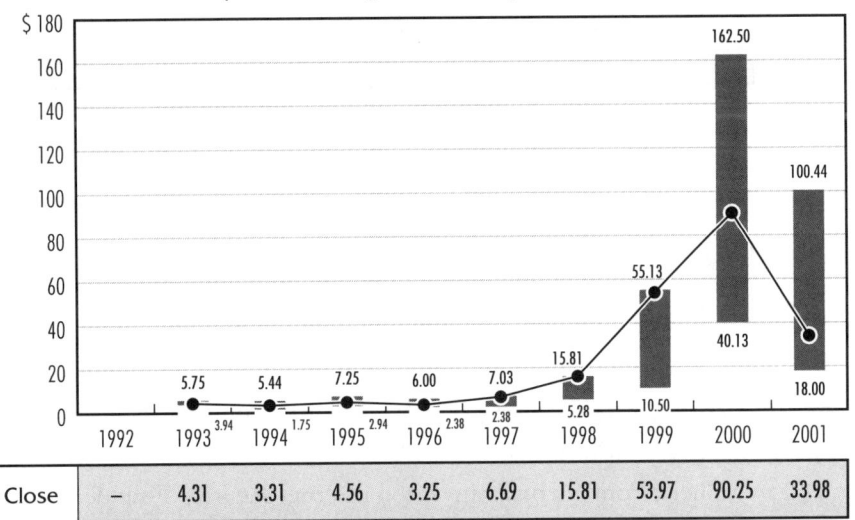

* Net income and EPS growth figures based on nine years.

CHECK POINT SOFTWARE TECHNOLOGIES LTD.

3 Lagoon Drive, Suite 400
Redwood City, CA 94065

Tel: (650) 628-2000
Fax: (650) 654-4233
www.checkpoint.com
Symbol: CHKP (NASDAQ)

Employees: 1,170
Founded: 1993
Listed: 1996

Chairperson and CEO: Gil Schwed
President: Jerry Ungerman

Share Price Growth	★ ★
Revenue Growth	★ ★ ★ ★ ★
EPS Growth	★ ★ ★ ★ ★
CHKP	**12**

About the Company

The biggest concern for businesses establishing an online presence or integrating local and wide area networks with the Internet is security. Sensitive data must be protected from the prying eyes of hackers. Transactions involving money transfer must be secure. And so business has turned in droves to Check Point Software Technologies for virtual private networks (VPNs), firewalls, and other leading-edge security solutions.

Check Point virtually invented Internet security. Founded by two Israelis, Gil Schwed and Marius Nacht, in 1993, today Check Point dominates the world of VPNs. A virtual private network connects local area networks together over a public network such as the Internet through encrypted connections. This is considerably cheaper than installing dedicated circuits for a true private network.

In 1997, Check Point launched the Open Platform for Security (OPSEC)—an open architecture that provides the framework for the integration and interoperability of solutions from over 300 industry partners. Products developed by members of the OPSEC Alliance go through rigorous testing before being approved as "OPSEC Certified" or "Secured by Check Point." These solutions are value-added products that conform to the Check Point Secure Virtual Network (SVN) architecture.

As of April 2002, Check Point has installed over 225,000 firewall and VPN solutions, as well as 125,000 VPN Gateway installations. Clients include 90 percent of America's 500 largest companies. It is the number one player in the VPN market with a 62 percent market share.

Check Point's software has won numerous awards, including Product of the Year for VPN-1 from *Network Magazine* (April 2001) and Editor's Choice Awards from *Network Computing* (December 2000) and *Communication News* (May 2001). It was also named Best Internet Infrastructure Company for 2001 by *Global Finance* and won Best Enterprise Security and Best Internet Security recognition from *Computerworld*.

Opportunities and Challenges

The brilliant OPSEC concept helps establish the proprietary Check Point SVN solution as the standard for network security. But there are challenges to Check Point's dominance in security. Microsoft now includes firewall features with Windows XP. And Cisco is including firewall software in almost all of its routers. Check Point must continually reinvent its VPN and firewall protocols.

The company introduced its latest products—VPN-1® Net and VPN-1® Pro in April 2002, improved variants in its VPN-1/Firewall-1 family. Also introduced was SmartDefense, a proactive solution that detects and defeats attacks on networks. This followed on the March introduction of its VPN-1/Firewall-1 VSX Internet security solution for service providers and corporate data centres.

Check Point made its name and its fortune with network security for corporations, but in September 2001 the company introduced its first product for the home user, its Safe@Home Security Management Platform. The product is targeted at Internet Service Providers who can offer it as a value-added service but is also offered at consumer retail stores.

Financial Highlights

Check Point had another record year in 2001, with revenues up 24.1 percent and earnings per share up 48.8 percent. While this looks great, it was actually less than anticipated as the tech spending freeze caught up with Check Point. And the company included deferred revenues from previous quarters to get there.

In the wake of Enron, anything even vaguely resembling fancy accounting disillusioned investors, and Check Point took a beating, dropping 12.9 percent on January 15, 2002 when its annual report was released. The stock continued to fall through the end of June 2002 when it started making modest headway again.

This is in stark contrast to the tech stock heyday when Check Point soared to $118 in October 2000. Like most of the Internet-related stocks, it got hammered down $21 in September 2001 and was making a solid recovery post 9/11. The company's growing revenues and earnings, as well as solid margins, indicate that there will be a turnaround in the stock sometime. Watch for an opportunity.

The hammer also knocked three stars from Check Point's share price appreciation.

Check Point Software Technologies Ltd. at a Glance

Fiscal Year-end: December
5-Year Return: 35.7%

	1997	1998	1999	2000	2001	7-Year Growth Average (%)	7-Year Growth Total (%)
Revenue (US$ mlns.)	82.9	141.9	219.6	425.3	527.6	106.3	5,427.4
Net Income (US$ mlns.)	40.2	69.9	95.8	221.2	321.9	110.9	6,541.6
Earnings/ Share (US$)	0.18	0.30	0.39	0.84	1.25	111.3	6,150.0
Dividend/ Share (US$)	–	–	–	–	–	–	–
Price/ Earnings	15.0 - 46.8	6.0 - 26.5	9.8 - 95.5	34.6 - 141.2	15.6 - 90.7	–	–

Table data courtesy of  www.shareowner.com

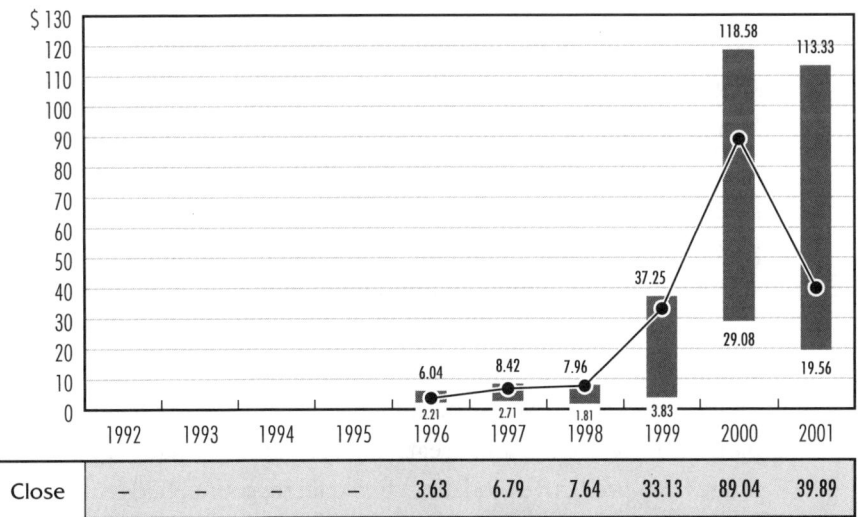

COGNOS INC.

3755 Riverside Drive
Ottawa, ON K1G 4K9

Tel: (613) 738-1440
Fax: (613) 738-0002
www.cognos.com
Symbol: CSN (TSX) (Also COGN-NASDAQ)

Employees: 2,600
Founded: 1969
Listed: 1986

CEO: Renato Zambonini
President and COO: Robert G. Ashe

Share Price Growth	★ ★ ★ ★ ★
Revenue Growth	★ ★ ★
EPS Growth	★ ★ ★ ★
CSN	**12**

About the Company

When the NASDAQ wanted to coordinate its comprehensive data to provide a useful analytical tool on its website, who did it turn to? When NASA was looking for a way to coordinate information on 20,000 employees working out of nine different field centres, who did it turn to? If you answered Cognos, you're right.

Ottawa-based Cognos is the world's largest and most successful business intelligence company. Its suite of software products operates on its Enterprise Business Intelligence (EBI) Platform to allow companies to coordinate and creatively use company data. These uses range from predictive modeling, financial reporting, budgeting, forecasting, analysis, and queries, to scenario creation and visualization.

The EBI Platform is not so much a product as an infrastructure that supports the manipulation of corporate data. Its applications vary from customer to customer.

Cognos' data platform incorporates the Internet to enable easy data sharing between various geographical operations of an organization. E-business solutions are also part of the company's activities.

In late 2000, Cognos entered the corporate portal market with its Enterprise Portal Partner (EPP) program. A portal program, such as the Plumtree Corporate Portal, integrates data from various programs and platforms into one customized common user interface or desktop. Cognos' EPP program enlists portal providers as partners to integrate Cognos' business intelligence software into their offerings.

More than 2.4 million Cognos Business Intelligence licences have been sold to over 20,000 organizations in over 135 countries. These include such major companies as Harrah's Hotels and Casinos, Otis Elevators, Future Shop, Red Robin Restaurants, Telus Mobility, Boeing, BC Ferry Corp., Nielsen Data Research, ABN AMRO Bank, BMW, Mercedes-Benz, Dow Chemical, Shell Oil, Nokia, Hewlett-Packard, Philips, Hydro Quebec, Bertelsmann Music Group, Siemens, and KLM.

Opportunities and Challenges

The Business Intelligence platform supports many functions in high demand from business today, including Customer Relationship Management (CRM), Enterprise Resource Planning (ERP), Data Warehousing, Supply Chain Management, and Human Resources Management. This has led to integration of key products in these fields to work seamlessly with the BI platform. Strategic partners include Siebel, SAP, Peoplesoft, Microsoft, PriceWaterhouseCoopers, Onyx, and more. What Business Intelligence does is provide the analytical tools to integrate and make sense of data provided by these other applications.

In April 2002, the company announced a new strategy to incorporate its products into what it calls a Corporate Performance

Management Framework, or CPM. This next generation of business intelligence software will improve functionality by facilitating the linking together of various departments and projects in a company and tying them to end goals. This shift in focus is expected to push the company to over US$1 billion in sales and give it an edge over rivals such as Business Objects SA of France.

Business analyst Summit Strategies estimates the portal market will reach US$14 billion by 2002, and business intelligence is seen as a killer application (meaning a superior or hot application that is much in demand) in this market. Five portal providers have now integrated Cognos solutions.

And in August 2002, Cognos announced it is moving into web services, which allows users to access the company's business intelligence software over the Internet or through wireless devices such as the BlackBerry pager and even through cash registers.

One of the challenges facing Cognos is a patent infringement suit launched by Business Objects, a suit that Cognos says is without foundation.

Financial Highlights

Cognos's revenues in Canadian dollars gained modestly by 3.8 percent in fiscal 2002 but was down in U.S.-dollar terms. Earnings per share dropped by 31.8 percent. The first quarter of fiscal 2003 (to May 31) showed continued growth with revenues up 11.2 percent and EPS of US$0.11 compared to a loss of US$0.13 the year before. Cognos has regularly beat expectations, and after collapsing to $20 in September 2001 from a high of $73 in November 2000, the stock soared to $48 in March 2002. A correction took it to the $27 area in August. The stock may fluctuate somewhat, but an improving economy should put Cognos back on a solid growth path. We knocked a star off its rating for EPS growth this year.

Cognos Inc. at a Glance
Fiscal Year-end: February
10-Year Return: 36.8%

	1998	1999	2000	2001	2002	10-Year Growth Average (%)	10-Year Growth Total (%)
Revenue ($ mlns.)	348.6	454.4	559.4	759.4	788.5	21.0	434.0
Net Income ($ mlns.)	72.2	92.8	85.3	101.0	67.5	–	–
Earnings/ Share ($)	0.79	1.04	0.97	1.10	0.75	–	–
Dividend/ Share ($)	–	–	–	–	–	–	–
Price/ Earnings	15.8 - 31.0	10.9 - 20.8	14.7 - 55.7	23.0 - 66.5	21.5 - 63.1	–	–

Table data courtesy of  www.shareowner.com

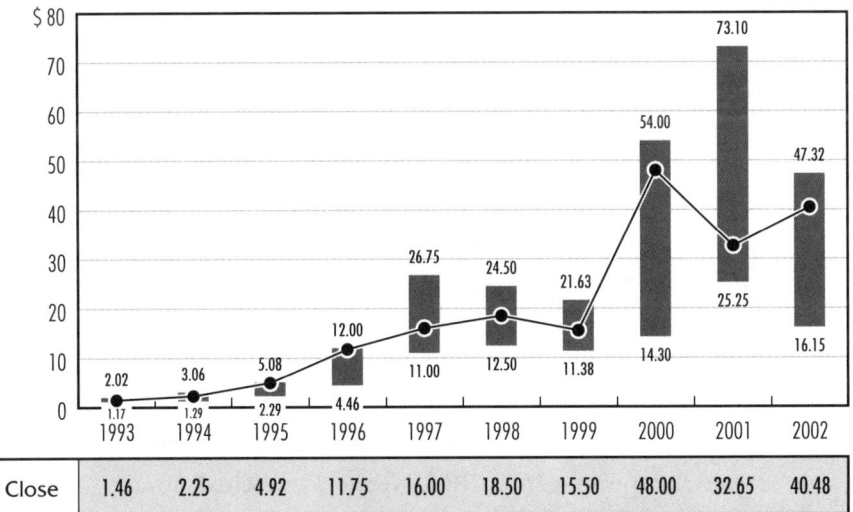

NETWORK APPLIANCE, INC.

495 East Java Drive
Sunnyvale, CA 94089

Tel: (408) 822-6000
Fax: (408) 822-4501
www.netapp.com

Employees: 2,200
Listed: 1995
Symbol: NTAP (NASDAQ)

Chairperson: Donald T. Valentine
CEO: Dan Warmenhoven
President: Thomas F. Mendoza

Share Price Growth	★ ★ ★ ★
Revenue Growth	★ ★ ★ ★ ★
EPS Growth	★
NTAP	**10**

About the Company

The amount of data flowing across the Internet and through corporate intranets is staggering. Where do you store all that stuff? Most of it (78 percent) is still stored in computer servers and hard drives sold by the major computer manufacturers, such as IBM, Compaq, and HP. But increasingly business is turning to specialized storage systems.

The two kinds of systems have exactly opposite acronyms. Storage area networks (SANs) are large integrated systems that compete with mainframes. The leader here is EMC Corporation, which effectively stole the top spot from IBM. Network-attached storage (NAS) integrates and stores files in specialized appliances, as they're called, and serves them over a network. Network Appliance is the leader in this field.

Network Appliance's filers and software solutions can integrate and store data across different platforms. For example, a company may have the computers in its accounting department running Unix and its sales department running Windows NT. Still other computers may be serving up information on the company website in HTML. Network Appliance's server can store all the data for these disparate systems in one place and make it accessible cross-platform. It does this with a specialized operating system called Data ONTAP.

The company also improves network response times with its Netcache appliance. Network traffic can be reduced up to 50 percent and web response time by a factor of 10, reducing what the company amusingly calls the "world wide wait."

Opportunities and Challenges

There is a marked shift from direct attached storage to networked attached storage, with an annual compounded growth rate for 2000 to 2004 estimated to be 45.7 percent. Network Appliance is at the forefront in serving this trend.

The reasons are several. Not only is networked storage faster, it is also cheaper. A study of storage systems by INPUT, an IT research firm, shows that NetApp's solutions reduce the cost of ownership by 70 percent over competitors such as Compaq, EMC, and Hitachi Data Systems. The study analyzed total expenditures including purchase, installation, maintenance, management, and staffing.

NetApp also introduced NearStore™, a centralized rapid recovery and backup consolidation solution, in December 2001. This suite of products adds business continuance and near-instant restore functionality. This was followed up by further alliances in data protection with Computer Associates' new BrightStor Enterprise Backup system, McAfee's NetShield anti-virus software, Advanced Digital Information Corporation, Spectra Logic, and Legato

Systems. NetApp introduced its own SnapVault™ data protection software in March 2002.

The years 2001 and 2002 saw several new alliances, including Xelus Enterprise Service Management solutions, which facilitate historical usage analysis and third-party ERP software, eMed Medical Imaging Solutions, and further collaboration with SAP. The company also won Microsoft Windows Media Certification.

NetApp Netcache servers have been incorporated into Anadarko's oil exploration operations and facilitated the transfer of Canada's @Home subscribers to Shaw Cable High Speed Internet Service with superior service to that afforded before.

Rival EMC Corporation decided to take a run at Network Appliance and overtook NetApp in the first quarter of 2001 in the NAS field. But with the market for NAS expected to rocket to US$6 billion in 2005 from US$1.89 billion in 2001, there is lots of room for both EMC and Network Appliance to grow and profit in this field. And NetApp is not taking the competition lying down. It is forging ahead with research and new product development as noted above.

Financial Highlights

Network Appliance saw revenues slip 20.7 percent in fiscal 2002, with earnings off 79.3 percent as the cutbacks in computer-related spending took its toll. That's an earnings drop to US$0.06 a share from US$0.29. Although NetApp fails to meet all of our criteria because of this blemish, we are making an exception in this case because we believe the demand for storage will pick up again as the economy recovers.

The company lost five stars this year, one for share price and four for earnings growth.

Network Appliance, Inc. at a Glance
Fiscal Year-end: April
6-Year Return: 37.3%

	1998	1999	2000	2001	2002	8-Year Growth Average (%)	8-Year Growth Total (%)
Revenue (US$ mlns.)	166.2	289.4	579.3	1,006.2	798.4	88.7	5,295.8
Net Income (US$ mlns.)	21.0	35.6	73.8	105.1	21.0	–	–
Earnings/ Share (US$)	0.07	0.12	0.21	0.29	0.06	–	–
Dividend/ Share (US$)	–	–	–	–	–	–	–
Price/ Earnings	25.2 - 66.7	33.3 - 139.6	46.9 - 590.5	39.4 - 526.7	100.0 - 491.7	–	–

Table data courtesy of  www.shareowner.com

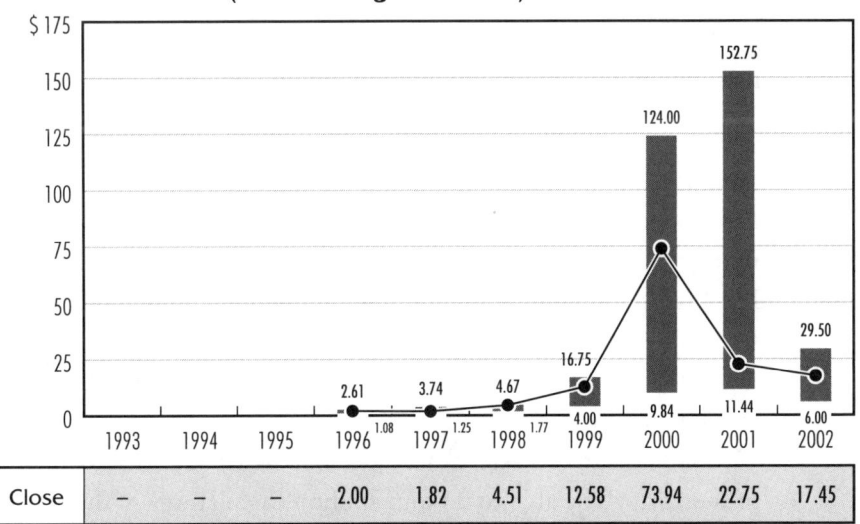

INTEL CORPORATION

2200 Mission College Boulevard
P.O. Box 58119
Santa Clara, CA 95052-8119

Tel: (408) 765-8080
Fax: (408) 765-9904
www.intel.com
Symbol: INTC (NASDAQ)

Employees: 80,000
Founded: 1968
Listed: 1971

Chairperson: Andrew S. Grove
President: Craig R. Barrett
CEO: Paul S. Otellini

Share Price Growth	★ ★ ★ ★ ★
Revenue Growth	★ ★ ★
EPS Growth	★
INTC	**9**

About the Company

Faster than a speeding bullet! More powerful than a locomotive! Able to leap tall buildings in a single bound! Well, not really the last two. But Intel Labs has developed a new transistor just 20 nanometres in size. By around 2007 this will enable the creation of microprocessors with a billion transistors running at speeds approaching 20 gigahertz at less than one volt.

How fast is that? Faster than a speeding bullet! This future microprocessor will be able to do four million calculations in the time it takes a bullet to travel one inch—a billion calculations in the blink of an eye. Each transistor switch will be able to turn on and off more than a trillion times a second.

Intel co-founder Gordon Moore coined a maxim in 1965 called Moore's Law: The number of transistors that can be put in an integrated circuit will double every 18 months. He expected this rate of growth to last until 1975, but it remains true today and, with the development of the tiny transistor noted above, will hold for another 10 years.

To give you an idea of what a phenomenal investment Intel has been over the years, US$10,000 invested when it first went public in 1971 would be worth over US$7.75 million today (at $20 a share). Although Intel's core business is still microprocessors for computers, it also produces components for wireless devices—mobile phones, PDAs, and so on—and it builds chips for networking—embedded circuits for hubs, routers, switches, and servers.

Opportunities and Challenges

Intel is always on the cutting edge. Current programs are focused on nanotechnology, networks, wireless communications, the Internet, speech synthesis, and voice recognition, and of course, constant research on upgrading the microprocessor. Latest innovations include the Xeon™ and Itanium® processors, as well as upgrades to the Pentium line.

Intel Capital is the company's strategic investing program and one of the largest corporate venture capital programs in the world. It has injected capital into several hundred small and mostly private companies whose products support Intel's own initiatives and emerging trends. This input of cash is meant to foster growth from start-up to the IPO or acquisition stage. The investments are constantly monitored and eventually sold with proceeds reinvested.

Although the clear industry leader, Intel is not without competition. Applied Micro Devices (AMD), makers of the Duron and Athlon microprocessors, have been gaining ground and are no slouches. Nevertheless, Intel, with its size and clout, not to mention its US$4 billion a year R&D budget, should meet and beat the competition.

Financial Highlights

Intel's revenues dropped in 2001 to US$26.5 billion from US$33.7 billion, or 21.3 percent. It was the first annual decline in revenues in the last 10 years as the slowing economy and reduction in spending on technology took its toll. Earnings were hit even harder, with diluted earnings per share dropping to US$0.19 from US$1.51—a drop of 87.4 percent. Ouch!

The first half of 2002 showed signs of recovery, with sales up modestly at 0.7 percent but more significantly, EPS doubled to US$0.20 from US$0.10.

Intel shares suffered with the rest of the technology market, declining to a low of US$18.96 in September 2001 from a high of US$75.81 in September 2000. The stock scrambled back to over $36 by the end of 2001 and started a slow descent through May to $28. Then the roof fell in. A revenue warning in June knocked $10 off the price in a few days. The company and the stock should be showing signs of recovery through 2003 as corporate America and domestic consumers start upgrading their computers again.

Because of its lacklustre 2001, Intel lost four stars for EPS growth and one for revenue growth in our ratings.

Intel Corporation at a Glance

Fiscal Year-end: December
10-Year Return: 33.1%

	1997	1998	1999	2000	2001	10-Year Growth Average (%)	10-Year Growth Total (%)
Revenue (US$ mlns.)	25,070.0	26,273.0	29,389.0	33,726.0	26,539.0	20.1	354.1
Net Income (US$ mlns.)	6,945.0	6,218.6	7,587.9	9,205.1	2,407.7	21.9	119.0
Earnings/ Share (US$)	0.97	0.88	1.09	1.32	0.35	21.3	118.8
Dividend/ Share (US$)	0.03	0.03	0.05	0.07	0.08	33.9	700.0
Price/ Earnings	16.4 - 26.3	18.7 - 35.8	23.0 - 41.1	22.6 - 57.4	54.2 - 110.3	–	–

Table data courtesy of  www.shareowner.com

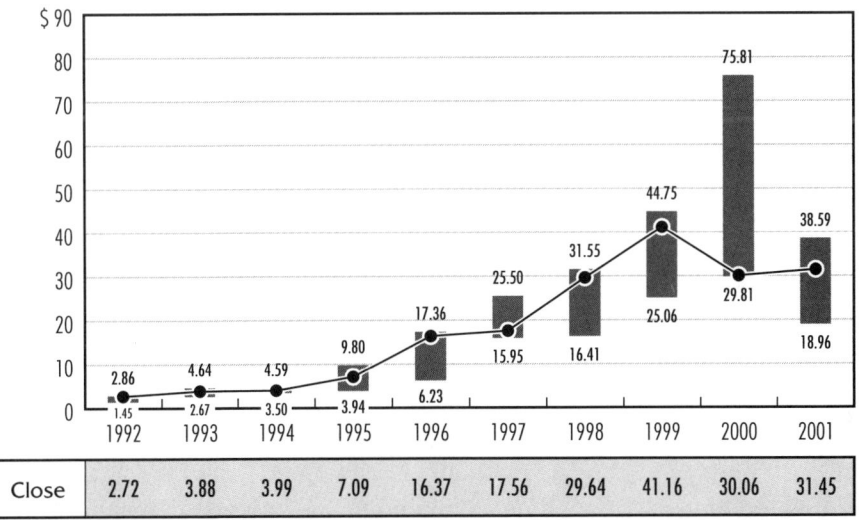

TELECOMMUNICATIONS

Aastra Technologies Ltd.
Comverse Technology Inc.
Aeroflex Inc.
Scientific-Atlanta Inc.
DALSA Corporation
Cygnal Technologies Corporation

AASTRA TECHNOLOGIES LTD.

155 Snow Boulevard
Concord, ON L4K 4N9

Tel: (905) 760-4200
Fax: (905) 760-4233
www.aastra.com
Symbol: AAH (TSX)

Employees: 200
Founded: 1991
Listed: 1998

Chairperson and CEO: Francis N. Shen
President and COO: Anthony P. Shen

Share Price Growth	★ ★ ★ ★ ★
Revenue Growth	★ ★ ★ ★ ★
EPS Growth	★ ★ ★ ★ ★
AAH	**15**

About the Company

Aastra Technologies makes telephones. Sounds like a simple enough business, and perhaps that's why it has been so successful. Aastra specializes in developing and distributing home telecom equipment including telephones, handsets, caller ID adjuncts, and Internet-enabled phones.

In 1999, 2000, and again in 2001, the company made the Deloitte & Touche Technology Fast 50 list as one of the fastest-growing companies in Canada. Aastra came in as the 19th fastest-growing company in Canada on *Profit Magazine*'s Profit 100 list for 2001 with a 4,415 percent jump in revenues from 1995 to 2000.

In December of 1999, Aastra purchased some of Nortel Networks' telephone manufacturing assets, including over 20 design patents and numerous trademarks such as Vista, PowerTouch, Nomad, Maestro, and Symphony. It also has the exclusive licence to market telephone products under the Bell trademark, serving all the major North American telcos, most of which also carry the Bell name. This is a huge franchise.

Seventy-three percent of Aastra's sales are exported outside Canada, primarily to the U.S. Its products are sold through all major North American telephone companies, as well as through retailers such as Radio Shack and Wal-Mart.

On April 20, 2001, Aastra was added to the S&P/TSX Composite Index. The company spent 5.2 percent of revenues on research and development in 2001.

Opportunities and Challenges

While former telephone manufacturing giants like Nortel and Lucent decided to chuck these "boring" products to seek their fortune in network equipment, Aastra has been buying up these and other assets and making money. As for the giants, well, they were getting hammered in the tech wreck.

In May 2001, Aastra acquired Nortel's Meridian Business System Centrex and ISDN product portfolio. The acquisition included manufacturing tools, equipment, patents, contracts, and inventory. In September 2001, it acquired Lucent Digital Video, an MPEG-2 encoding technology for broadcast, cable, and video networking. This expands Aastra's market to cable operators and network service providers.

Yet another acquisition was Ericsson's cable modem group and its patented Pipelock® in December 2001, making Aastra a leading supplier of high-speed modems for the cable industry.

With its latest acquisitions, Aastra is expanding beyond voice to video. The company believes that, just as the last 10 years has seen a transformation of networks from voice to data, so the next 10 years will make extensive video networks a reality. These acquisitions put Aastra in a good position to participate in this evolution.

Aastra's biggest challenge is its client base—a small number of large customers. The top five accounted for 48 percent of revenue in 2001, down from 55 percent in 2000. The loss of a significant customer could adversely impact the company. The company also contracts out the manufacturing of its products to companies in Asia, Australia, and Mexico. A default by a supplier could also have negative impact.

Financial Highlights

Aastra's sales dropped substantially in 2001—23.2 percent. But earnings per share held their own, dropping just slightly to $1.27 from $1.29. EPS held steady because of increased margins. Margin in 1998 was 16.7 percent. That moved up to 17.9 percent in 1999, 24.2 percent in 2000, and 35.3 percent in 2001. This was partly because of the acquisition of high-margin products from Nortel and Lucent. But look at the first half of 2002. Revenues were up 48.7 percent and earnings per share were up 36.8 percent.

Aastra stock fairly exploded from October 1999 to March 2000, jumping to $17 from $5. The stock then fell to $8 by October 2000. That was followed by a surge to $14, even as many tech stocks were falling in the first half of 2001. After a short correction in the fall of 2001, Aastra has gone on to new multi-year highs, topping $25 in April 2002. While most tech stocks crashed in the summer of 2002, Aastra hung tough above the $22 level. Even at new highs, the company's P/E ratio remained a modest 16 to 17. There is no change in our rating.

Aastra Technologies Ltd. at a Glance

Fiscal Year-end: December
4-Year Return: 115.4%

	1997	1998	1999	2000	2001	9-Year Growth Average (%)	9-Year Growth Total (%)
Revenue ($ mlns.)	13.1	37.2	97.1	188.7	144.9	85.7	8,146.2
Net Income ($ mlns.)	-0.4	1.3	5.2	17.2	18.6	–	77,495.8
Earnings/ Share ($)	-0.05	0.16	0.51	1.26	1.27	–	12,600.0
Dividend/ Share ($)	–	–	–	–	–	–	–
Price/ Earnings	-1.3 - -32.7	3.8 - 21.9	6.4 - 30.2	4.0 - 13.9	6.5 - 15.5	–	–

Table data courtesy of ✓Canadian Shareowner   www.shareowner.com

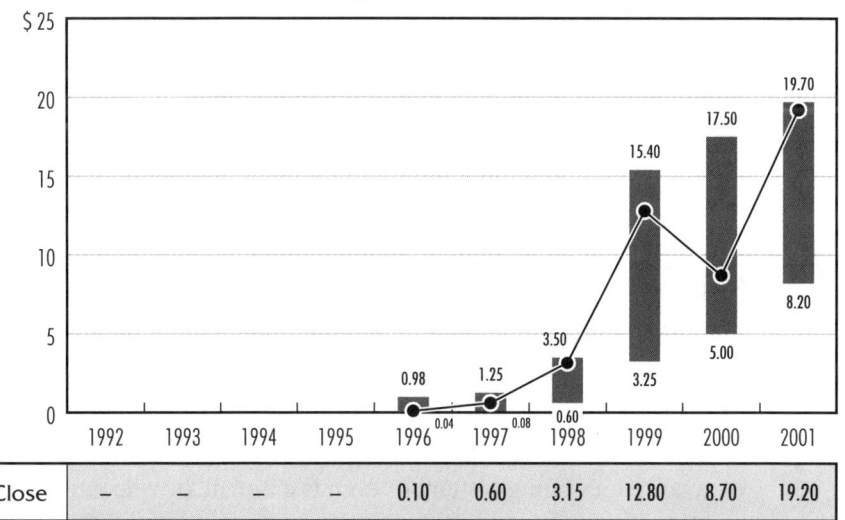

Stock Growth (Fiscal Year High-Low-Close)

* Data for the years 1993–97 from company reports.

COMVERSE TECHNOLOGY INC.

170 Crossways Park Drive
Woodbury, NY 11797

Tel: (516) 677-7200
Fax: (516) 677-7355
www.cmvt.com
Symbol: CMVT (NASDAQ)

Employees: 6,000
Founded: 1984
Listed: 1986

Chairperson and CEO: Kobi Alexander

Share Price Growth	★ ★ ★ ★
Revenue Growth	★ ★ ★ ★ ★
EPS Growth	★ ★ ★ ★
CMVT	**13**

About the Company

In two words—voice mail. Comverse does it so well that it is the world's leading provider of software and systems for messaging services. The company operates three main business divisions: Comverse Network Systems, Verint Systems (formerly Comverse Infosys), and Ulticom, as well as a number of specialty subsidiaries.

The top dog, generating the bulk of revenues, is Comverse Network Systems. It supplies unified messaging services for major telecoms around the world. If you use your telephone company's call answer service, voice messaging system, or even fax, e-mail, or video messaging services, chances are you are using Comverse technology. And, of course, there are corporate networks—we all hate calling up a company and getting those annoying "If you want Accounting, push one, if you want Sales, push two, if you want the president of the company, hang up and don't try again later" messages. Nevertheless, Comverse sells a lot of these systems.

Verint Systems is in the digital video security and surveillance, communications interception, and business intelligence fields. Verint's solutions are installed in government facilities, airports, transportation systems, prisons, customer service centers, major corporations, and anywhere that security is a concern. This includes digital recording and monitoring systems used by law enforcement agencies.

Ulticom is involved in intelligent network services. Even though it generates only 4 percent of the company's revenues, Ulticom's services are ubiquitous, deployed by over 250 carriers in 90 countries, serving 80 percent of the world's population. Network services include global roaming for cell phones, prepaid calling, calling cards, Internet call waiting, and a host of others.

Its Persay subsidiary is a leader in voice verification systems, while Wydeband is a joint venture with Radware to provide a flexible, scalable platform to manage broadband value-added services.

Comverse is truly a giant in its field, with revenues exploding to US$1,270.2 million in fiscal 2002 from US$15.8 million in fiscal 1991.

Opportunities and Challenges

With the terrorist attack on America in September 2001, the demand for security and surveillance equipment is on the rise. Comverse is well positioned to meet this demand with its Verint Systems security and surveillance systems. And its Persay subsidiary is a world leader in voice verification systems, also likely to be in increasing demand.

This is on top of the growing demand from telecoms for services to enhance revenue. In fact, 64 percent of Comverse's sales are generated outside the U.S. and Canada. In May 2001, Comverse was selected as the exclusive provider of short messaging systems and voice mail in China.

The company's services cover all carrier systems from wireline to wireless, local networks to the Internet. Through its Wydeband joint venture with Radware, it is prepared for convergence as the world moves to broadband applications such as streaming video services and picture messaging. When video stores start supplying movies for download over phone lines, Comverse will be there with the systems to make it happen. There's a lot of future potential here.

In fact, Comverse formed an alliance in May 2002 with Liberate Technologies, a provider of software platforms for enhanced television, to integrate their services to allow two-way messaging through the home television set.

Verint was spun off in an initial public offering in May 2002.

Financial Highlights

Despite a slowing economy in 2001, Comverse managed to increase revenues by 3.7 percent but earnings per share took a hit, declining 41.5 percent. In the first half of 2002, revenues plummeted 44.7 percent and the company sustained a loss. The technology rout on the stock market was not kind to Comverse, dropping the stock to US$70 from US$120 in 2000. The stock managed to climb back to new highs by January 2001, only to crash hard in two waves that year to level out at around US$20. From January to September 2002 it drifted slowly down to the US$8 level. As the economy recovers, so should Comverse's fortunes.

We knocked two stars off its rating this year, one for earnings and one for price appreciation.

Comverse Technology Inc. at a Glance

Fiscal Year-end: January
10-Year Return: 16.1%

	1997	1999	2000	2001	2002	10-Year Growth Average (%)	10-Year Growth Total (%)
Revenue (US$ mlns.)	280.3	696.1	872.2	1,225.1	1,270.2	52.1	3,287.3
Net Income (US$ mlns.)	43.5	111.5	191.6	279.5	160.4	61.1	3,180.7
Earnings/Share (US$)	0.54	0.78	1.08	1.47	0.86	34.4	760.0
Dividend/Share (US$)	–	–	–	–	–	–	–
Price/Earnings	19.4 - 33.9	12.6 - 36.6	20.1 - 73.4	42.2 - 84.9	17.5 - 134.4	–	–

Table data courtesy of  www.shareowner.com

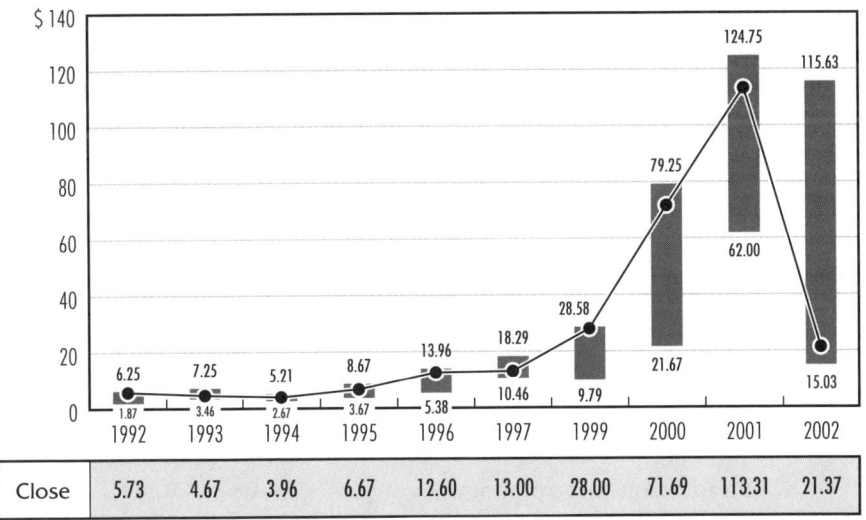

* As of fiscal 1999, the company's fiscal year-end changed from December to January. January 1998 is not included in these data.

AEROFLEX INC.

35 South Service Road
Plainview, NY 11803

Tel: (516) 694-6700
Fax: (516) 694-4823
www.aeroflex.com

Employees: 1,250
Founded: 1937
Symbol: ARXX (NASDAQ)

Chairperson and CEO: Harvey R. Blau
President: Michael Gorin

Share Price Growth	★ ★ ★ ★ ★
Revenue Growth	★ ★
EPS Growth	★ ★ ★ ★ ★
ARXX	**12**

About the Company

While major telecom companies like Lucent, Cisco, and Nortel Networks were seeing business dry up as the technology boom ended in 2000 and 2001, one small New York company in the same arena was growing revenues and profits. That company was Aeroflex. Its secret? Diversification.

Aeroflex designs and manufactures a wide range of microelectronic, integrated circuit, interconnect, and testing products to support communications systems, networks, and automatic test systems. It creates enabling technologies for fibre optics, broadband cable, and wireless and satellite communications. It also manufactures systems to isolate vibration and control motion.

The company operates in three distinct areas. Aeroflex Microelectronic Solutions has been operating since 1974 and has grown steadily both internally and through acquisition—(Marconi Circuit Technology in 1994, MIC Technology in 1996, certain equipment, inventory, licences, and patents from Lucent in 1997). Further acquisitions took place from 1999 to 2001. It manufactures such things as fibre optic amplifiers, modulator drivers, and optical switches used in fibre optic networks; multi-chip modules for air, sea, and space, as well as ground-based avionics and telecom systems; passive thin film circuits and interconnects used in wireless, satellite, and microwave systems; and integrated circuits for avionics and space applications.

The test solutions segment focuses on test systems and instruments for computer networks and embedded devices, microwave, and RF, and noise monitoring on broadband networks, as well as motion control products including electro-optical scanning devices used in infrared night vision systems. And the isolator products division designs and makes severe shock and vibration isolation systems used primarily in defence applications.

In fiscal 2001, 29 percent of sales went to the U.S. government or prime defence contractors and subcontractors to the government. This was down from 33 percent in 2000 and 42 percent in 1999, as the company sought to concentrate on the commercial market.

Aeroflex spent US$18.9 million on research and development in 2001, 8.1 percent of revenues and an increase of 63 percent over the year before.

Opportunities and Challenges

While Aeroflex does a lot of work for telecom and fibre optic networks, it also has numerous products and applications for satellite and microwave communications, as well as commercial and military avionics. This has helped Aeroflex avoid the rout in business of the large telecoms and avoid the huge associated losses.

This leaves the company prepared to ramp up sales and profits on two fronts going into 2003. One is the increased demand for military applications as the war on terrorism continues. Some US$15 million of new orders were placed in December 2001 alone. The other is the very likely resurgence of the economy in 2003, with attendant rising demand for fibre optic and cable networks. Aeroflex's multi-chips facilitate ultra-high-speed processing.

Acquisitions continue with the company's bid for IFR Systems Inc. in April 2002.

The company's primary challenge is the temporary slump in fiscal 2002 with the tailing off of the economy and drop in demand for networking equipment. The latter half of 2002 and 2003 should see things back on track again.

Financial Highlights

Net sales for Aeroflex increased 23.3 percent in 2001, with fully diluted earnings per share up 25 percent. But for fiscal 2002 (which ended on June 30) the numbers were not good. Revenues were down 13 percent and profit turned to loss.

The stock grew steadily through the '90s, correcting sharply in the first wave of the technology rout in 2000 before soaring 200 percent by year end. The tech crash sent the stock plummeting back down again with the final wave in the summer of 2002, knocking it down to the $5 level. Business should pick up in fiscal 2003 for reasons noted above.

Aeroflex Inc. at a Glance
Fiscal Year-end: June
10-Year Return: 34%

	1997	1998	1999	2000	2001	10-Year Growth Average (%)	10-Year Growth Total (%)
Revenue (US$ mlns.)	94.3	118.9	157.1	185.9	232.8	16.2	268.8
Net Income (US$ mlns.)	4.4	8.4	13.3	14.8	23.1	62.6	3,085.8
Earnings/ Share (US$)	0.13	0.20	0.28	0.23	0.38	39.4	850.0
Dividend/ Share (US$)	–	–	–	–	–	–	–
Price/ Earnings	9.6 - 18.8	8.5 - 29.8	8.9 - 28.4	9.2 - 124.3	18.6 - 100.5	–	–

Table data courtesy of ✓Canadian Shareowner   www.shareowner.com

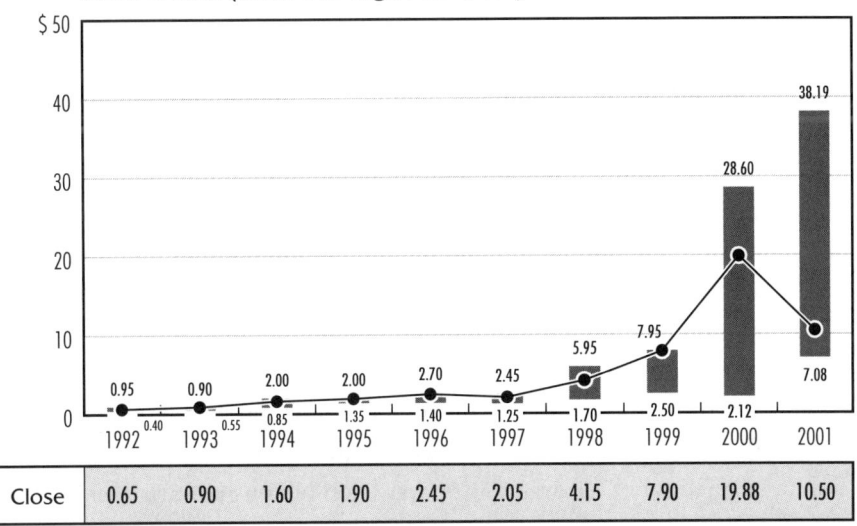

Stock Growth (Fiscal Year High-Low-Close)

| Close | 0.65 | 0.90 | 1.60 | 1.90 | 2.45 | 2.05 | 4.15 | 7.90 | 19.88 | 10.50 |

SCIENTIFIC-ATLANTA INC.

5030 Sugarloaf Parkway
Lawrenceville, GA 30044-2869

Tel: (770) 236-5000
Fax: (770) 236-6777
www.sciatl.com
Symbol: SFA (NYSE)

Employees: 8,000
Founded: 1951
Listed: 1959

Chairperson, President, and CEO: James F. McDonald

Share Price Growth	★ ★ ★ ★
Revenue Growth	★ ★ ★
EPS Growth	★ ★ ★ ★
SFA	**11**

About the Company

Coming soon to a television near you! Video-on-demand! Interactive TV! You'll be able to watch the program you want to watch, when you want to watch it. You'll be able to pause, rewind, or skip ahead in the program. You'll be able to buy merchandise related to the program or chat online with friends while watching the program. Convergence with a vengeance. And Scientific-Atlanta (SA) is in the forefront of this revolution.

The company was started in 1951 when seven associates of the Georgia Institute of Technology decided to set up an electronics company. Capitalization? Each chipped in a hundred bucks. That's right—this company with a market cap of over US$3 billion got started on US$700!

For years Scientific-Atlanta has been a leading supplier of amplifiers, tuners, modulators, satellite decoders, and other high-end products for cable television operators and television networks and stations. Scientific-Atlanta is in the forefront of digital development as well. Companies from CNN to the Disney Channel, as well as the major television networks, use SA satellite and broadband digital solutions.

But the company has transformed into a mass market company in the last few years with the development of its Explorer line of set-top boxes for interactive digital television. Video-on-demand television from Scientific-Atlanta is starting to come onstream as well. These units are the world's first complete home entertainment package for cable, including television, multiple digital recording and playback, and data.

Opportunities and Challenges

The company's digital footprint expanded to 254 cable systems installed in fiscal 2001. About 4.8 million Explorer set-top boxes were shipped in fiscal 2001, bringing the total to 7.2 million shipped. It is the best selling product line in Scientific-Atlanta's history.

The company also introduced its own line of cable modems in fiscal 2001 and now ranks among the top five cable modem suppliers.

The company continues to invest in research and development and has developed a new high-end Explorer product, the 4000 model, that combines the set-top box with an internal cable modem—the next step in convergence. It will be a home gateway, capable of communicating with computers and other household devices through wireline and wireless connections. The Explorer 8000 includes an internal hard-drive for digital recording. This is the unit that will make video-on-demand a reality, and it starts shipping in fiscal 2002. SA believes the Explorer 8000 will become the home media server, managing all home communication needs simultaneously.

Challenges? The market weakness that hit North America from 2000 through 2002 is starting to affect SA as well. There is likely to be continuing consolidation in the cable market, and there is competition from Direct Broadcast Satellite (DBS) as well as other set-top box manufacturers such as Motorola and Gemstar.

Financial Highlights

Scientific-Atlanta's fiscal year runs from July 1 to June 30, and fiscal 2001 was a banner year for the company. Revenues were up a whopping 46.4 percent—almost US$800 million. Fully diluted earnings per share were up 90.1 percent. But the slowdown in the economy did show up in fiscal 2002. Revenues were off 33.5 percent and EPS dropped 66.8 percent.

The stock moved up steadily in the first half of the '90s, then traded flat until the end of 1998 when it took off like a rocket to $90 in August 2000 from $7.50 in October 1999. It then crashed with the rest of the technology issues to $16.50 in September 2001. A sharp move up to $30 by December gave way to a flat trading range between $20 and $27 for the first half of 2002 before falling away to around $12 in 2002's summer slump.

Watch for things to pick up as the economy recovers and video-on-demand is rolled out in earnest.

Scientific-Atlanta Inc. at a Glance

Fiscal Year-end: June
10-Year Return: 22.7%

	1997	1998	1999	2000	2001	10-Year Growth Average (%)	10-Year Growth Total (%)
Revenue (US$ mlns.)	1,168.2	1,181.4	1,243.5	1,715.4	2,512.0	19.1	332.5
Net Income (US$ mlns.)	57.2	68.9	64.5	150.3	290.3	46.0	1,477.9
Earnings/ Share (US$)	0.37	0.43	0.41	0.91	1.73	42.5	1,230.8
Dividend/ Share (US$)	0.03	0.03	0.03	0.04	0.04	3.7	33.3
Price/ Earnings	16.2-31.8	16.3-30.4	14.3-48.5	18.6-85.6	16.9-54.3	–	–

Table data courtesy of ✓Canadian Shareowner   www.shareowner.com

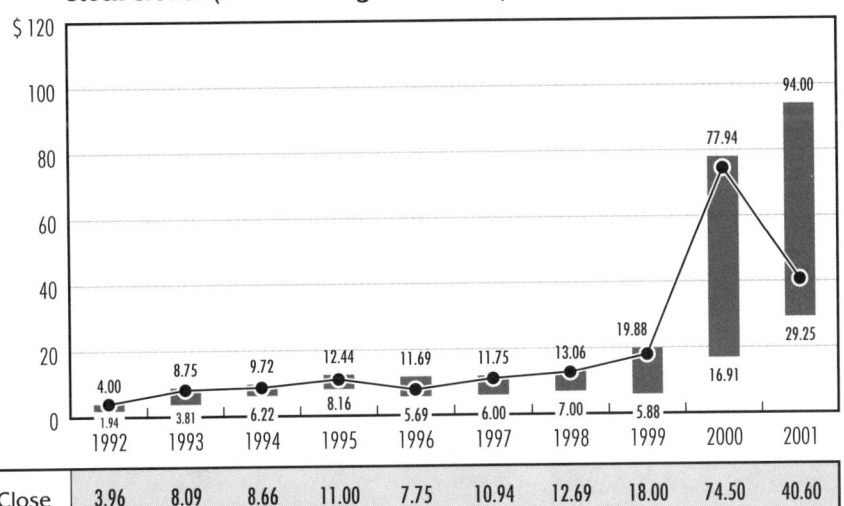

Stock Growth (Fiscal Year High-Low-Close)

| Close | 3.96 | 8.09 | 8.66 | 11.00 | 7.75 | 10.94 | 12.69 | 18.00 | 74.50 | 40.60 |

DALSA CORPORATION

605 McMurray Road
Waterloo, ON N2V 2E9

Tel: (519) 886-6000
Fax: (519) 886-0185
www.dalsa.com
Symbol: DSA (TSX)

Employees: 600
Founded: 1980
Listed: 1996

Chairperson and CEO: Dr. Savvas G. Chamberlain
President: Brian C. Doody

Share Price Growth	★ ★
Revenue Growth	★ ★ ★ ★ ★
EPS Growth	★ ★
DSA	**9**

About the Company

DALSA Corp. was founded in 1980 by imaging pioneer Dr. Savvas Chamberlain, a former Professor of Electrical Engineering at the University of Waterloo. Chamberlain developed image sensors using Charge Coupled Devices (CCD) and Complementary Metal Oxide Semiconductors (CMOS), two technologies that capture light and transform it into digital electronic signals.

The year 1987 saw the company receive its first patents on line-scan image sensors. The following year saw the company grow to 10 employees and its first million dollars in sales.

Today the company is a recognized leader in digital imaging technology, with its camera and image sensing products used in postal and parcel sorting, robotics, mammography, genomic analysis, DNA sequencing, and image sensing equipment used in line manufacturing. DALSA's cameras and sensors provide the electronic eyes used to operate the Canadarm2 on the International Space Station.

DALSA's imaging technologies are more than just ordinary cameras. They are advanced, specialized, high-speed imaging sensors that can capture a picture of the markings on a bullet in flight.

Steady growth brought the company to 300 employees and $56.98 million in sales for fiscal 2001. But growth has really taken off in 2002, with strategic acquisitions and internal growth pushing the employee number to 600 with estimated revenues of between $114 million to $126 million.

The company maintains two offices in the U.S., as well as one in Germany and one in Japan.

Opportunities and Challenges

DALSA has grown strongly through strategic acquisitions in the last few years. These include Silicon Mountain Design of Colorado Springs in 1999, MedOptics of Tucson, Arizona in 2000, the Zarlink wafer foundry in Bromont, Quebec in February 2002, and the Philips CCD Business Unit in Eindhoven, the Netherlands, in April 2002.

The Zarlink foundry acquisition enabled DALSA to become a fully integrated manufacturer of technologically advanced imaging products. It also lets the company provide outsourced manufacturing for Original Equipment Manufacturers and fabless (a term used to describe technology companies that design equipment but out source manufacturing) semiconductor manufacturers.

Philips is a particularly good fit with DALSA's imaging technology. Philips' expertise in area scan technology augments DALSA's expertise in line scan and TDI (time delay and integration) technology. And Philips' fabrication process platform will improve DALSA's foundry capabilities.

The company's mission statement included a target of $100 million in annual sales by the end of 2002, a target now reached. Its next target is $1 billion in sales by the end of the decade.

Financial Highlights

Semiconductors and electronics manufacturers have taken a beating the last two years, but Waterloo, Ontario's DALSA Corporation has managed to buck this trend and is forging solidly ahead. While revenues for fiscal 2001 climbed a modest 5.8 percent and earnings per share slid 35.7 percent, the first half of 2002 was another story. Revenues jumped 65.9 percent and EPS grew by a phenomenal 142.9 percent. The stock price also soared.

With losses in 1999 and 2000, DALSA does not meet the minimum requirements for this book. But it is just starting to come into its stride and so we are making an exception. DALSA is a late add to the book and our star rating for price appreciation is based on performance to September 2002.

DALSA Corporation at a Glance

Fiscal Year-end: December
6-Year Return: 2.8%

	1997	1998	1999	2000	2001	10-Year Growth Average (%)	10-Year Growth Total (%)
Revenue ($ mlns.)	27.0	29.4	38.0	53.3	56.4	30.1	964.2
Net Income (US$ mlns.)	3.4	4.1	-0.4	-11.1	4.0	19.6	400.0
Earnings/ Share ($)	0.31	0.36	-0.03	-1.00	0.33	15.5	266.7
Dividend/ Share ($)	0.00	0.00	0.00	0.00	0.00	–	–
Price/ Earnings	14.8 - 30.6	12.5 - 33.6	-158.3 - -316.7	-6.0 - -10.1	12.4 - 24.2	–	–

Table data courtesy of  www.shareowner.com

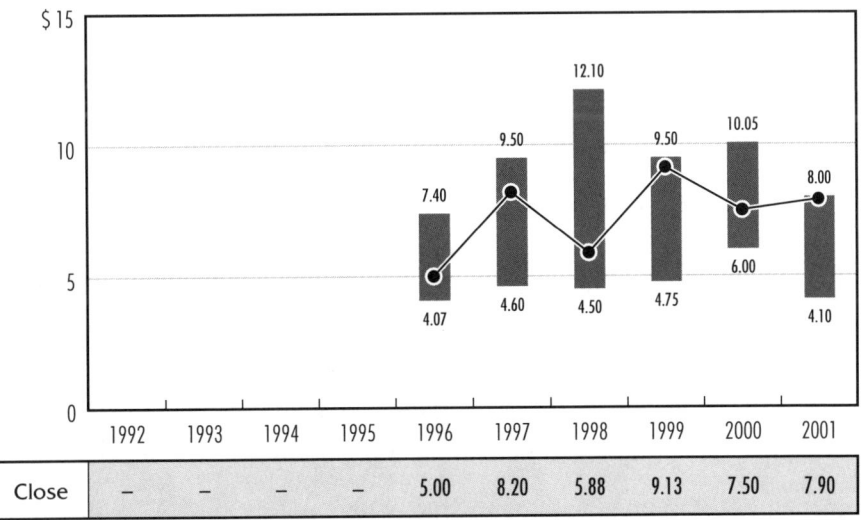

CYGNAL TECHNOLOGIES CORPORATION

1350 Thornton Road S.
Oshawa, Ontario L1J 8C4

Tel: (905) 436-8888
Fax: (905) 436-1075
www.cygnal.ca
Symbol: CYN (TSX)

Employees: 500
Founded: 1998
Listed: 1999

Chairperson: Gerald S. Hurlow
Vice-Chairperson and CEO: J. Douglas Young
President and COO: Kieron J. Dowling

Share Price Growth	0
Revenue Growth	★ ★ ★ ★ ★
EPS Growth	★
CYN	**6**

About the Company

Cygnal Technologies Corporation was named the fastest-growing company in Canada in the *Profit Magazine* Profit 100 list published June 2001. The five-year growth rate, a whopping 112,519 percent, is the largest in the history of the Profit 100. What does Cygnal Technologies do? It designs, builds, integrates and manages wired and wireless broadband, data, and telecommunications networks.

The company's roots go back to 1992 with the formation of Comlink Systems. Comlink launched subsidiary In-Flight Phones the next year to provide cellular phone service to airline passengers. That did not fly, so to speak, though Comlink continued as an Oshawa, Ontario-based distributor of cable network equipment.

In 1997, the present company evolved with the merger of Normex Telecom, a builder of private wired and wireless infrastructure in Quebec, and Comlink. In its first reporting year, 1997, the company had revenues of $6.7 million.

In April 1998, it changed its name to Cygnal Technologies and proceeded on an aggressive growth path. It acquired White Radio Ltd., a national value-added reseller of audio and video telecommunications products. This was followed by the takeover of Polycables National Inc., a cable installer in Quebec, in 1999. The company began trading on the Toronto Stock Exchange in October that year.

The next two years saw further expansion through acquisition with the purchase of Accord Communications, Integrated Cable Systems, West Technical Technologies, Saltel Electric, and Lasertel Communications.

The company has expertise in all facets of telecommunications infrastructure, including satellite, coaxial cable, fibre optics, twisted pair, and microwave. Its clients include cable companies, telephone companies, broadcasters, utilities, and other businesses wanting to install telecom networks. These include such companies as AT&T, Bell Expressvu, CBC, Rogers Cable, Cogeco, IBM, Ontario Hydro, and Wal-Mart.

Opportunities and Challenges

Cygnal has competitors in voice, data, and video, but it is the only company that can handle complete end-to-end installation and management of all three types of telecom infrastructure. Like many of the other companies in this book, Cygnal benefits from a trend to outsourcing. Telephone and cable companies as well as broadcasters can save by contracting out complex installations to Cygnal.

The company's Integrated Cable Systems group earned Silver Certification from Cisco Systems in March 2002, giving it special benefits as an installer of Cisco networking solutions.

The company took a step towards further expansion with the appointment of Kieron Dowling as president in March 2002. He brings 20 years of experience with Alcatel, Celestica and Nortel Networks to the job.

The key challenge for Cygnal will be to integrate its various business units and leverage these assets for greater profitability. In April 2002, the company moved to eliminate about two-thirds of its long-term debt with the sale of its Burlington distribution centre, which was tied into a 12-year lease back agreement.

Financial Highlights

Cygnal Technologies continues to grow, with revenues up 39.4 percent in 2001 and earnings per share up 40 percent. The first half of 2002 showed continuing growth with revenues up 30.9 percent and diluted earnings per share more than doubling from $0.03 to $0.07 a share.

Cygnal does not meet all of our criteria, as it had losses in its first two years (1997 and 1998) but has been seeing growing profits since then. Although the company was listed as Cygnal on the TSX in October 1999, it was publicly traded in its earlier incarnations going back to 1994. It traded as high as $42 back then but we are only considering share price growth from the time of its TSX listing. The stock soared from $2.10 at its TSX listing to $9.75 in March 2000 at the height of the technology boom. It then fell to a low of $1.75 in September 2001. It moved up sharply for the rest of 2001 and entered a prolonged downtrend for the first eight months of 2002. But growth prospects and strategic alliances point to possible strong growth for 2003.

Cygnal Technologies Corporation at a Glance

Fiscal Year-end: December
4-Year Return: 3.3%

	1997	1998	1999	2000	2001	3-Year Growth Average (%)	3-Year Growth Total (%)
Revenue ($ mlns.)	–	–	59.9	101.8	141.8	54.7	136.9
Net Income ($ mlns.)	–	–	0.7	1.8	2.3	92.2	227.6
Earnings/ Share ($)	–	–	0.09	0.11	0.15	29.3	66.7
Dividend/ Share ($)	–	–	–	–	–	–	–
Price/ Earnings	–	–	13.3 - 43.3	26.4 - 88.6	9.1 - 26.5	–	–

Table data courtesy of ✓Canadian Shareowner www.shareowner.com

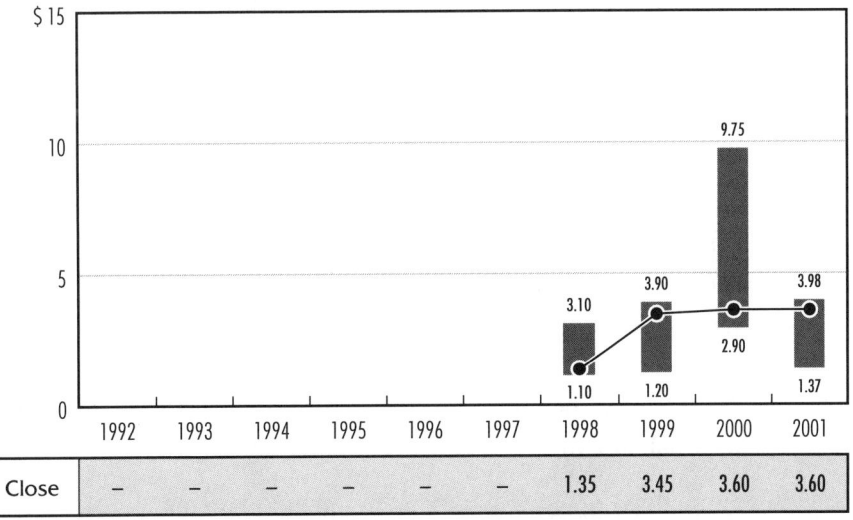

Stock Growth (Fiscal Year High-Low-Close)

| Close | – | – | – | – | – | – | 1.35 | 3.45 | 3.60 | 3.60 |

GLOSSARY

These definitions explain the terms used in the tables and charts accompanying each company profile, and what financial measures the figures represent.

Dividend per Share The cash dividends per share paid to investors during the reporting period. This item has been adjusted to reflect all stock splits and stock dividends.

Earnings per Share (EPS) Calculated by dividing net income by the fully diluted shares outstanding (allowing for the exercise of all warrants and options outstanding). This item has been adjusted to reflect all stock splits and stock dividends.

Fiscal Year-end The last day of this month is the end of the company's 12-month accounting year.

Growth, Average An average year-over-year growth rate.

Growth, Total A simple rate calculated using the starting and ending values only.

Net Income The income, or loss, reported by a company after costs, expenses, and preferred dividends have been subtracted from all revenue for the fiscal year. This data item excludes the effect of all special, discontinued, and extraordinary items.

Price-to-Earnings Ratio (P/E) Ownership of a share of stock means ownership of one share's worth of a company's earnings per share. A stock's price-to-earnings ratio indicates how much an investor is willing to pay to become the owner of $1.00 of a company's earnings per share.

This ratio is calculated by dividing the company's fiscal year high and low share prices by its earnings per share for the corresponding period. The data are presented as a range starting with the fiscal year low price-to-earnings ratio and ending with the fiscal year high price-to-earnings ratio.

Return A compound rate reflecting monthly price appreciation (ending May 2001) plus reinvestment of dividends and the compounding effect of dividends paid on reinvested dividends.

Revenue The dollar amount of annual sales, reduced by discounts and returned merchandise. It is the "top line" figure from which costs are subtracted to determine net income.

Definitions courtesy of  www.shareowner.com

THE 50 BEST SCIENCE & TECHNOLOGY STOCKS IN ALPHABETICAL ORDER

Company	Stars	Page
Aastra Technologies Ltd.	15	228
ADF Group Inc.	11	136
Aeroflex Inc.	12	236
ArthroCare Corporation	7	52
ATS Automation Tooling Systems Inc.	7	172
Axcan Pharma Inc.	12	80
Bennett Environmental Inc.	12	60
Biovail Corporation	14	68
Bombardier Inc.	10	140
BW Technologies Ltd.	10	144
CAE Inc.	6	176
Calpine Corporation	13	102
Canadian Hydro Developers	11	114
Canadian Medical Laboratories Ltd.	7	56
Cangene Corporation	9	84
CGI Group Inc.	15	190
Check Point Software Technologies Ltd.	12	210
Cognos Inc.	12	214
Comverse Technology Inc.	13	232
Cygnal technologies Corporation	6	248
DALSA Corporation	9	244
DuPont Canada Inc.	7	168
Enerchem International Inc.	13	106

Company	Stars	Page
Forest Laboratories, Inc.	13	72
Gennum Corporation	9	152
Goldcorp Inc.	12	118
Groupe Laperrière & Verreault Inc.	9	156
Intel Corporation	9	222
Magellan Aerospace Corporation	4	184
Magna International Inc.	14	128
MDS Inc.	8	48
Merck & Company, Inc.	6	96
Mercury Interactive Corporation	13	206
Microsoft Corporation	15	194
Network Appliance, Inc.	10	218
Paladin Laboratories Inc.	9	88
Pason Systems Inc.	13	110
Patheon Inc.	13	44
Pfizer Inc.	9	92
Scientific-Atlanta Inc.	11	240
Siebel Systems, Inc.	15	198
Silent Witness Enterprises Ltd.	12	132
SNC-Lavalin Group Inc.	10	148
Stantec Inc.	8	160
Taro Pharmaceutical Industries Ltd.	13	76
Tesma International Inc.	6	180
THQ Inc.	14	202
Trican Well Service Ltd.	10	122
Winpak Ltd.	8	164
Zenon Environmental Inc.	11	64

INDEX

A
Aarnio-Wihuri, Antti, 164
Aastra Technologies Ltd., 228–231
Abgenix, 50
Accord Communications, 249
Adelphia, 4
ADF Group Inc., 136–139
Adtranz, 141
Advanced Digital Information Corporation, 219
Advice for Investors, 36, 37
Aeroflex Inc., 34, 236–239
Aeroflex Microelectronic Solutions, 237
Agilent Technologies, 50
Alberta's Fastest Growing Companies, 38
Alexander, Kobi, 232
Alfa Laval Celleco, 157
A.L.I. Technologies, 15
Allen, Paul, 194
Amazon.com, 10
Andrx Corp., 70
annual earnings growth, 24
AOL Time Warner, 13, 34
Applied Micro Devices, 223–224
Aqua Guard Technologies, 60
Arthrocare Corporation, 52–55
Ashe, Robert G., 214
Associated Consulting Engineers, 162
ATI Technologies, 13
ATS Automation Tooling Systems Inc., 41, 172–175
average growth, 252
Axcan Pharma Inc., 80–83

B
BAE Systems Flight Simulation and Training, 177
Baker, Michael A., 52
Baker Hughes Inc., 157
Bakshi, Rajeev (Rob), 132
Ballmer, Steven A., 194
Barrett, Craig R., 222

BCE Inc., 14, 34
bear market, 7–8
Beaudoin, Laurent, 140
Beloit, 157
Benedek, Andrew, 64
Bennett, John A., 60
Bennett Environmental Inc., 60–63
Big Charts. *See* Advice for Investors
biomedicine
    Arthrocare Corporation, 52–55
    Canadian Medical Laboratories Ltd., 56–59
    category of, 11
    MDS Inc., 48–51
    Patheon Inc., 44–47
Biovail Contract Research, 69
Biovail Corporation, 68–71
Biovail Pharmaceuticals U.S., 69
Black Clawson-Kennedy Ltd., 157
Blau, Harvey R., 236
Blau companies, 180
Blodgett, Henry, 5–6
Bombardier, J. Armande, 40, 140
Bombardier Inc., 140–143
Bovis Lend Lease LMB Inc., 137–138
Branham 300, 38
Break Out Report, 31, 37, 38, 40
Bristol Aerospace, 185
Brown, Robert L., 140
Burney, Derek H., 176, 177
Busicom, 9
buy-and-hold strategy, 27
buy right, 23–26
BW Technologies Ltd., 31, 144–147

C
C-MAC Industries, 13
Cabot Market Letter, 38
CAE Inc., 176–179
Calpine Corporation, 10, 29, 102–105
Canada Iron, 157
Canadair, 141
Canadian Biotech News, 36, 38

Canadian Explosives Ltd., 169
Canadian Hydro Developers, Inc., 10, 114–117
Canadian Industries Ltd. (CIL), 169
Canadian Medical Discoveries Fund, 49
Canadian Medical Laboratories Ltd., 56–59
Canadian Oilfield Stimulation Services, 123–124
Canadian Pharmacists Association, 90
Canadian Shareowner. See Advice for Investors
Cangene Corporation, 84–87
CANSLIM approach, 23–25, 30
Capital d'Amerique, 150
Carlson Online. See Advice for Investors
Cartwright, Peter, 102, 103
Cassidy, Donald, 6, 26, 27, 28
Celestica, 13
Center for Disease Control and Prevention, 86
CGI Group Inc., 34, 35, 190–193
Chamberlain, Savvas G., 244
changes, 33–36
Check Point Software Technologies Ltd., 34, 210–213
Chênevert, Georges, 148
Chesapeake Biological Laboratories, 85, 86
Cipher Pharmaceuticals, 57, 58
Cobbe, Murray L., 122
Cogeco Cable, 150
Cognos Inc., 35, 214–217
Colcleugh, David W., 168
Comlink Systems, 249
Computer Associates, 219
Comverse Network Systems, 232–233
Comverse Technology Inc., 232–235
contrarian investing, 22
convergence, 34
Cree Inc., 14
current quarterly earnings growth, 24
Cybermedix Health Services, 56
Cygnal Technologies Corporation, 34, 248–251

D

DALSA Corporation, 15, 34, 35, 244–247
DC DiagnostiCare, 57
Decarson Rentals, 108
Decoma, 130
den Ouden, Marco, 40–41
Dent, Harry S., 8
Desjardins Credit Union, 191–192
DiPietro, Nick, 44
diversification, 21–23

dividend per share, 252
DJ Pharma, 69
Dobranowski, Anthony E., 180
Donnelly Corporation, 130
Doody, Brian C., 244
Dorr-Oliver Canada, 157
Dow Jones Industrial Average, 26–27
Dowling, Kieron J., 248, 250
Dr. Tomorrow, 36
du Pont, Lammot, 168
DuPont Canada Inc., 168–171

E

e-commerce, 35
earnings per share (EPS), 252
Edwards, N. Murray, 184
Egyptian Canadian Company for Chemical Industries, 107
E.I. du Pont de Nemours, 169
Eli Lilly, 70
Ellard Croft Design Group, 162
EMC Corporation, 13, 218, 220
Encal Energy, 103
Enerchem International Inc., 106–109
energy sector
  Calpine Corporation, 102–105
  Canadian Hydro Developers, Inc., 114–117
  category of, 11
  Enerchem International Inc., 106–109
  growth industry, 35
  Pason Systems Inc., 110–113
English Harper Reta Architects, 162
Enhance Packaging Technologies, 170
Enron collapse, 3–5, 7, 103
environment
  Bennett Environmental Inc., 60–63
  category of, 11
  Zenon Environmental Inc., 64
Equity Research Center, 37
Eralmetall, 180
Erhart, Charles, 37
Erker, Dennis M., 114
Ethicon, 53
Excel Bestview, 56

F

Falk, Herbert, 80
Farrell, Brian J., 202
Fast 50, 38
Fast 500, 38
Finbow, John, 144

Index

fiscal year-end, 252
Fleet Aerospace, 184
Fleet Industries, 185
Fleming, Alexander, 93
Forest Laboratories, Inc., 69, 72–75
Fortune 100, 38
Franceschini, Anthony P., 160
Future File, 36
FutureStock Review, 38

G

Galephar Pharmaceutical Research, 57
Gates, Bill, 41, 194
Gennum Corporation, 35, 152–155
Gilmartin, Raymond V., 96
Gingl, Manfred, 180
GlaxoSmithKline, 70
Globeinvestor.com, 14, 36, 37
glossary, 252–253
Godin, Serge, 41, 190
Goldcorp Inc., 118–121
Good Gambling Guide, 30
Goodman, Jonathan Ross, 88
Goodman, Kenneth E., 72
Gorilla Game (Moore), 22
Gorin, Michael, 236
Gosselin, Léon F., 80
Green, Peter A.W., 44
Groupe Laperrière & Verreault Inc., 156
Grove, Andrew S., 222
Grupo Ferrovial/Cintra, 150
Gyyr, 133

H

H. Lundbeck, 72
HAC Corporation, 181
Hager Technology Research, 38
Haley Industries, 186
Hamilton Powder Company, 168
Hill, Jim, 110
house advantage, 29–33
How to Make Money in Stocks (O'Neil), 23–24
Hoye, Bob, 8
Hurlow, Gerald S., 248

I

IBM, 9
IBM Life Sciences, 50
Imbeau, André, 41, 190
IMRglobal, 191
In-Flight Phones, 249

industry
 ADF Group Inc., 136–139
 ATS Automation Tooling Systems Inc., 172–175
 Bombardier Inc., 140–143
 BW Technologies Ltd., 144–147
 CAE Inc., 176–179
 category of, 11
 DuPont Canada Inc., 168–171
 Gennum Corporation, 152–155
 Groupe Laperrière & Verreault Inc., 156
 Magellan Aerospace Corporation, 184–187
 Magna International Inc., 128–131
 Silent Witness Enterprises Ltd., 132–135
 SNC Lavalin Group Inc., 148–151
 Stantec Inc., 160–163
 Tesma International Inc., 180–183
 Winpak Ltd., 164–167
information technology
 category of, 11
 CGI Group Inc., 190–193
 Check Point Software Technologies Ltd., 210–213
 Cognos Inc., 214–217
 Intel Corporation, 222–225
 Mercury Interactive Corporation, 206–209
 Microsoft Corporation, 194–197
 Siebel Systems, Inc., 198–201
 THQ Inc., 202–205
innovation, 8–9
institutional sponsorship, 25
Integrated Cable Systems, 249
Intel Corporation, 8–9, 222–225
Interfalk, 80
Internet research, 36–38
Internet Security Systems, 13, 35
IT Corporation, 61
It's When You Sell That Counts (Cassidy), 6, 26, 28

J

Janna Systems, 199
JDS Uniphase, 5, 20
Jouveinal Inc., 81

K

K-Line Pharmaceuticals, 77
Keating, J. Ross, 114
Keating, John D., 114
King, Stephen, 207
Kyosaki, Robert, 22

L

L-3 Communications Holdings, 14
Laboratoire du Lactéol du Docteur Boucard, 82
Lamarre, Jacques, 148
Landan, Amnon, 206
Langley Aerospace, 185
Langstaff, John, 84
Lasertel Communications, 249
last year's picks, 16–20
Laurentian Bank, 34–35
LaValley Industries, 157
Lavery, J. Robert, 164
leadership, 25
Legato Systems, 219–220
Levitt, Aaron, 76
Levitt, Barrie, 76
Lewitt, Wilfred G., 48
Liqui-Box Corporation, 170
Lohnerwerke GmbH, 140
Lucent Technologies, 34, 229, 237

M

Maffin, Tod, 36
Magellan Aerospace Corporation, 184–187
Magna International Inc., 23, 35, 128–131, 180
Magna Steyr, 129, 130
Maple Group, 180
Marconi Circuit Technology, 237
market direction, 25
Marvel Comics, 204
McAfee, 219
McDonald, James F., 240
McEwen, Robert R., 118, 119
McGinn, Richard, 34
McKeough, Pat, 14
McKinnell, Henry A., 92
McWalter, Ian L., 152
MDS Capital Corporation, 49
MDS Inc., 48–51
MDS Pharma Services, 49
Med-Chem Health Care, 56
medical breakthroughs, 35
medicine
    Axcan Pharma Inc., 80–83
    Biovail Corporation, 68–71
    Cangene Corporation, 84–87
    category of, 11
    Forest Laboratories, Inc., 72–75
    Merck & Company, Inc., 96–99

    Paladin Laboratories, 88–91
    Pfizer Inc., 92–95
    Taro Pharmaceutical Industries Ltd., 76–79
MedOptics, 245
Meeker, Mary, 6
Melnyk, Eugene N., 68
Mendoza, Thomas F., 218
Merck & Company, Inc., 96–99
Merck Frosst Canada, 96
Mercury Interactive Corporation, 35, 206–209
Merrill Lynch investigation, 5–6, 7
MIC Technology, 237
Microsoft Corporation, 194–197, 200
MIT Technology Review, 36
Moore, Geoffrey, 22
Moore, Gordon, 40, 41, 223
Mull, John D., 56
Muzyka, Doug, 168

N

Nacht, Marius, 210
nanotechnology, 35
Negroponte, Nicholas, 34
Neill, Richard A., 184
Nenniger, Emil, 148
net income, 252
Network Appliance Inc., 218–222
news, 24
newsletters, 38
Normex Telecom, 249
Nortel Networks, 20, 229
Noyce, Robert, 40

O

Ogden, Frank, 36
O'Neil, William, 23–25, 30–31
Online Investor Toolbox, 15
Onyx Environmental Services, 61
OptimaPharma, 77
Oracle, 200
Orenda, 185
Otellini, Paul S., 222
outsourcing, 34–35, 45, 191

P

P/E ratio, 253
Paladin Laboratories, 88–91
Paschini, Jean, 136
Paschini, Pierre, 136
Pason Systems Inc., 110–113

Patheon Inc., 35, 44–47
Pentacore Inc., 162
Pfizer, Charles, 92
Pfizer Inc., 92–95
Pharmacia Corporation, 94
Pharmascience Inc., 88
Philips CCD Business Unit, 245
Phillips, Larry B., 106
Phoenix International Life Sciences, 49, 50
PMC Sierra, 13
Polycables National Inc., 249
Poole, William S., 68
Preventive Technologies, 181
Profit 100, 38

R
Radware, 233
Rainbow Studios, 203
Red Herring, 36
Red Lake Mine, 118–119
Re$earch Infosource, 38
Research in Motion, 13
resources sector
    category of, 11
    Goldcorp Inc., 118–121
    Trican Well Service Ltd., 122–125
return, 253
revenue, 253
Rhône Poulenc Rorer, 69
Rich Dad's Guide to Investing (Kiyosaki), 22
Richardson, Peter, 60
risk minimization, 11
Roach, Michael, 190
The Roaring 2000s (Dent), 8
Rogers, John A., 48
Rothschild, Nathan, 3

S
Saint-Pierre, Guy, 148
Saltel Electric, 249
Sankyo Pharma, 73
Sapient, 13
Schreiner Aviation Training, 177
Schwab, Charles G., 208
Schwed, Gil, 210
science and technology stocks, 9–11
Scientific-Atlanta Inc., 34, 240–243
security, 34
Sedar. *See* Advice for Investors
sell right, 26–28

selling strategies, 27–28
September 11 attacks, 2–3, 6–7, 16, 233
Shen, Anthony P., 228
Shen, Francis N., 228
Sherman, Bernard C., 84
Short Brothers PLC, 141
Siebel, Thomas M., 198
Siebel Systems, Inc., 35, 198–201
Silent Witness Enterprises Ltd., 34, 35, 132–135
Silicon Mountain Design, 245
SimuFlite Training International, 177
Site Consultants Inc., 162
Site Management Organizations (SMOs), 58
Slater, Cody Z., 144
SNC Lavalin Group Inc., 148–151
Society of Obstetricians and Gynecologists, 90
Solectron, 13
Solomon, Howard, 72
Spectra Logic, 219
The Spink Corporation, 162
Spitzer, Eliot, 5
Stanley, Don, 160
Stanley Technology Group. *See* Stantec Inc.
Stanley Works, 134
Stantec Inc., 160–163
Steyr-Daimler-Puch, 129
stock chart channels, 28–29
stock lists, 38
stock selection, 11–16
Stronach, Belinda, 128, 129
Stronach, Frank, 41, 128, 129
sub-sectors, 22
Successful Investor, 38
Superior Cementers, 123
supply and demand, 25
Surveyor, Arthur, 148

T
T-Net 100, 38
Taggart Engineering, 162
Tapp, Lawrence G., 172
Taro International, 77
Taro Pharmaceutical Industries Ltd., 76–79
Taro Research Institute, 77
Technology Review. *See* Advice for Investors
Tedford, Robert C., 44
telecommunications
    Aastra Technologies Ltd., 228–231
    Aeroflex Inc., 236–239

category of, 11
Comverse Technology Inc., 232–235
Cygnal Technologies Corporation, 248–251
DALSA Corporation, 244–247
Scientific-Altlanta Inc., 240–243
Terry, Heath, 203
Tesma International Inc., 35, 130, 180–183
Teva Pharmaceuticals, 69
Thode, H. Patrick, 152
Thomson Corporation, 14
THQ Inc., 202–205
Tipton & Kalmbach, 162
Top 500 Stocks on TSX, 38
Toronto Stock Exchange. *See* Advice for Investors
total growth, 252
Trican Well Service Ltd., 35, 122–125
Triffo, Ronald P., 160
Trysol Canada, 106, 108

U
Ulticom, 232, 233
Ungerman, Jerry, 210

V
Valentine, Donald T., 218
Valmarine, 177
Verint Systems, 232, 233
Verreault, Laurent, 156
Vivendi, 61

W
Wahl, Paul, 198
Walker, Donald J., 180

Walkerton, Ontario, 65
Warmenhoven, Dan, 218
Warner Lambert, 93
Wellum, Jonathan, 46
Wescam, 14
West Technical Technologies, 249
Wharf Mine, 119
White Radio Ltd., 249
Wihuri Oy, 164
Wilson, Lynton R., 176
Winpak Ltd., 164–167
Wired, 36
Wise, Ted, 88
Woerner, Klaus, 41, 172
World Trade Center attacks, 2–3, 6–7, 16, 233
WorldCom, 4
Wyeth-Ayerst, 69, 81

X
Xelus Enterprise Service Management, 220

Y
Yahoo!, 13
Young, J. Douglas, 248

Z
Zambonini, Renato, 214
Zarlink wafer foundry, 245
Zenon Environmental Inc., 23, 64

also in
for **CANADIANS**
series

The 50 Best Stocks for Canadians

Lori Bamber and Gene Walden
ISBN 1-55335-02-0

Every portfolio needs a core of blue-chip stocks. Build your portfolio with these 50 proven low-risk, long-term winners, and prosper over the long haul.

The 50 Best Small Cap Stocks for Canadians

Lori Bamber and Gene Walden
ISBN 1-55335-021-9

Small cap stocks offer greater risks and also greater rewards. Add small cap stocks to your portfolio, and cash in on those rewards!

The 50 Best Global Stocks for Canadians

Lori Bamber
ISBN 1-55335-023-5

Canadian investors can place up to 30% of their RRSP investments in non-Canadian securities, yet many do not. This book applies the *50 Best* criteria and measurement standards to companies around the world.

Did you know...

Canadians are buying stocks with commissions as low as

$1 per trade!

Do you know where...

www.Investments.ShareOwner.com/Best

Member Canadian
Investor Protection
Fund

Member Investment
Dealers Association
of Canada

Participant in the
Canadian Depository
for Securities Ltd.

121 Richmond Street West, 7th Floor · Toronto ON M5H 2K1 · (416) 595-7200